KEVIN LEE
WITH CATHERINE SEDA

Search Engine Advertising

Buying Your Way
to the Top
to Increase Sales

SECOND EDITION

lew

Search Engine Advertising
Buying Your Way to the Top to Increase Sales, Second Edition
Kevin Lee with Catherine Seda

New Riders
1249 Eighth Street
Berkeley, CA 94710
510/524-2178

Find us on the web at www.newriders.com
To report errors, please send a note to errata@peachpit.com

New Riders is an imprint of Peachpit, a division of Pearson Education

Copyright © 2009 by Kevin Lee with Catherine Seda

Notice of Rights

Notice of Liability

Trademarks

Printed and bound in the United States of America

ISBN 13: 978-0-321-49599-0
ISBN 10: 0-321-49599-3

9 8 7 6 5 4 3 2 1

Project Editor
Nancy Peterson

Development Editor
Robyn G. Thomas

Technical Editor
Steven Baldwin

Production Coordinator
Hilal Sala

Copy Editor
Darren Meiss

Compositor
Danielle Foster

Marketing Manager
Glenn Bisignani

Indexers
Joy Dean Lee
John Sleeva

Cover Designer
Aren Howell

Cover Compositor
Mike Tanamachi

Interior Designer
Kim Scott

Dedications

This book is dedicated to all the clients I've had in the last 15 years whose challenging business objectives forced my teams and me to constantly overcome search marketing obstacles through the application of technology, smarts, and sometimes brute force. In addition, I could not have become the expert I am nor finished this book without the support and patience of my wife Allison who patiently observed as month after month, laptop on my knees, I toiled away chapter after chapter. The support of my business partner Dave Pasternack has also been invaluable as has the constant pressure from Didit's competition. Succeeding is sweeter when there are at least some capable competitors forcing you to work even harder and smarter for clients.

Kevin Lee

Acknowledgments

Every Didit employee has in some way helped shape this book. My employees help clients overcome the daily challenges of search marketing. The most challenging of client objectives often result in my involvement in strategy, and that's great. The shared desire of my team to solve the clients' problems and achieve those objectives has enabled us all to grow into highly experienced and seasoned search engine advertising experts. For that I'm truly grateful.

About the Authors

Kevin Lee, Founder, Chairman, and CEO of Didit, has been an acknowledged search engine marketing (SEM) expert since 1995. Kevin's years of SEM expertise provide the foundation for Didit's proprietary Maestro search campaign technology. Didit's unparalleled results and client profit lift have earned Didit recognition not only among marketers but also as part of the 2007 Inc. 500 (#137) as well as a #12 position on Deloitte's Fast 500. His first book, *The Eyes Have It: How to Market in an Age of Divergent Consumers, Media Chaos and Advertising Anarchy* (Easton Studio Press, 2007) was followed by another widely praised book: *The Truth About Pay-Per-Click Search Advertising* (FT Press, 2009). *The Wall Street Journal, Business Week, The New York Times, Bloomberg, CNET, USA Today, San Jose Mercury News,* and other press quote Kevin regularly. Kevin lectures at leading industry conferences.

In 2008, Kevin Lee and partner David Pasternack launched a social entrepreneurship venture, www.We-Care.com, that generates passive donation revenue for nonprofit causes.

2008 also marked the launch of a Didit subsidiary, PowerProfiles.com, the official Dun & Bradstreet Online Business Directory.

Kevin earned his MBA from Yale School of Management in 1992. He lives in Manhattan with his wife (a New York psychologist) and children.

Catherine Seda is a 14-year Internet marketing strategist. She wrote the first edition of *Search Engine Advertising* (New Riders, 2004), which sold over 10,000 copies worldwide. She is also author of *How to Win Sales & Influence Spiders* (New Riders, 2007), which is now available in Chinese, Japanese, and Polish.

As a popular speaker, Catherine has presented at eBay Live!, eBay University, Entrepreneur magazine, DMA, Search Engine Strategies, and UC San Diego Extension. She shares practical tips in her articles for publications such as *Entrepreneur* magazine, *Leader* magazine, *Yahoo! Small Business Insights*, and *U.S. SBA's Small Business Success*. She is also frequently quoted in eWeek.com, CNET news.com, eBay Radio, American Public Media's Marketplace, and other news outlets.

Catherine teaches business professionals how to attract new customers, search engine spiders, and the press simultaneously. Her unique approach enables entrepreneurs to increase their business by up to $100,000 in 30 days. Corporate brands can increase their revenue by $1 million a month or more.

Catherine loves Internet marketing because she loves speed. In fact, she survived skeleton training at the Utah Olympic Park during which she raced down an icy bobsled track, head-first, on a sled, at 70 MPH. For companies looking to bring speed and power to their Internet marketing performance, Catherine is the perfect match.

To get Catherine's free "Top 10 Internet Marketing Mistakes" report, and find out more about her services, visit www.CatherineSeda.com.

Authors' Notes

People often ask me why I'm so passionate about search engine advertising. The reality is the whole industry was made for me, or perhaps I was made for the industry. I loved economics and majored in it as an undergraduate then went on to Yale School of Management for my MBA and became as passionate about marketing as I was about econ. When in late 1997 GoTo.com announced that it would auction off clicks from a search results page (at the time only its own), I was fascinated. That fascination grew into delight as paid search advertising proved itself and I realized I could help marketers take a great form of advertising and make it work even harder through the application of best practices and technology.

Since founding Didit in 1996, my level of passion has increased. Who would have thought that paid search would validate the concept that highly valuable advertising inventory could be auctioned off in real time much like financial instruments and commodities. Finally, all my economics training combined with my love of advertising (I spent a couple of years on Madison Avenue after grad school) allowed me to help assure advertisers that their paid search and auction-based media dollars were being spent both optimally and wisely.

The diversity of backgrounds for the early search advertising professionals is amazing. Catherine Seda and a handful of early pioneers in search engine advertising helped put in place the best practices that thousands of marketers follow today. I can't tell you how pleased I was when Catherine asked me to pick up where she left off in 2003 by writing an updated version of this book. Catherine has been a client and friend and has co-presented at conferences, and now I'm pleased that Catherine was able to provide guidance to me as I penned this book.

Kevin Lee
Internet marketing strategist
www.KevinLee.net

Search engines have come a long way since I used WebCrawler in 1994. Search engine marketing, specifically pay per click (PPC), has also evolved since I wrote *Search Engine Advertising* in 2003. Although a few of the PPC fundamentals are the same, the strategies needed to make PPC profitable are a lot more advanced.

PPC is still one of the fastest ways to reach a targeted audience on the web. It's also one of the fastest ways to blow your budget, if you're not careful. That's why I have chosen Kevin Lee, co-founder of Didit, to write the second edition of this book.

I've always been impressed by how much valuable information Kevin shares. His use of statistics and case studies, along with practical tips, will help you protect your profits while achieving greater success—whether you're a new or experienced PPC advertiser. I also know firsthand the results Didit can achieve for clients.

In 2002–2003, Didit helped me catch click fraud and broken tracking links in my clients' accounts. These problems, along with many others, could cost you a fortune. Don't worry; you'll learn how to avoid, catch, and fix PPC problems in this book. You'll also learn how to maximize your results. Ready to get started?

To your online success!

Catherine Seda
Internet marketing strategist
Author of *Search Engine Advertising*, First Edition (New Riders, 2004)
Author of *How to Win Sales & Influence Spiders* (New Riders, 2007)
www.CatherineSeda.com

Contributors

Technical Editor and Contributing Writer

Steve Baldwin, Didit Editor-in-Chief, has been writing about interactive media since 1990 for *PC Magazine*, *Computer Shopper*, *ZDNet*, and Time, Inc. Steve has co-authored three books about the New Economy: *Netslaves: True Tales of Working the Web* (McGraw-Hill, 1999), *Netslaves 2.0: Tales of "Surviving" the Great Tech Gold Rush* (Allworth Press, 2003), and *The Eyes Have It: How to Market in an Age of Divergent Consumers, Media Chaos and Advertising Anarchy* (Easton Studio Press, 2007). Steve is a regular columnist for MediaPost's *Search Insider* and has lectured at NYU, Columbia, Vassar, and at the Piet Zwart Institute in Rotterdam. He is a graduate of Fordham University and lives in Brooklyn, New York.

Contents

Foreword

Advertisers pay millions to put their messages on the traditional broadcast systems of television, radio, and print. These systems let advertisers reach a wide audience. The drawback, aside from the expense, is inevitably the message reaches a large number of consumers who simply aren't interested.

Search engines are also a form of broadcast, but a unique system where the normal rules are flipped around. Instead of advertisers broadcasting their messages to consumers, the "reverse broadcast network" of search engines lets millions of consumers each day tell advertisers exactly what they want. These consumers needn't be convinced to buy a particular product, such as a new car, DVD player, or washing machine. They're already looking. When they search, they're looking for someone who stands ready to fulfill their needs. As an advertiser, you simply need to know how to tune into this consumer desire. This great book from Kevin Lee and Catherine Seda shows you how.

Both Kevin and Catherine are long-time veterans of the paid search space. They were speaking and writing about the topic before Google became a household word and before many of today's ad programs had matured. They can tell stories about actively working in systems that required buying ads on a keyword-by-keyword basis, or having to actively watch for costly "bid gaps" (similar to the "I walked through the snow eight miles to school each day" stories parents tell their children). Features we now take for granted in ad programs didn't exist when they started; in part, the reason we have them today is because of the pioneering work they did to win support and changes through industry education.

Their educational work continues in this book. You'll learn how to get started with search engine advertising at a very basic level, yet you'll find a full education about advanced issues available to those who want them.

Though search engines are a broadcast network, they don't require millions of dollars to get started. Any business can start with a budget of only tens of dollars. You'll learn quickly just how powerful search engines can be, if your experience is like that of the many other advertisers who are spending enough to make search engine advertising into a multibillion dollar industry.

So enjoy the book, then dive in and get started with search engine advertising! No other advertising medium provides such immediate, measurable results. Once you try search engine advertising, you'll wonder why it took you so long to discover it—and you'll hope your competitors never find out.

—*Danny Sullivan*
Editor, SearchEngineLand.com

Search—More than the New Yellow Pages

These days, chances are that it's been quite awhile since you used the printed Yellow Pages when searching for a local business. If you are like most people in the USA (and globally for that matter), you have replaced the printed Yellow Pages with Google, Yahoo, MSN, or your favorite search engine. Perhaps you occasionally use an online Yellow Pages site. However, search engine use goes far beyond replacing the printed Yellow Pages, and consumers and business-to-business (B2B) purchasers use search engines to research travel options, make online or offline purchases at stores they already know and love, learn about news stories, entertainment, and stocks, and much more. Search engines have become a gateway to information, which makes them critically important to marketers and business owners. Being able to provide *your* product and services information to searchers at the appropriate time is clearly an opportunity for you to influence that searcher's eventual purchase decision.

It's no surprise therefore that search engine marketing (SEM), also known as *paid search*, is a powerful new advertising channel that simply did not exist just a decade ago. In 2007, marketers spent more than $12 billion on paid search advertising campaigns, and forecasters project that spending on search advertising will double by 2011 to more than $25 billion (Source: SEMPO's 2007 *State of Search Marketing* survey).

Paid search engine advertising campaigns are made up of keywords that trigger text link listings at the top and down the right side of a search engine results page (SERP). Advertisers bid for position in those results, paying when a click occurs on their ads linking to their website. As you might expect, this performance-based advertising model is quite attractive. Unlike Yellow Pages advertising, which charges a fixed annual fee; or radio, TV, or print advertising, all priced at a variant of cost-per-thousand (CPM) impressions (those who are exposed to an ad); or direct mail advertising, where postage and printing costs are involved, search delivers potential customers on a per-click basis, which is one of the primary reasons that paid search was propelled to $12 billion in ten years.

Search advertising and the old-fashioned printed Yellow Pages share a common theme: people who are searching for information and are in a unique state of mind. Having entered their desires, needs, and wishes into a little search box, these searchers are giving the search engines (Google, Yahoo, Microsoft, Ask, and others) an unprecedented level of information. That information translates into advertising revenue, as the search engines auction off visibility in the search results to marketers. What marketer wouldn't want to be in front of a potential customer an instant after he or she expressed a need or desire that matched with the product or service? In this respect, paid search advertising updates the longstanding model of the printed Yellow Pages, which engages potential customers at a very opportune point in time, yet provides marketers much greater control over searchers' experience after they click your ad.

Business interest in SEM is strong, widespread, and growing, from search conferences such as SES (Search Engine Strategies) to Fortune 500 boardrooms to the entrepreneur down the street. The major search engines—Google, Yahoo, and Microsoft—are working hard to recruit marketers to join the roughly 800,000 businesses, organizations, and individuals now running paid search campaigns there. After all, millions of business owners use Google, Yahoo, Microsoft, and Ask to do their searches, and they understand the power of search firsthand. Some marketers choose to manage their search engine marketing campaigns themselves; others use their ad agencies or specialized SEM agencies.

Of course, it is to be expected that the search engines are banging the drum about the virtues of SEM, a practice and a discipline that should be understood by any entity that has an online business presence. But SEM is also an exceedingly complex field, and new marketers learning about SEM's promise should be equally aware of the pitfalls—some not so obvious—that can trip up the unwary. The search engines (that naturally want as many marketers advertising as possible) don't stress the pitfalls for fear of scaring people away, leaving many marketers to learn the hard way, either through inefficient budget allocations or through missed opportunities.

As a result of the buzz and the promise of search engine marketing success, marketers continue to flock to SEM. The search engines have made it easy—perhaps too easy—for anyone to log onto Google AdWords, Yahoo Search Marketing, or Microsoft AdCenter, pay $5 to open an account, and start buying keyword-targeted search engine traffic.

What is difficult, however, is designing and executing paid search campaigns that deliver consistent, sustainable results, and that is why I have written this book. It reflects the lessons I've learned from founding and running a paid search agency for more than 10 years, helping clients, both large and small, get the most out of SEM, and studying the problems that I've seen marketers run up against. Most importantly, this book provides many of the effective solutions for search-related marketing problems. My hope is that this body of knowledge can help you, whether you're in charge of an SEM team at a major corporation, at an ad agency whose clients are increasingly asking you how to buy search media, or if you are using SEM for your own small or home-based business or consultancy.

The last edition of this book predates both the current Yahoo and Microsoft systems, and Google's system was in its relative infancy at the time as well. The search engines make many changes to their systems, often several within a year. However, the significance of the changes has slowed dramatically, allowing this book to focus on the common best practices and areas that have solidified within the last several years as well as providing a foundation of knowledge that will apply to the newest changes to the offerings in paid search.

Be warned: This book will not be all things for all people. I have tried to cover many areas in a way that even absolute beginners will benefit, but if you are a neophyte to paid placement SEM, spend some time learning the basic mechanics of SEM by attending a conference or two or by diving into the major SEM-oriented websites and bulletin boards, such as ClickZ.com, SearchEngineWatch.com, and SearchEngineLand.com.

Profiting in a Google Economy

According to the Microsoft Atlas Institute's study *Paying for Navigational Search*, "Navigational search from branded keywords and repeat visits account for 71% of sponsored search links." This means that consumers are relying on search engines not only to answer questions and discover new solutions to the problem of finding information, but also as a mode of navigation. This is both an opportunity and a curse. You may find yourself paying Google, Yahoo, Microsoft, and others to recapture existing customers who already had the intent to find and do business with you. Many marketers think of this as a *toll* collected by the search engines. Failure to pay the toll will often lead to a reduction in visitors and revenue as some of your current customers find your competition in either the paid or unpaid results. Conversely, you may be able to augment your existing visibility in the unpaid search results with paid search ads tuned specifically for your target audience. When you review your paid search advertising invoice, remember that the engines essentially collect a toll between the user searching for a given product or service and the business providing it. Even brand names and domain names are bid on by their owners, their channel, and their competition. No matter who is doing the bidding and the buying, the search engines cash the checks.

Since competitors can often bid on branded and trademarked terms in some engines, many merchants will also take advantage of situations where they can harvest demand created by their competition. I talk more about some of these strategies and tactics later in this book.

The success of the search engines in changing user behavior for informational, purchase, and navigational searches has essentially put many marketers between a rock and a hard place. Marketers can only ignore having a presence in the search results at their own peril, because it is likely that their competitors are already actively mining the search marketplace, and the consumers are in control. The power of Google's brand in just 10 years is a testament to the control they have gained in the marketplace. Milward Brown ranked Google's brand as the most valuable in the world in its 2008 BrandZ report: "Google tops the list again with a brand value of $86.1 billion followed by GE at $71.4 billion and Microsoft at $70.8 billion."

Marketers will need to adapt to the "Google Economy," where some forms of advertising become nearly mandatory if the marketer wants to maximize revenues and profits.

However, the situation of having to pay significant media and advertising dollars to talk to existing customers isn't unique to search. Much of the advertising consumers see is for products or services they already buy. Marketers are always looking to strengthen their brands and continue to communicate their messages to consumers. Coke and Pepsi spend hundreds of millions of dollars promoting products nearly everyone knows quite well. The same is true for the automotive, banking, consumer products, travel, and retail sectors.

Ironically, for traditional offline advertising, the better targeted the media is to the audience, the greater the number of existing customers will see the ad. This is because a marketer's best next customer probably shares a significant amount in common with the current customer. The key goal for the CMO (Chief Marketing Officer), marketing VP, or business owner is not eliminating duplicate advertising but maximizing the impact of the advertising touching those consumers who are undecided or are open to switching from the competition. Search engine marketing reaches existing customers, reinforcing the brand, and prospective customers, potentially influencing them favorably towards purchase. A well-crafted campaign influences both new and returning consumers positively even if the dollars spent feel like a toll being paid to a toll-taker. The key to success in the "Google Economy" is understanding the ecosystem and deploying monetary and human capital resources in the best possible mix across all marketing and media.

How This Book Is Organized

Most marketers and business owners treat their paid search campaigns the same way they treat a new piece of software or a new piece of computer equipment. They jump right in and don't take the time to read the directions. Even if they read the directions, they often don't know enough to absorb much of the content.

For this reason, I've included information on paid search fundamentals, as well as hands-on information for making existing campaigns more effective or providing a great launching pad for new campaigns. However, this isn't simply a how-to book. I spend a lot of time on the "why" as well, in order to create a balance between tactical guide and strategic owner's manual.

When appropriate to illustrate a point, I use graphics, screenshots, or charts. However, the bulk of the material is textual, with a focus on what you'll need to rapidly gain expertise in search engine advertising, particularly paid placement search engine advertising.

Why 80% of This Book Is About Paid Placement

Paid placement is the form of pay-per-click (PPC) search engine visibility that most marketers consider when they think about search engine advertising. After all, when you or anyone on your team does a search on Google, Yahoo, or Microsoft, you see the paid placement listings. Although there are other forms of online search advertising, the majority of opportunity and the majority of budgetary risk falls into the area of paid placement. Every marketer and advertiser wants to be at the top of the *free* search engine results (often called *natural* or *organic* search engine listings). The quality control teams at Google, Yahoo, Microsoft, and every smaller search engine are focused on relevance. Search engine optimization (SEO) is the practice of improving position and visibility in organic/natural results.

Much of what it takes to have pages listed at the top of the free listings in the search engines for the most coveted keywords and phrases is not under the marketer's control. Like in public relations, learning the best practices on organic SEO and the rules of the game improves your chances, but there are no guarantees that your efforts to improve ranking on targeted keywords will succeed. Even if you have success, the level of this success is difficult or impossible to predict. Yet in the same way that having a good PR team or agency may enhance your firm's visibility, there's good reason to explore SEO, particularly if your site is the most relevant for specific search queries and is nowhere to be found in the results page.

There are entire books, sites, conferences, and courses devoted specifically to SEO, a practice which operates as a parallel discipline alongside SEM or paid search. SEO is an important subject in and of itself, and creating the best, most navigable, and most compelling content on your website is a critical task for two important reasons. First, you want to be able to take advantage of the free organic traffic delivered by the search engines; and second, you want the site that is the target of your PPC ad to be the most relevant, most compelling offer possible to maximize the chances that *your clickers* will convert. Several websites, including Search Engine Watch, ClickZ, and SearchEngineLand, provide useful information on SEO and search marketing in general, as do the various online learning centers (incorporated within the ad management web pages) and help sections of the major search engines themselves.

What's in Each Chapter: Not Just for Novices

Whether your search engine marketing campaigns were set up five years ago, six months ago, or you plan on setting them up while reading this book, the reality is that they're rarely in optimal shape the first, second, or third time around. With that in mind, after

Chapters 1 and 2 cover some introductory topics on the landscape and industry; Chapters 3 and 4 cover foundation and strategic review; Chapters 5 through 11 help you double-check each of your existing campaigns' compliance with best practices; Chapters 12 through 14 discuss venues beyond search. You may have missed nuances in your campaign structure that can result in a far more profitable campaign with just a few adjustments. Therefore, even if you consider yourself a seasoned search engine marketer, I encourage you to at least skim the earlier sections of this book dedicated to campaign setup, then concentrate on the more advanced strategies covered in the latter portions of the book.

 **PART I**

Paid Search Fundamentals

Part I

Introduction

According to a late-2008 Microsoft adCenter study of 400 small business owners, "7 in 10 small-business owners who participated revealed that they would rather try to do their own taxes than start a paid search marketing campaign." So, topics that a search engine marketing professional considers to be "fundamental" may in fact be sophisticated and daunting to many. Therefore, I've allocated a significant level of coverage in this book to paid search fundamentals. My objective is to put you at ease with search engine advertising and marketing elements that may seem arcane and complex. With sufficient explanation, they will become clear and manageable.

Chapter 1

Search Engine Advertising Overview

Although you are likely familiar with search engine advertising, the true power of paid search advertising may not have become apparent to you yet. This overview will provide you with an understanding of the fundamentals of search engine marketing, setting the stage for you to tap this important source of potential customers. Depending on your level of experience with search engine advertising, this overview may also bring to light important nuances and strategic drivers that relate to your business and your campaign.

Customers Raise Their Hands

Search engine marketing (SEM) has rapidly become the foundation of any interactive marketing or media plan. Consumers and prospects are in lean-forward mode, ready to make a decision, when reviewing and selecting search engine results, which can include your ad. Every time someone enters text into the search box on Google, Yahoo, or one of the Microsoft search engine brands, or he or she uses a toolbar from a vendor, that searcher volunteers a critical piece of information to the search engine that allows it to display relevant advertising. It is a rare moment indeed when the marketer can tune the message so specifically to the current expressed needs of the consumer.

Imagine how much more powerful that direct mail catalog distribution would be if you could use a "psychic mailman" who waited outside the door of your best customers' homes with hundreds of different offers and rang the doorbell only at the moment your customer started thinking about researching or purchasing a specific product or service. When the customer was thinking about a new down ski jacket, the psychic mailman would tear out the appropriate page from your catalog and hand it over. SEM can be your psychic mailman, delivering the perfect offer, tuned to the specific need of searchers. Every time a searcher enters a search term, he or she is entering *hunt* mode—looking for information, a solution to a problem, or perhaps something to buy. The best news is that many of the proven direct marketing and catalog marketing practices you have used over the years to drive profit and revenue can be adapted to SEM.

Pay-per-click SEM is unlike traditional forms of advertising, marketing, and promotion. One of its most important characteristics is its nonintrusive nature. Unlike advertising that uses time-honored techniques to distract or interrupt prospective customers from whatever they're doing (reading a magazine, watching TV, listening to the radio, driving down the highway, and so on), SEM is an elective, opt-in form of marketing. Nobody forces users to click on search ads. Ads on search engine results pages (SERP) are always clicked voluntarily, which means that the person who sees the ad has affirmatively decided to initiate a conversation with the marketer who has paid to run the ad in the search results.

Paid search advertising provides an efficient way for businesses, both small and large, to reach groups of people most likely to be interested in their products and services. Unlike advertising in traditional media that typically requires the marketer to pay the publisher for messages that may not be seen, much less acted upon by readers, viewers, or listeners, SEM is laser-targeted. It is designed to appeal just at the instant in time when the individual is most receptive and most likely to take advantage of, or *convert* to, a marketing offer. In fact, in SEMPO's 2007 annual *State of Search Engine Marketing* survey, 54 percent of marketers rated paid search as the best-performing online advertising method, followed by SEO (50 percent), and email marketing (39 percent), with other forms of marketing trailing significantly.

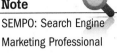

Note

SEMPO: Search Engine Marketing Professional Organization

Paid placement SEM is measurable in a highly granular way that has never before been possible in any advertising medium. Unlike traditional media, where campaigns are based on estimates, sometimes dubious research, and focus groups, online media and paid search offer the opportunity to optimize campaigns around real results. With the right technology and tools, marketers can see where their clicks came from, where they are going, and whether the users behind these clicks are taking advantage of their offers, converting to sales online and potentially even tracking offline behavior. Marketers can do all of this in near real time, which enables them to make course corrections while a campaign is in-flight, a huge benefit providing for both the elimination of waste and the exploitation of opportunities.

What Is a SERP and Where Are the Paid Ads?

The search engine results page (SERP) is the page a consumer sees after performing a search. SERPs used to be purely textual, but increasingly, the search engines are mixing text results together with image results, video results, and in some cases links to audio files. This recent phenomenon, called *universal search*, describes mixing different sections/categories of graphical, textual, and potentially rich-media (video) results all on the same page. For many years, the search engines had separate search tabs for news, images, maps, video, and products. However, when the search engine algorithm believes that a searcher may want to see results from more than one tab, instead of simply highlighting the tabs where users can find additional relevant information, the search engines are now mixing the results together in the primary SERP. In the example in **Figure 1.1,** you can see the sponsored links both at the top and the right *rail* (area to the right of the main results). The SERP also includes results from the local computer (due to having Google's desktop/toolbar installed), as well as a Google map, which has local business results overlaid with accompanying hotlinks. As marketers, we can control our paid advertising listings but have only a small amount of control on the unpaid listings (in the map as well as below the map). The ads you see on the top and right rail are part of Google's pay-per-click (PPC) search engine advertising system, AdWords. A similar system currently exists on Yahoo and across the Microsoft properties (adCenter).

Figure 1.1

Google search display results, a SERP

Getting Ready for a Real-Time Auction

Auctions work well for the owner of an asset (by maximizing the prices paid by the buyers) when there is a valuable, scarce commodity or product and sufficient demand to justify running an auction. Many of us think of traditional auctions for valuable common items such as paintings, antiques, cars, and estates. Governments use auctions to allocate wireless spectrum (via the FCC). Real-time auctions are also used to trade financial instruments such as stocks, bonds, options, and commodities (such as pork bellies, gold, and crude oil).

In 1997, Bill Gross of IdeaLab founded a company called GoTo.com. The premise was simple: placement in the search results on GoTo.com would be auctioned off in real time on a keyword-by-keyword basis. The highest bidder at the instant a searcher searched would get the higher spot in the SERP, and bids started at a penny. It ended up that the paid placement model was great, and the few early marketers to try it (including my firm Didit, which now focuses almost exclusively on paid search) loved the high response rate of visitors. However, GoTo.com didn't have enough of a brand to convince the millions of searchers to search on GoTo.com instead of their current favorites (at the time Lycos, AltaVista, Excite, Infospace, HotBot, and Yahoo) and so instead changed its strategy to one of syndicating the paid results out to other search engines, primarily Yahoo. After going public with a new name, Overture, the syndication model continued to prove itself, and Yahoo eventually bought the company. In the meantime, a tiny company named Google started building a huge user base and decided to make a major improvement to the idea of paid placement (auctioned ad placements in the search results) by factoring in the relevance of the ad, not just the bid. Such an auction system that makes decisions based on non-price factors such as relevance is known as a *hybrid* auction system.

Google's change to a hybrid auction system had two major implications, one being that it was able to earn more from a search results page than search engines using simpler auction models because a hybrid auction maximizes revenue. Such systems also put the onus on search engine marketers to make sure their ads and keywords were highly relevant to the searches being done. The mechanics of this hybrid paid placement system are covered in the next chapter.

The search engines sell keywords to marketers in a real-time, auction-driven marketplace in which the instantaneous values of any given word or word combination are subject to significant price fluctuations. Some of these fluctuations are obvious, secular, and predictable—for example, the value of the term *flowers* rises predictably around Valentine's and Mothers' Day, and the phrase *ski vacation* becomes premium-priced in the fall in the U.S. and the spring in the southern hemisphere.

If you've bought media ads before, you know that prices for ad units, whether they are in print, radio, TV, or other media, are established well in advance. This makes designing a media plan as simple as entering figures in a spreadsheet. But the search marketplace is constantly changing as competitors freely enter and exit the marketplace, and it's often impossible to know in advance how much you must spend on individual clicks to reach your objectives or maintain specific positions.

Search engines will automatically recommend specific budget levels for your search campaigns, based on the amount you're willing to pay for keywords and the expected traffic from them. However, this does not mean that you can afford to simply go along with the search engine's automatic budget recommendations and hope everything will work out. We spend time on the topic of setting budgets later in the book, particularly in Chapter 8, "Campaign Setup: Titles and Descriptions." You need to plan to be successful in search marketing. In fact, you must create a plan that is far more sophisticated than yesterday's simple media plans. This book will show you how you can create a forward-looking search media plan, test its operation, and refine it so that it consistently operates at maximum efficiency.

Ten Years and Ten Billion Dollars

As you may have guessed, the highly targeted nature of search engine advertising combined with surges in consumer use of search engines have resulted in the dramatic growth of the industry. Escalating click prices, increases in the number of search advertisers, and a surge in overall click volume have all combined to take a relatively new business to well over $10 billion in 10 years. Google, which was virtually unknown for the first year after being founded in 1998, is now a company with a market capitalization larger that Cisco, Intel, Oracle, or Coca-Cola. But a case can be made that Google's real growth years lie ahead of it. In fact, many Wall Street analysts are predicting that the paid search ad revenues will double again in just a few more years. This historical growth and the optimism among analysts with regard to continued growth is a testament to the value of the search advertising click and the power that players like Google have amassed in a short period of time.

Click prices have risen in recent years, but even with the costs for search engine advertising clicks rising, many marketers continue to find that relative to other forms of advertising, PPC SEM continues to be affordable. In some ways, paid search levels the playing field for marketers with small budgets but who learn and apply best practices. There are no minimum spends or high fixed unit costs, such as those accompanying the purchase of a newspaper or TV ad. You can start out buying a handful of keywords, run a campaign for a few days, shut it down, and take the knowledge gained from this experience to refine your approach before restarting it.

However, the perceived ease of PPC search is misleading because in a real-time auction you need to know how best to allocate your budget across a multitude of simultaneous choices, bidding against an ever-changing mix of competitors that also want access to the same searcher you have identified as the perfect prospect or customer. The higher the bids go and the more your competition discovers the power of search engine traffic, the more savvy you will need to be to beat out those waiting to grab any customers you miss.

Why Google Comes First

In the SEM industry, *query share* is a closely watched metric, reporting the percentage of overall searches occurring in one search engine versus the total number of queries occurring across all search engines. A *search query* represents a searcher asking a search engine for a result by typing in a keyword or phrase. More queries or a higher percentage of queries occurring on one engine or another is similar to one TV station (or TV show) having a higher viewership than another or a greater percentage of total viewers (a Nielsen rating). Similarly, radio uses Arbitron ratings, and magazines and newspapers deliver audiences to advertisers in different size buckets as reported by the Audit Bureau of Circulation (ABC). The makeup of audiences, of course, differs *demographically* (location, age, gender, or income) and *psychographically* (beliefs, attitudes, and behaviors) among shows, newspapers, and magazines. However, for any advertising venue to be of interest to a marketer, advertiser, or agency media buyer, some minimum audience size is important. When managing a traditional ad campaign, more effort and attention is paid to the portion of the campaign that delivers the greatest relevant, targeted audience.

In the United States, and most of the world for that matter, as you may have guessed, Google leads in total number of queries and query share. **Table 1.1** shows October 2008 data on search query share within the U.S. as reported by some online ratings agencies. As you can see, the share of search data vary somewhat, but Google is always far in front, followed by Yahoo and Microsoft.

Table 1.1 October 2008 Search Engine Percent of Search Data Share

Search Engine	comScore	Hitwise	Nielsen Online	Compete.com
Google Sites	63.1	71.7	61.2	68.4
Yahoo Sites	2.05	17.74	16.9	18.3
Microsoft Sites	8.5	5.4	11.4	9.3
Ask Network	4.2	3.53	2.3	2.7
AOL	3.7	n/a	4.3	1.1

Internationally, the data vary by country, with Google trailing in some countries in Asia. If you aren't located in the U.S., you can look up the current data by visiting the websites of the companies mentioned or, of course, doing a search for *Google query share Japan*, for example.

However, Google's advertising business model isn't purely about selling search engine advertising through its SERPs. Google also supplies the advertising results to several smaller search engines, giving them some or all of the paid ads. This places Google's effective query share higher still.

For this reason, this book spends more time on Google than on the other search engines. Also, the smaller search engines use essentially the same ad and campaign structure standards as Google, making Google the de facto standard.

Chapter 2

The Engines: Google, Yahoo, Microsoft, and Beyond

The search engines appear very similar from the perspective of the searcher, but for the search marketers there are some important distinctions. The mechanics of search engines and search engine advertising drive strategy and provide the foundation for the tactics you'll use, therefore it is critical that you understand the options and the way the engines work.

Paid Placement vs. Paid Inclusion vs. Directory Inclusion

When most people talk about paid search engine advertising, they are discussing the paid placement ads that are obvious to the searcher on the top five or ten search engines. These paid placement search ads are only one of three basic ways that advertisers can generate search engine traffic. So in the interest of accuracy and comprehensive review, let's discuss all the forms of paid search advertising even though many advertisers will focus almost exclusively on paid placement.

Paid Placement

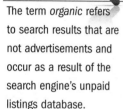

Note

The term *organic* refers to search results that are not advertisements and occur as a result of the search engine's unpaid listings database.

The majority of search engine ad spending occurs in the form of paid placement, otherwise called pay-for-placement (PFP) programs. The 2007 SEMPO *State of Search Marketing* survey illustrates that paid placement represents 87.4 percent of overall search engine marketing spending—and that includes *organic* SEO, not just paid search advertising. If you look at advertising-only segments, the domination of paid placement is even greater—well over 99 percent of the total paid search ad dollars. **Figure 2.1** shows the specifics:

Figure 2.1

Market size data from the SEMPO (Search Engine Marketing Professional Organization) *2007 State of Search Marketing Survey.*

2007 North American SEM Industry Size Estimate, by Tactic

RESEARCH HIGHLIGHTS

	2007 Advertiser SEM Spending	Share of Total	Share of Tactic
Paid Placement	**$10,648,350,000**	**87.4%**	
Search Media Firms	$9,597,200,000	78.8%	90.1%
SEM Agencies	$308,640,000	2.5%	2.9%
In-House	$742,510,000	6.1%	7.0%
Paid Inclusion	**$85,290,000**	**0.7%**	
Search Media Firms	$76,760,000	0.6%	90.0%
SEM Agencies	$8,530,000	0.1%	10.0%
Organic SEO	**$1,279,210,000**	**10.5%**	
SEM Agencies	$263,510,000	2.2%	20.6%
In-House	$1,015,700,000	8.3%	79.4%
SEM Tech	**$171,690,000**	**1.4%**	
Leasing	$12,470,000	0.1%	7.3%
SEM Agencies	$61,540,000	0.5%	35.8%
In-House	$97,680,000	0.8%	56.9%
Total	**$12,184,540,000**		

Source: Search Engine Marketing Professional Organization survey of SEM agencies and advertisers, Dec 07-Jan 08. Global Results. Copyright © 2008

SEMPO radarresearch

Source: Radar Research Forecast, North America, 1/08

1

These real-time paid placement search engine ad platforms allow you to outbid competing advertisers on a keyword-by-keyword basis to attain higher positions in the search results. It's an ongoing auction where your competitors, as well as algorithms in the search engines, set the going keyword cost-per-click bid rate required to participate or to achieve a specific position. Google is the largest of the search engines that have paid placement programs, but it's not the only game in town, at least not yet. Yahoo and Microsoft also have paid placement search engine advertising programs and systems.

Paid placement programs can seem easy and affordable for businesses to start driving high-quality traffic to their websites almost immediately. But both entrepreneurs and corporate advertisers need to be aware of the challenges to manage their campaigns effectively, as there are many best practices as well as pitfalls that can turn an otherwise profitable campaign into a money-loser.

Paid placement is the fastest and easiest way for advertisers to get started in paid search, and for most advertisers it continues to be the most important form of paid search marketing.

Paid Inclusion

Paid inclusion is a process by which you can guarantee that the search engines are including at least some portion of your site in their search results. However, unlike paid placement, the search engine provides no guarantees with respect to your site actually showing up in the results.

The oldest form of paid inclusion is paying Yahoo a fee to have your site included in the Yahoo directory. Yahoo charges a flat fee of $299 to review, on an expedited basis, a single commercial website for inclusion in its directory; if accepted, an additional annual fee of $299 is charged to maintain such a listing (a $600 one-time/$600 annual recurring charge is assessed for adult-oriented websites). Many practitioners believe that it is worth paying Yahoo for the listing because doing so will hypothetically improve their unpaid organic search positions. Consequently, having such a listing in Yahoo's directory may help Google and Microsoft rank your site higher in the unpaid search results. Plus, Yahoo still includes its own directory results in regular organic search results. Depending on the size of your business, paid directory inclusion may still make sense, but it certainly isn't tops on many to-do lists within the search marketing professional's laundry list. Remember though that this is a listing for your overall site, so it doesn't help much if you have tons of products and services because a single listing can only cover so much. Google and Microsoft don't have paid directory inclusion programs.

Aside from directory inclusion, Yahoo also has a form of paid inclusion that lets you make sure specific pages from your site are included in the Yahoo search index (the database that includes not just sites, but specific pages). For small sites, Yahoo's Search Submit Basic program charges $49 annually to include up to 5 URLs per domain within Yahoo's nonpaid results. (A *URL* is your website domain name plus any additional navigational elements denoting a specific page or section.) Program participants receive frequent visits from Yahoo's search spider (the software program that adds sites to the Yahoo index), performance reports, and access to tools allowing them to optimize their sites for search engines.

For larger sites, Yahoo's Search Submit Pro provides more extensive features and controls. Designed for sites with a large number of pages that may be created dynamically (hence making them difficult for search engines to index), this program bills marketers on a cost-per-click basis. Technically speaking, your site's data are transmitted to Yahoo in an automated fashion via XML. If your site has lots of unique landing pages (for example, pages containing specific product information), XML paid inclusion may be worth considering; however, it's unlikely to represent a significant percentage of your ad buy or drive a significant number of sales in comparison with other paid search ads.

Are paid inclusion programs for you? Many people within the industry believe that an operator of a site that is well-optimized for inclusion within the organic/unpaid results of a search engine shouldn't need to pay for paid inclusion because Yahoo doesn't give any inherent position boost to a paid inclusion listing over one that is already in the index. So you might find yourself paying for a click you would have gotten anyway or (in the case of the per-URL annual fee) paying for inclusion when you might already be included for free. If you think either of the Yahoo Search Submit submission products is right for you, try learning about keywords and ad copy using paid placement first and then apply what you've learned to your inclusion program.

Keyword Bidding

Many marketers, agencies, and search engines themselves refer to the process of paid placement search engine advertising as *bidding on keywords*. Although the process you go through feels very much like bidding on keywords, in actuality a well-run search engine marketing and advertising campaign is about bidding to gain visibility among a specific *audience* that is searching on these keywords. Marketers often refer to buying *clicks* or *traffic*; what they really want is to attract human prospects and customers to their websites using very targeted and effective paid search ads. Advertising is about educating, communicating with, and influencing potential customers and turning them into profitable paying customers. Search marketing is a means to that end.

Campaign Elements

In the search engine advertising interfaces, you have an opportunity to specify several campaign elements to provide instructions to the search engine as to when and which ads you'd like shown to searchers. Five of these campaign elements follow:

- The keyword(s): Keywords and phrases are the triggers for an ad. Your ad will not be shown on a search results page unless you specify that these keywords and phrases are to be displayed. There are nuances to this selection process, which are covered in the specific tactical chapters later in this book. However, the important thing to understand at this point is that the search engines use keywords to target the ads.

- The text ad itself: The ads are made up of three visible elements and one "invisible" element. Current standard text ad formats specify a title of up to 25 characters (including spaces) followed by either two lines of 35 characters each or one line of up to 70 characters (spaces included). These two options may seem identical at first, but because the 35-character limit per line must include a complete word on each line, the line break in the ad can make a difference in what fits under the two standards.

- **The display URL:** The URL is your website domain name plus any additional navigational elements denoting a specific page or section you might wish to show to a searcher. Some search engines do not show the display URL, but because users prefer the additional information before clicking, most engines do display the URL.

- **The destination URL:** This URL specifies where the search engine sends the searcher after he or she clicks. Later chapters discuss how to use tracking destination URLs in order to better understand which keywords and ads are working in a campaign and what sections of a campaign are not delivering value and profits.

- **The bid (also called *max bid*):** Search advertising is billed on a *cost-per-click* (CPC) basis. Consequently, bids are taken on a CPC basis. The search engine will use your bid as part of the formula to determine when and where (position) to show your ad. Bids can be controlled at the keyword level and at higher levels (called *ad groups* or *campaigns*), allowing bids to be globally assigned to all campaign elements within a group. There are reasons why you might want to control bids at the ad group or campaign level, but it's generally worth the time to bid separately because the profile of people searching for keywords may differ from those searching for phrases. This is similar to a decision to pay different amounts for ads in different magazines (even if the circulation numbers are identical).

In cases where several keywords and phrases may share the same ad or the same bid price, there are many ways to structure campaigns. In addition, different search engines offer a variety of additional targeting and management options. Later chapters cover how to use these additional targeting and management options both during campaign setup and as levers to optimize a campaign and maximize profits. Some of these additional campaign settings include:

- Language

- Geography (at the country, region, or city level, or sometimes a custom level)

- Daily or monthly budget (depending on the search engine, but it is easy to use multiplication or division to determine either one)

- Ad distribution or syndication network settings (as previously mentioned, Google and some other engines also supply ads to other search engines)

All the search engines now use a similar algorithm to rank ads based not just on the cost-per-click bid but also on relevance, or more precisely, the predicted *click-through rate* (CTR; the percentage of instances that a searcher is likely to click on an ad). It's easiest to use Google as the example showing exactly how bidding on keywords translates into your ad showing up in the search engines.

How Google Does It

These next few sections can get a bit mathematical. However, the key takeaway after reading these sections on Google's paid placement algorithms (formulas) is that the price you are willing to pay per click (your bid) is only one determinant of the final position of your ad. This evolutionary change from the early straight paid-placement search advertising auctions has become a major competitive advantage for Google and a significant aggravation for marketers.

Google added significant innovations to the idea of paid placement. When determining which ads to show (chosen from all the advertisers whose bids and campaign settings match a particular query), the bid is only one factor. Google and the other search engines now all use additional factors, particularly predicted click-through rate, when deciding the order in which to place ads.

Google multiplies the max bid by the predicted CTR to arrive at a formula called AdRank (max bid × CTR = AdRank). The reason for this is twofold. Search engine representatives love to claim that the primary reason the predicted CTR is used is because ads that have gotten high CTRs in the past for a particular search prove that the combination of the ad and the advertiser are considered most relevant by searchers. After all, given a mix of text ads rotated randomly on a search engine results page, consumers will more often select the ads they feel are relevant. The search engines consider higher CTR rates to be "positive votes" by searchers, whereas low CTR rates indicate that the ad is less relevant to the search. This all makes sense, and it's a way to keep results weighted more towards the relevant ads. First and foremost (although the search engines may not admit it) is that the search engines want to make the most money. When a searcher skips over an ad (or ads) due to low relevance, the opportunity for the search engine to make money on that specific search is gone, forever. So, the search engines can balance relevance and profit simultaneously with the AdRank-based system. A less relevant ad can still appear over a more relevant ad, but one must bid proportionately more (see **Table 2.1**).

Note

eCPM is defined by Google as "effective cost per thousand impressions." This metric is used to provide a normalized method by which CPC-billed ads and CPM-billed ads may compete within the same search ad auction. eCPM is computed using a number of factors, including the ad's bid price and click-through rate.

Table 2.1 Google Display Rank Determination

Bid	Predicted Normalized CTR (Percent)	Predicted eCPM	Displayed Rank
$ 0.82	1.2	$ 0.98	1
$ 0.98	0.8	$ 0.78	4
$ 0.81	1.07	$ 0.87	2
$ 0.88	0.88	$ 0.77	5
$ 0.78	1.1	$ 0.86	3

This Is How It Works

Imagine the following scenario. You pick a keyword to advertise on. Google puts your ads into a rotation, taking a best guess as to how relevant your ad will be in comparison to the competing ads already in rotation. After several searches have occurred, causing ads (including yours) to display in one or more positions, Google will have collected some data. Your ad either got clicked or it did not for each and every search. Similarly, the performance of the neighboring ads were also watched by the Google system. For future searches, Google will begin to use a formula similar to the one used to calculate AdRank (max bid × CTR = AdRank) to determine if your ad qualifies for display at all, and if so, at what position. In addition to the data in

Table 2.1, the position and frequency is also determined by additional factors such as whether or not you have a daily or monthly budget cap set in the AdWords system for the keyword campaign (budget caps automatically shut off the display of ads once a certain spending threshold has been met or modify the ad display frequency to maintain spending near the budget).

The AdRank formula and concept can make even a math whiz's head spin, particularly if you go beyond the oversimplified data in Table 2-1 and look at how Google (or the other search engines using similar formulas) actually comes up with a predicted normalized CTR. Essentially, the better the search engine is at predicting how much higher your ad's CTR will be (compared to all the other ads that could potentially be shown for a specific search), the more effectively the search engine can make money. The normalization process is one in which Google (et al) always factors in the position your ad happens to be at the instant you do get a click versus the higher or lower positions at which your competitors' ads are showing. Google and the other engines know that being higher up in the results automatically means your ad will get clicked more often. This process of adjusting for position is called *normalization* of CTR.

Because AdRank depends on two factors, you can get a fairly high AdRank by excelling in only one side of the equation. If you're paying enormous sums of money, you still stand a chance of getting a good AdRank, even if your ad doesn't get many clicks. If you're getting a phenomenal number of clicks, you stand a chance of getting a very good AdRank even if you're paying next to nothing for every click (this happens to be one of the key goals of account optimization, as well as a reason that correct account setup is so important).

Even throwing money at an ad with a low CTR eventually stops working because the engines set minimums on the predicted CTR that even high bids per click can't overcome. If your AdRank drops, the frequency with which your ad appears drops, and finally your ad disappears. So, clearly the best solution is to run a relevant targeted ad that gets good click-through rates and a reasonable bid that still generates a good AdRank.

There are two keys to PPC search campaign optimization: buying the right clicks at the right price and then knowing how to maximize the return on each click after you have bought it.

Keyword Targeted Contextual Ads

When setting up paid placement search engine advertising accounts, you will have an opportunity to opt in (or opt out) of contextually targeted advertising. If you do any significant surfing around, particularly on *blogs* (web logs, which are like online diaries of sorts), you've seen the contextual ads running adjacent to editorial content. These ads are often text-based and labeled "Ads by Google." You should start your campaign with this setting turned off.

Is contextual inventory a good thing or not? Questions from marketers abound: What exactly is all this contextual inventory? How does this inventory differ from the search engine results inventory we love, but hate to pay for? Will this contextual inventory affect us?

Essentially, the contextual inventory attempts to match user interests to the ads being served through contextual relevance. Some examples of contextual relevance:

- Editorial content about a specific topic is matched with in-page, text-based advertising units that look much like the search listings you see in portals. The contextual ad engine boils down the essence of the page to a search term and serves up ads that marketers have purchased for that keyword/term. The number of test listings varies by implementation.

- Registered domains, not in use (also known as "parked" domains) when visited due to a typo or casual visitor, are covered in advertising links that may or may not relate to the implied topic of the domain. Some of these ad listings relate to words used as part of the domain name, and others are just popular search terms organized in a directory format in an attempt to get visitors to click forward, earning revenue for the domain owner.

Effective implementation of contextual inventory placement hinges on a really accurate mapping technology that extracts the "true essence" of a page or site and then finds the phrase that most accurately describes that essence. You hope for a truly impartial contextual algorithm that will not include the price paid for clicks in its mapping decision.

Google's Content-Targeted AdWords system is based on the first of the two examples in the list (ads placed within a publisher's page). They are syndicated across an ever-growing set of content sites, including HowStuffWorks and Blogger (surf around on HowStuffWorks for examples of the ads, often at the bottom of the pages). According to Google, its famously accurate relevancy algorithms determine the best matching keywords and phrases based on what the Google system understands about a page. In reality there's a significant amount of wiggle room, particularly if the page on which the ad is being served is a news story or is otherwise ambiguous.

Based on the results of testing the top three search engines and several second-tier search engines, their contextual inventory shows promise for some marketers. As a general matter, it is far more important to focus on regular search traffic first, because a lower percentage of humans interacting with contextual advertising are actually in-market for products or services in the way they are with search. If you need additional reach and are willing to manage a campaign against branding metrics and not just direct response metrics, then contextual inventory is far more likely to be a fit for you. If you are primarily using search, focus on those prospects and consumers who are already looking for a specific solution, and leave the contextual option off until you have the time to really test it.

Keyword Targeted Behavioral Ads

In the next decade of digital advertising, behavioral targeting will make great strides, which are expected to include the application of behavioral targeting (BT) methodologies to the search marketing arena. Behaviorally targeted keyword advertising uses information about what a specific computer/individual searched on in the past and uses that non-personally identifiable information to target advertising. Although there is some risk of governmental or regulatory actions taking the steam out of behavioral targeting unless current privacy concerns are thoroughly addressed through industry self-regulation, there is a good chance that some form of search-centric BT will be available to you as a marketer. One of the first places you should consider tapping the power of behavioral targeting is within search.

For advertising that is shown anywhere other than a SERP, prior user (searcher or visitor) behavior often provides a better way to target an ad than using contextual methods. For example, when you read news sites, most of the stories you are reading don't tell Google, Yahoo, or Microsoft's ad servers much about your interests other than the fact that the story you are reading was sufficiently interesting to bring you to the page. You may not even be engaged in reading the story, or you care only about the headline and first couple of sentences.

Given that you can buy searchers directly from the SERP, you may wonder why you should be interested in targeting them later by following them around and showing them text links or other ad formats. The reason is simple: Most of the searchers didn't click on your ad, and even among those who did, the vast majority didn't convert to meet any of your primary success metrics within a given browsing session or even during that day. So, if you happen to have an amazing 20 percent click-through rate on your search engine ads, and you converted an amazing 10 percent of visitors to a lead or order (in e-commerce the average is under 3 percent), you'd still have an interest in reaching all the rest of the interested searchers who, for whatever reason, weren't ready or willing to commit. That's still 98 percent of the searchers you didn't convert yet (you converted 10 percent of the 20 percent you saw.) You'd certainly be willing to pay a decent CPC rate to capture that searcher even when he or she isn't searching that minute. Behaviorally retargeting against search behavior creates a win-win-win scenario. The publisher makes more money on inventory that was difficult to sell at a reasonable return; the prior searcher (now a surfer) sees a really relevant ad instead of another irrelevant one. Most important, we marketers have an opportunity to retarget a person who's in-market for our product or service.

My team and I have had success by working directly with several online ad networks to allow for behavioral retargeting of searchers. On these ad networks, you can retarget your prior visitors based on searchers who have visited your site already, either through paid or organic search. This kind of retargeting is perfect, because those who see the ads already know who you are. The downside of the network model is that you get to display ads only to those searchers you already displayed ads to before. This only gets you access to the 20 percent or fewer who visited your site. Most likely, the second way you'll be able to take advantage of behavioral search is through the search engines themselves on a CPC basis. I'm excited by the possibilities behaviorally targeting searchers will provide for marketers, which is why we've been testing it. By being able to reach your searchers after they complete their review of SERPs, you may be able to realize significant increases in reach and scale while maintaining or improving profitability. For example, web-based email is currently low-value inventory that could serve as an attractive location for behavioral search ads. All three search engines have huge email bases (Gmail, Hotmail, and Yahoo Mail), as well as large content areas that they either own or control. Should they choose to deploy behavioral search retargeting within their own properties in an easy-to-use CPC environment, marketers will be empowered to more effectively exploit these traditionally low-value areas.

Second-Tier Engines

In the North American market, some pay-per-click text ad vendors try to pass themselves off as search engines when in fact little if any of their advertising is served in response to consumer-generated search queries. Aside from some so-called "vertical marketplace" search engines where all the listings and content are about a specific industry or niche topic, if you don't see a search engine listed among the top ten engines in a report issued by one or more of the major tracking services, they probably don't have very much pure search engine traffic, even if the search engine vendor is an aggregator. Of course, once your paid placement marketing spend in Google, Yahoo, and Microsoft exceeds several hundred thousand dollars (or local equivalent), you may find that you are running out of available high quality pure search inventory, in which case even smaller players can make sense. To keep track of who is biggest and who is worthy of your time, search for the term *search engine* followed by one of these terms: *Hitwise*, *comScore*, or *Nielsen NetRatings*. Each of these vendors regularly update their lists of the most popular search engines.

Local Search and the Internet Yellow Pages

Think about your own search engine use. Many of the searches you perform have local intent, even if those searches occur in an international, multipurpose search engine such as Google. Differing research firms and analysts place the percentage of searches with local intent at between 15 and 40 percent. Regardless of where the actual percentage lies, local searches are sure to climb as mobile devices get more Internet-friendly. Later chapters discuss how to advertise in the major search engines when you have a local offering and also how to exploit IYPs (Internet Yellow Pages) and local directory offerings that may also make sense for your business.

Chapter 3

Essential Pre-Planning

Resist the temptation to jump directly into paid placement search engine marketing because if your site is not ready, you'll be wasting money. Just like a retail store being ready to accept traffic generated by flyers and mailings, your online presence must be ready to make the best possible use of visitors. Failure to be ready is an opportunity cost, a missed opportunity, as well as a poor reflection of your brand on visitors.

Is Your Site Ready?

Searchers are different from other visitors to your website. Searchers have a specific need, desire, or interest, and failure to reinforce and meet that need can cause the dreaded Back button click. You'll struggle to keep site abandonment or Back-click percentage as low as possible for online marketing. However, even though this book is about paid search advertising, there are many reasons to think of your site as an extension of the advertising you do in the search engines. Searchers begin their interaction with you at the ad level but end up on your site. Until your site is presentable, you must resist the temptation to open the floodgates of traffic or even start testing with your toe in the water.

Later in the book, Chapter 6, "Campaign Setup: Structuring Your Listings," is devoted entirely to landing pages and optimizing the user experience. However, many marketers need a head start when it comes to making any changes to their web presence. Frequently, web development initiatives take months, if not years, to get accomplished. If that's the case, you have some options, including microsites, which are small stand-alone websites dedicated to a subset of products or services or perhaps to a specific campaign or promotion.

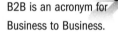

Note

B2B is an acronym for Business to Business.

One reason for recommending a microsite strategy is that it could be that you are trying to sell your customers from headquarters, and that's no good for either you or your customer. If as a potential customer you walked into the headquarters of the Gap, GE, Citigroup, or Verizon, your experience would be very different from that provided by a dedicated selling environment such as a retail store. Those retail stores, business unit sales offices, bank branches, and cell phone retailer outlets have been painstakingly designed to cater to your needs while simultaneously moving you toward an eventual purchase. Superfluous messaging is removed, and if the business has done its job, they have found a balance between too much information or not enough in both retail and B2B touch points.

Yet, nearly every search engine marketer is using their existing site to "sell" to searchers right there along with everyone else who archives at the site with a diverse mix of objectives, not just purchase intent. Same site, same navigation, same look, and so on. This approach may not seem bad for a Gap.com, which is first and foremost an online store. But if your site has evolved from static brochureware, it's difficult to shake off the trappings of that original site, particularly when a web presence has to serve multiple constituents.

Your site may have been originally designed (and perhaps redesigned several times) to address the information needs of prospects, returning customers, the press, analysts (investment or industry), your reseller and/or distributor channel, your in-house staff (as a resource), investors (if public), and perhaps influencers (who don't purchase but can influence the sale).

Search is critically important for most businesses, because people are increasingly using search at every stage of the buying cycle. If search is important to your business, you should probably stop selling to your search visitors from your headquarters. Start thinking like them, and design a user experience that balances your needs to sell against their needs to select the best solution for their needs.

Although nearly every marketer understands this argument, internal obstacles often conspire to prevent them from taking appropriate action. Many protest that their IT departments and tech teams are resource-constrained and that it might take years to get any additional pages put up on the site. Fortunately, microsites allow you to provide a more personalized user experience without imposing any real burden on your internal operations.

What Is a Microsite?

A microsite is a search-specific web presence that includes features and functionality appropriate for targeting searchers. It's highly likely that you've seen some microsites yourself, particularly if you've searched within education, credit card, mortgage, cable/satellite, or cell phone markets. B2B and general lead-generation markets are also chock-full of highly focused microsites providing minimal distractions and just enough information to get visitors excited.

Microsites need not involve your IT department at all (assuming you have the latitude to test marketing campaigns without their blessing). Most search marketing agencies have departments, technology, and expertise specifically designed to help marketers develop such microsites. Even if your IT team is fully behind your microsite project, it may still make sense to use the tools and technologies developed by your search agency instead of pulling together what you need from different technology vendors and having your IT team integrate everything together for the first time.

Search marketing agencies aren't the only players offering expertise in deploying microsites. Performance-based and lead-generation firms have made great strides in developing them. Many affiliate marketers have also become quite accomplished at developing and deploying microsites.

Is Your Competition Brilliant or Bogus?

The high visibility offered by top rankings in the search engine results pages (SERPs) of Google, Yahoo, and Microsoft search has interested top executives because of the upside potential for increased sales, market share, and other tangible benefits to your organization. Such interest has highlighted the importance of search engine marketing and your organization's position within the SERP relative to your competition. Because rankings in the sponsored listings portion of the SERP are driven by a real-time, pay-per-click (PPC) auction, competitors whose listings might be less relevant to the interest of searchers can elbow their way to the top if they are willing to spend enough. This results in an interesting scenario. At the top of sponsored PPC search results sit two kinds of marketers: brilliant ones and total lunatics. Which do you want to be?

In the early days of PPC auctions, it was relatively easy to keep track of what your competitors were paying for keywords, because the search engines publicly disclosed keyword prices. But today, the bid landscapes have become nearly completely opaque "black boxes." Now, you don't have the same information about how changes to your bid will influence position within the search results or even if changes you see are due to your actions, the search engine algorithm, or the actions of your competition. Consequently, knowing what you are paying and knowing your own return on investment (ROI) doesn't tell you whether you're bidding against a brilliant marketer or a total lunatic. Even if you could look at the competitive bid prices, you won't have enough information to evaluate your competitors' strategies. They might or might not have good reason to bid as highly as they do for certain keywords.

One typical scenario is this: Every time you raise your keyword listing cost per click (CPC) bids in an attempt to get a higher position in the results (an action that usually results in additional clicks) while also keeping the bid increases modest (to maintain your ROI), your competition raises its bids, too. They might be acting irrationally (by maintaining a reserve CPC price significantly above yours), or their results might be considered more relevant by the search engine, and thus be the beneficiary of lower click prices provided by the search engine algorithm. (Google awards such a benefit when a marketer's paid search listings have what it calls a high *Quality Score*.)

To learn which is the case, you'd need to know a number of things, such as actual billed CPC (which may differ from your bid due to the search engine policies of "auto discounting" to charge you only enough to archive the position you qualify for), conversion rate from click to lead or sale, the quality of the customer the keyword generates, the profit margin on the kinds of goods or services your competitor sells, and whether it's factoring in offline conversion when it allocates budget to spending on search engines. Your competitor may have done an analysis to determine how searchers typing in a given keyword are influenced to move down the conversion path (increased awareness, purchase intent, or lagged conversion analysis). Another bid behavior influencer is the size of your competitors' keyword lists. Smaller lists allow them to concentrate on fewer alternatives and therefore spend a larger percentage of their budgets on each word.

To truly evaluate your competitors' campaign performance in all three engines, you'd also need to know the competition's CTR by position and whether they set a daily budget cap below the maximum inventory available for that keyword per day (meaning that there might be 400 clicks available that day but they have set a daily budget sufficient to only buy 200 and are therefore only being served half the time). Plus, it would help to know if the keyword was purchased on a broad, phrase, or exact-match basis. With enough information, you might be able to at least estimate the price your competitors pay to be one position above or below you. If you could get all of this data, you'd probably still not have enough information to determine their rationality, so you need to have a strategy that works either way.

The brilliant marketer knows how much to bid on every keyword and why he's bidding for that price/position combination. The search marketplace is filled with choices in bid, keywords, and targeting variables, such as those governing when (day-parting) and where (geo-targeting) a given paid listing will be displayed. When an additional dollar is available to spend, you should know ahead of time where that dollar should be put for maximum return. Some campaign management solutions can predict the relative return of moving bids around, but it's not an easy calculation because of the rational and irrational bidder mix.

The lunatic almost always makes bid decisions based purely on position, even in hybrid auctions such as AdWords where bid is only one factor influencing position. (Predicted click-through rate [CTR], what Google calls a Quality Score, also drives position.)

What drives irrational bidders to bid for position, and are they really irrational? That's an interesting question to ponder.

Reasons a company might bid to extreme prices on certain keywords might include:

- The CEO/president/marketing VP says they have to be number one (or two or three) in the search results for this *power* keyword. Usually, this decision is made without factual backup, so it qualifies as an irrational bid choice.

- The marketer has a large marketing budget and "going all out" on all his keywords represents a fraction of the cost of television, radio, or print advertising. A million here, a million there, no big deal. This strategy may seem irrational, but television and other mass media ad effectiveness is shrinking. One rationale for such excessive spending might be that the increase in branding and/or engagement received from top-ranked listings is well worth the money spent.

- The marketer has a very small list of keywords that precisely target his desired audience. Given a small list, a marketer may feel he has no choice but to bid very aggressively on those keywords.

- The ad agency is managing the campaign, and the traditional or interactive agency media team knows very little about search, so it simply tells the search engine sales or account reps to manage to a specific position or to use simple bid management technology that adjusts your bids in the search engines automatically based on settings or formulas to maintain a given position. Agencies often don't have the workforce allocated to truly understand the nuances of a real-time auction marketplace for clicks, where all clicks are not created equal.

- A marketer or agency is running the campaign as a portfolio. As long as there are high-yield keywords in the campaign, it's willing to act very irrationally on other keywords on their list simply to maintain scale, even if the marginal profit on some keywords is negative. The negative profit will be concealed in the averages reported to the executives and therefore hidden from view.

A truly brilliant marketer with a direct ROI and profit-maximizing campaign strategy may in some cases look like a lunatic, based on his bidding behaviors. If he has great conversion, profit, and lifetime customer value and has built a media mix allocation model (which calculates the value of all advertising in concert as well as the individual impact of each element of media) that is constructed with an understanding of the buying cycle, he may be willing to dramatically escalate bids.

Whether the competition is an empowered brilliant marketer or a total lunatic, the problem is the same. If you want to improve your search results based on a keyword but a bid increase made to gain position always results in a bid war, consider your options:

- Investigate keywords that won't stimulate bid wars.

- Seek opportunities in other engines. Yahoo, Microsoft, and Ask are not your only options. You have others—not as many as you'd like perhaps, but some.

- Get better CTR from your ads. Sometimes getting a better CTR is more powerful than raising a bid. Today, all major search engines use hybrid auctions that use a predicted CTR to calculate position, so don't overlook the economic benefits provided by making your ad and landing page as relevant to your searchers as possible.

With hundreds of thousands of marketers in search campaigns already and more joining every day, it's increasingly important to control campaigns in a way that combines wisdom (strategic insight) and intelligence (the ability to see trends and learn quickly as data becomes available). All the major engines are moving to hybrid bidding systems. Consequently, it's ever more important to understand how buying clicks in an auction is unlike the buying processes of other media.

Metrics and Formulas in Marketing Goal Reviews

Clear objectives, effective measurement, and appropriate metrics are critically important for all marketing efforts. You can't run and optimize search engine advertising unless you know what you want to achieve, and if you have more than one objective (which isn't unusual in a marketing campaign), you will need to build blended goals and objectives.

Search engine marketers have additional campaign metrics challenges. Typical search engine marketing (SEM) campaigns involve tracking hundreds or thousands of keywords simultaneously. Tracking post-click behavior (what the searcher does after arriving at your site) is complicated because such behavior changes somewhat based on the position of the ad at the time of the click. In the case of campaigns running across multiple engines with different syndication networks of other sites or smaller search engines (which the search engines build to supplement the traffic they have themselves) delivering different audiences who may prefer AOL over Google, the precise context in which the click was made impacts the resulting searcher behavior.

As all marketers do, you'll learn fairly quickly that not all search-result click-throughs are created equal. Some visitors to your site find what they are looking for; others just leave, clicking that dreaded Back button after you've paid to get them to visit your site.

The challenge is to translate your site's business objectives into campaign objectives based on the right metrics. Metrics help you get the most out of your campaign, so make sure you understand how to pick those that fit your needs. The most common SEM and broader online marketing metrics are cost per order (CPO), cost per action

(CPA), return on advertising spend (ROAS), and return on invest-ment (ROI). In the interests of sharing best practices, let's review the common metrics, how they interrelate, and where they come from. However, keep in mind that all these metrics are observed and observable metrics. Much of the benefit of any marketing or adver-tising campaign is challenging to observe and measure for a variety of reasons. This means your true ROI may be significantly higher than your observed ROI.

CPO (Cost per Order)

Offline media, such as direct response television, direct mail, and print advertising, regularly use the CPO metric. Online banner cam-paigns are often judged based on this metric also. If you sell some-thing online, you might want to measure CPO and use the data to manage your campaign. You can measure CPO for a whole cam-paign or for individual keywords and engines. CPO targets can be set on a campaign-wide basis or even on a much more granular level, including by product or keyword.

Some marketers have a hard time setting a CPO target. It's not always easy. Since an order has an immediate profit value and an impact on the lifetime estimated value for a customer, you can use both the immediate profit and long-term value when you set your CPOs.

If you need a justification to set a CPO target higher, consider adding intangible values to your formula, such as brand building or gain of market share. In addition, if you know you often get phone or mail orders generated by your online efforts, adjust the measured CPO targets accordingly. By adding an adjustment factor to the measured CPO, the campaign can be managed closest to the actual CPO.

CPA (Cost per Action)

Orders are great as a metric, but tracking orders online is difficult, or even impossible, for some businesses. This may be because the business is a service, the item is not appropriate for online purchase, it's a high-involvement purchase (requiring many hours, days, or weeks of research), or the sales process for that product or service is complex. In this case, to differentiate between good and poor traffic, the campaign metric must be an action that correlates in some way to a future sale.

Actions that marketers may measure to determine traffic quality typically include registering for a newsletter, requesting information, downloading a white paper, reaching a particular page within the site, or visiting the "contact us" page. To select actions to measure, understand that those actions are proxies for what you're really after—revenue. Think about how your sales and revenue generation process works. If you have more than one action contributing to the likelihood of a sale, assign a weight to each action relative to the others.

ROAS (Return on Advertising Spending)

Measuring the ROAS is an appealing concept. It's the amount of revenue generated per dollar spent on advertising. For example, a ROAS of $1 means you're generating $1 in sales for every $1 spent on advertising; a ROAS of $10 means you generate $10 in sales for every $1 of spending. ROAS is a useful metric, but only for some marketers. If your profit margin is the same or very similar across products, the ROAS can be quite appropriate as a campaign metric.

With a predictable profit margin, it's easy to set a target ROAS. For example, if your profit margin is 25 percent and your ROAS is $4, you are breaking even (spending all your profit on marketing spend). If your ROAS is $8, half of your profit goes toward customer acquisition.

Of course, ROAS does not take into account lifetime value; it simply looks at the return for the initial order. When using ROAS and all these metrics, keep in mind that gross profit doesn't take into account your overhead, allowances for returns, bad debt, and so on.

ROAS starts to break down when there is a large variation in profit margin on products or if the sale of some products tends to predict a higher lifetime value. For example, an online office supply store may have a lower margin on office phones than on binders, but customers who buy binders may be more likely to order again. Neither factor is taken into account with ROAS.

ROI (Return on Investment)

It would be hard to find a more overused term in marketing than ROI. True ROI is difficult to accurately measure and calculate, and some marketers use revenue to calculate ROI, others use immediate profit (on a particular tracked sale), and others truly try to determine the holistic return on any invested dollar. Most marketers use gross profit when calculating ROI, and that is a great start, so feel free to start there, too. However, in the long run, if you really want to know the long-term profit generated by an investment in advertising, marketing, or any other activity, you need to capture all sorts of information that is more difficult to find because true return on investment means total return.

The slipperiest of variables is *lifetime value* (LTV), which is how much profit a particular customer or type of customer contributes to the bottom line over time. Then there are factors that could influence profit negatively, which sometimes get left out of a lifetime value formula that looks exclusively at revenue generated over time, such as how often that customer calls the tech support line or how often he or she returns items after purchase.

If you don't have access to more sophisticated data, leave out complicated metrics such as lifetime value, and use the immediate ROI based on the purchase transaction that occurs online (or offline).

The ROI formula is (profit − cost)/cost. For example, if you spend $100 advertising an electric stapler and sell $800 worth of staplers on which you make $300 in gross profit, your ROI using the immediate profit is ($300 − $100)/$100, resulting in an ROI ratio of 2 (some prefer to use percentages—in this case 200 percent). You put in a dollar and get out a net of two dollars.

ROI is often the metric used when setting CPO and/or CPA targets for a campaign. After all, you probably want to set your CPO or CPA at a level where the ROI is acceptable.

Putting It All Together

These metrics and formulas are tools allowing marketers to make better decisions about marketing by shedding light on the good and bad portions of a campaign. Marketers who understand and use these tools will outperform those operating in the dark. A campaign can have objectives that are measured using more than one of the discussed metrics. If you sell products but also have a monthly newsletter, you can set both CPO and CPA objectives and even meld the two together by assigning weights. If 1 in 20 people who sign up for a newsletter eventually place an order, a conversion from a newsletter subscription is worth 5 percent of a sale. I'll discuss the specifics and rationale behind blended or multivariable holistic metrics later in Chapter 5, "Direct Response and Branding Metrics."

Where Does Search Fit in Your Media Plan?

If you are like most marketers, you have separated your brand advertising, direct response advertising, and public relations budgets in your media plan. You may be wondering where to put PPC search. Most marketers put PPC search into the direct response budget. However, I propose that the current system of evaluating direct response media on a purely direct response (DR) basis and evaluating brand marketing based purely on lift in brand metrics or "demographic/psychographic fit" results in mismanagement of spending, poor budget allocation decision making, and failure to take media interaction effects into account. Media interaction effects describe the process of one form of advertising changing the impact of another form. These effects are especially important (and pronounced) in the context of search marketing, because consumers of nonsearch media such as TV, radio, and print often express a subsequent desire to learn more about a given advertised product by entering a query into a search engine.

Sure, the Holy Grail is a media mix model that analyzes the impact of all media on eventual sales, profit, and LTV. However, those models are too complex (perhaps needlessly complex) for most marketers to master. The practice of separating different marketing channels into discrete categories is called *siloing*, and it made sense when media was far less interactive than it is today. The first marketing silos that need to be smashed and obliterated are the brand budget silo and the DR budget silo, as well as any budgets for interactive media residing in another agency. Three budgets, three marketing agencies or teams, several sets of objectives, none of which fully reflect the way the consumer arrives at a purchase decision and finally becomes a customer (or returning customer). Could things get any crazier than this?

As if the mega-budget silos for brand, DR, and interactive weren't bad enough, there are additional budget silos for PR and promotions. Your web presence, and search in particular, aren't simply new forms of media. Search traffic (both organic and paid) is the result of consumer behavior that is more often than not stimulated through exposure to media, advertising, PR, or word of mouth (WOM). Nonsearch media, when purchased on a CPC basis, such as contextual or behavioral clicks, are also acted upon in a way representing consumer choice. In all CPC media, consumers who have better things to do with their time opt to click on your ads. The simple act of clicking on your ad is an expression of interest. So the landing pages you present, your site presence, and all the content you provide are critical to your marketing efforts. Failure is not an option, and in the same way that offline retail advertising drives consumers into a store to "check it out," and B2B advertising drives potential buyers to engage via phone, Internet, or in person, your website and all the media that drive visitors must be working in concert.

Brand marketing, direct response, PR, promotions, and search all share the same end-goal: a profitable enterprise that is acquiring new customers and is maximizing the revenue and profit from all customers (*high share of wallet*). The philosophies for the different marketing disciplines diverge primarily with respect to the best way to accomplish goals and measure the effectiveness of a current campaign.

No single media, ad, or marketing discipline generates purely direct response or branding impact. All media and advertising deliver some combination of marketing value to the organization. In search and online auctioned media, using either direct response or brand metrics alone results in a non-optimal campaign because the bid prices and the advertising messages are lopsided. Specific campaign budgets will fail to take into account metrics that actually lead to eventual purchases or increases in profit and long-term revenues.

The reason PPC search marketers must be among the first to take an integrated approach to marketing is that in an auction media marketplace, failure to bid appropriately when your competition is behaving more holistically means they will win in the long term. The solution is not a simple portfolio campaign in which your high ROI keywords subsidize those keywords with lower conversion rates or ROI. The correct way to address your campaign planning is to be customer-focused. Only by understanding the way your customers buy can you hope to spend your money effectively by positively influencing these customers.

The holistic search solution is about much more than appropriate bidding: It's also about messaging. Someone who isn't ready to buy responds negatively to call-to-action messages targeted towards late-stage, buy-funnel prospects. Early-stage buyers need information, and they need to be educated about why your product or service should be "top of the list" in their final consideration. If you are a value, service, luxury, prestige, or price player, your messaging should be consistent throughout the buy cycle.

If you look at the SERPs and find that your competitors are ahead of you, it may not be because they have better conversion rates or are irrational bidders. They may just have a more holistic approach to search marketing, having moved beyond a "search engine sales," direct response-only budgeting process to a holistic brand/DR hybrid.

Tracking and Bidding

Now that you know generally how the PPC search engine advertising systems work, you know how to categorize your budget and (at least initially) how you'll measure your return. It's time to think about just how you'll track and then how your tracking data empowers your bidding strategies.

The most common way to manage bids (manually or in an automated, real-time basis) is through tying post-click behaviors to the listings that brought visitors to your site. (I say listings, not keywords, because there are many ways to set up a keyword-triggered search ad, which is covered in the remainder of this book.)

Earlier in this chapter, I discussed some metrics you might want to use to measure and define success in your search advertising campaign. Many of those metrics can be tied to online behaviors, particularly for e-commerce marketers. E-commerce marketers can track online behaviors with a remarkable level of precision, typically by programming web analytics or campaign management software to set a cookie (a tracking ID) in the searcher's browser when that search arrives at the marketer's site. This cookie is anonymous but can be tied back to the listing on which the searcher clicked. By monitoring all the clicks, the current prices paid for listings, and the resulting behaviors, a human or a software program can begin to understand the relative profitability of one listing over another. The search engines often provide such marketers with built-in web analytics functionality, but many marketers feel far more comfortable using an independent third-party campaign management solution or web analytics platform because they prefer to keep sensitive details about their commerce operations completely private.

The diversity of formulae that can be applied to your bidding strategies is fairly significant. In a nutshell, through either a manual or automated means, you should understand the following data for a listing:

- A listing's ability to deliver against your metric (ROI/ROAS/CPA)

- A listing's volume potential (if you bid more or had a higher position, would there be significant volume increases?)

- A listing's elasticity (do competitors respond to increased bids on your listing, or can you gain position through aggressive bidding?)

There is more that you could factor in. You could include a more comprehensive tradeoff analysis of one listing versus the other that would require both the marginal profitability of the clicks coming in as well as an estimate of what other opportunities were available.

The simplest way to think about buying clicks (that are in fact humans doing searches) is by thinking of the process in the way that a gambler would about the odds of obtaining a payout from a slot machine. No slot machine pays out after every pull. But a gambler would naturally prefer to use those machines more likely to provide a positive ROI. Good keyword-search advertising listings are like those slot machines. However, to get more clicks you have to bid more, which reduces marginal profit but may increase scale dramatically as well.

Chapter 4

Marketing Campaign Foundation

You can't build a great pay-per-click marketing campaign without a strong overall marketing plan and campaign foundation. If you have a business plan, you've probably already outlined your marketing foundation: mission statement, target market, unique selling points, and call to action. If you haven't, take just 15 minutes, or several weeks for a more comprehensive marketing plan, to discuss the following sections with your team.

To provide you with a consistent reference point, I'll be using a live campaign to illustrate both the strategic and tactical elements of a search marketing campaign. The venture I'll be using is www.We-Care.com, a venture my business partner and I co-founded as a way to give back to the nonprofit community. Although We-Care.com is a for-profit venture, it serves the nonprofit community at no cost to its members. You'll learn a bit more about We-Care through illustrations and examples.

Mission Statement

Your overall marketing mission statement is often derived from your company mission statement, or it might be exactly the same. What's the "30-second elevator speech" you'd tell someone who asked what your company does? Include the main benefit to your customers as well as a description of your product or service.

For example, "Company A saves medical clinics millions of dollars by providing access to a centralized patient database." Or, "Company B designs flower arrangements at wholesale rates for weddings and special events." Remember, every person who reads or hears your mission statement is a potential customer, referral source, or partner. Keep your message short. Include the chief benefit your company provides that will encourage potential customers to ask for more information.

Here's a sample mission statement for We-Care.com:

> *"We-Care.com is dedicated to empowering nonprofit causes to harness the purchasing power of their supporters to deliver millions of dollars of no-cost donation revenue through the application of technology and marketing."*

Goals Become Objectives

Your senior management (or perhaps you) has overall goals for the organization. Often the goals of an organization are an extension of the mission and are statements defining the outcome that the organization is trying to accomplish. For example, your marketing goal may be to become recognized as a leader in the online search engine marketing industry. Or the goal for We-Care.com might be to empower as many nonprofit causes as possible to supplement their donation revenue using passive, no-cost donation revenue.

Unlike goals, objectives are precise and measurable outcomes and always have a deadline associated with them. Essentially, objectives are the targets for actions taken to support the completion of a goal.

Converting goals into marketing objectives for a search engine marketing campaign may seem simple, but there are often many measurable metrics, all of which contribute in some way to the achievement of the overall goal you have set. Therefore, the best way to accomplish this conversion is to break the goals down into quantifiable stages and steps while also assigning a time period to the stage or step.

So, assume that We-Care.com will have paid search ad campaigns running both to attract and acquire nonprofit causes to sign up for its free online marketplace, while also advertising for new users to select a cause from the listed nonprofits and either register or make a purchase. In this case, several objectives could be created for different segments of the campaign, or the objectives could even be used in tandem on the same campaign. Consider the following objectives:

- Acquire 300 new nonprofit partners at a cost of $30 or less per new registered cause during 2009.

- Maintain a cost-per registered new shopper/supporter of $2 or less for the entire month of December.

Both of these objectives are tangible, measurable, and time-limited. The first has a fixed cost associated with its achievement; the second, although open-ended in terms of its final cost, is a concrete objective that can serve as a benchmark against which the health of the search campaign can be measured.

Chapter 9, "Campaign Setup: Conversion Pages, Bids, and Budgets," will cover more about how technology analytics and campaign management platforms can both measure objectives and (using more sophisticated technology) maintain your campaign within your stated objectives.

Target Market Definition

Describe your preferred buyers, customers, or prospects. To help you with this, look at your current customers (or those of your competitors, if you have a new business). Consider demographics such as sex, age, marital status, job title, and job industry, if applicable.

Also consider psychographics, which are the lifestyle behaviors and attitudes of your ideal customers. This information gives you an understanding of your prospects' potential buying decisions and patterns. Armed with this insight, you'll be better able to address any concerns or questions and then guide site visitors through your site, either leading to a directly measureable online purchase or other positive event. Indicators as to which psychographic categories your prospects may fall into may include activities and purchases made in relation to business/education, health/fitness, and recreation/leisure.

Both demographics and psychographics can provide you with additional color on the people you are trying to reach. More information is always better when designing an effective advertising campaign. Your entire campaign would be dramatically different if you market a car to 16 to 25 year-old men who play extreme sports, as opposed to 35 to 45 year-old married women, with children, who subscribe to parenting magazines. Depending on your business, it's likely that you'll have multiple target markets, and often each will require a slightly different strategy and perhaps even different messages.

The more you know about your ideal customers, the better you can communicate with them and develop a relationship. Relationships are key to both initial and repeat sales.

Sample target markets for We-Care.com might include:

- Nonprofits with more than 300 supporters
- Online shoppers who spend more than $2,000 per year on travel and products
- Corporations that support nonprofit causes

Each of these target markets has the potential to deliver a specific revenue source to the venture, yet effectively reaching these three markets requires a different plan. Rarely will one form of media or advertising effectively reach each of several target markets, so tactically and strategically any plan must be evaluated against its ability to reach one or more of the groups.

Call to Action

What do you want people to do on your website once they get there? Do you want different visitors to do different things based on the target market they are within, their demographic/psychographic profile, or the search terms they select? Isolate your primary business goal to determine your primary *call to action*. A call to action is the next step you want your visitors to take; it'll more than likely be revenue-oriented, which means getting visitors to buy something, register, or contact you.

Under your primary call to action, list secondary ones. Think about levels of visitor communication that enhance your business, even if immediate traceable sales aren't produced. For example, consider the following as possible, important secondary objectives: increasing subscriptions to your online newsletter, contact by the press that results in articles in the media, new distribution partnerships or reseller channels for your products, visits to your site's "contact us" page, phone calls, or brochure requests. Every business will be different and so will every site. Prospects and customers have different points of interaction with every business. These are often called *touch points*. Use the touch points you establish to enhance your branding or otherwise strengthen relationships with your prospects and customers.

A sample call to action list for We-Care.com suitable for use in a search marketing campaign could include:

- Primary objective: Increase percentage of visitors who exit through to a merchant from 4 percent to 6.5 percent within the next month.

- Calls to action:

    - Primary: Shop at Target.com (a participating online merchant) and get free shipping today.

    - Secondary: Support your nonprofit cause, find a merchant among 700 top online stores.

    - Secondary: Register for specials email newsletter.

Review the designated calls to action before, during, and after you execute a keyword text link campaign on search engines. Individual search engine ad listings can be created for each call to action (or you could combine a few actions into one listing). For each call to action, your keywords, ad copy, and landing pages can all be modified to continually improve your campaign performance. By tracking the performance of each ad listing, you'll be pointed to the ones you'll want to re-evaluate. Rework poor performers; emulate high-performing ones. There isn't a lot of room in a paid search ad for discursion, so it is important to keep focused on the benefit and call to action that you believe will resonate best.

You can identify primary and secondary calls to action for nearly every page of your entire site. To achieve the best results from your online marketing efforts, however, apply this list to each major content page of your website.

The Buying Funnel and Search

A call to action works only when the consumer or searcher is ready to answer this call. But ask yourself this: Are you always ready to buy, register, call, or subscribe? I didn't think so. Neither is your target audience. Remember Marketing 101 and those sales books that talk about the buying cycle? They have a point well worth heeding when it comes to search marketing: Not every visitor is ready to buy all the time, even after they have searched to solve a very specific need or to find a very specific product. This doesn't mean these people are worthless visitors to you, however. They may actually be very close to becoming valuable customers or are several months away from becoming them.

One useful construct for representing the movement of people from casual consideration to commitment/conversion is the buying funnel. What is extraordinary in search is the degree to which it is possible to infer the location of searchers in this funnel based on their selection of keywords. (This topic is discussed in additional detail in the "Qualitative Method" section.)

Normally, I rant and rave about measuring conversions so you can optimize your campaign around orders, conversions to leads, or other monetizable actions that bring you a tangible return on the money you spend acquiring visitors. However, metrics such as ROI, ROAS, cost per order (CPO), cost per action (CPA), and lifetime value are just the beginning of the story for effective marketers. Effective marketers are mastering the buying funnel (the concept that describes the stages that purchasers go through on their way to making the final purchase decision) and how search delivers influence at every stage by educating site visitors, raising awareness, and improving the chances that your product, service, or company are still in consideration as the purchase decision process evolves. Marketers must embrace the reality that all the stages of the buying cycle must be taken into account when planning and executing search marketing campaigns, not just the final conversion. The evolution to this holistic view of the influence of advertising (search ads as well as others) will take time and be empowered through technology.

Different Phases of the Buying Cycles

As mentioned earlier, prospects within your target audience go through phases in the buying cycle online, just as they would in the offline world. To ignore this fact results in an inefficient site and an inefficient media campaign, regardless of traffic source (for example, search traffic, traffic from banners, or traffic from other media). Depending on your role within your organization, you may think differently about these "not ready to buy" phases.

Sales enthusiasts define the buying cycle as a continuum extending from attention, interest, conviction, desire, to close. Some marketers prefer to use a definition of the *marketing cycle* or *marketing life cycle*, and they use the acronym AIDA (attention, interest, desire, and action). Marketers are more likely to include branding metrics in their definition of stages while sales managers or VPs talk about the elimination of poor leads and the focus on those who are closer to making a purchase.

CRM marketers (those with an interest in maintaining relationships with pre-existing customers) have their own steps—reach, acquisition, conversion, retention, and loyalty—while brand-oriented marketers use lift in metrics such as *unaided awareness* and *purchase intent.*

Although the labels applied to the location of prospects within the buying cycle/buying funnel are varied, note that all these metrics are attempting to quantify, measure, or at least acknowledge that the customer goes through buying cycle/buying funnel stages, and that to be an efficient marketer you need to keep the buying process in mind when planning and executing campaigns. The same is true for search campaigns—and perhaps even more so, because CPCs are getting expensive and you need to know if they are worth it.

As a manufacturer, brand marketer, or marketer with a distribution consisting of retailers, resellers, online merchants, or other distribution outlets, you definitely want to reach consumers in the early stages of their buying cycle. As a retailer, your preference may be to catch consumers after they have passed through the early stages of the cycle and are ready to buy, or at least ready to register for a newsletter that will allow you to further market to them. So the extent to which you take the early stages of the buying cycle into account depends on your overall marketing objectives. There are two ways to factor in the early stages of the cycle—one is more quantitative, the other more qualitative.

Quantitative Method

The *quantitative method* of factoring the buying cycle in a search engine marketing (SEM) campaign involves the use of survey data or other information about post-click user behaviors to determine which stages of the buying cycle the visitor is in.

The next chapter will discuss blended post-click behavior metrics and the concept of branding proxies such as the Branding Effectiveness Index (BEI) that I created. This index lets you assign values to different post-click behaviors based on their impact on the visitor's likelihood to buy (and therefore their value to you). By using this blended metric as the objective around which you optimize your search campaign, and adjusting the values of the different measured activities, you can adjust the price or position of each listing in your campaign based on the traffic's true value to you. Each listing will deliver a mix of immediate buyers and those in earlier stages of the buying cycle (as well as a few completely disinterested people who clicked on a listing without reading it carefully).

By taking buying stages into account, you can optimize for the true value of a campaign. The challenge is in setting the values of actions so they accurately reflect the value to your organization. Brand marketers might do a site *intercept survey* (a sample of site visitors who receive a survey invitation while visiting your site) to determine what actions on their sites resulted in a lift in purchase intent or awareness. A direct marketer might use hard data, attributing a value to a catalog request or a newsletter registration based on how many of those requestors actually make purchases.

Qualitative Method

The *qualitative method* to address the early-stage versus late-stage visitor involves using linguistic logic. As mentioned earlier, powerful inferences may be made about visitors' location within the buying cycle/buying funnel based on the keywords used to access information. Some keywords will likely indicate the mindset of the searcher sufficiently to adjust your CPC for that keyword to reflect early-stage visitors whom you still value at some level. For example, let's illustrate a typical search marketing campaign containing a variety of keywords:

- *laser printer*: This is a generic term attracting a population of searchers that is likely a mix of early- and late-stage visitors.

- *laser printer review* or *laser printer compare*: Selection of these keywords likely indicates that these searchers are not quite ready to buy; however, they may be susceptible to marketing messages that concern the benefits of a particular type of laser printer.

- *cheap laser printer*: These searchers are probably close to the purchase stage but are demonstrating price sensitivity.

- *best laser printer*: These searchers are likely not quite ready to buy; however, they may be susceptible to marketing messages that concern the benefits of a particular laser printer.

- *hp 1200 laser printer*: These searchers may be close to purchase due to the specific model number in the query.

Valuing Site Visitors

Should you start valuing your site visitors differently? The answer depends on your business and if you are likely to be the beneficiary of the attitude or preference changes you facilitated during the early buying stages. You don't want to contribute to moving visitors through the buying cycle if they ultimately buy from your competition, but you may want to do so if you are a multichannel retailer and have data indicating that research done online results in an offline purchase through your retail outlet. Of course, manufacturers benefit along with their distribution channels when they use SEM, regardless of whether you consider this benefit in terms of branding, building awareness, lifting purchase intent, competitive positioning, or facilitating the sales cycle.

So, take a moment to think about your marketing objectives. Review how much emphasis you would like to place on the earlier stages of the buying cycle. Then determine how best to modify your current campaign objectives to include early-stage visitors. Addressing the needs of early-stage buyers may be one of the best investments you can make.

Successes You Can't Measure

You can measure an amazing diversity of post-click behaviors, and it's particularly easy to link the behavior of site visitors coming in from paid search listings to online conversions. However, there are a bevy of successes that are occurring as a result of your paid search campaign that you can't measure easily. Often these conversions are happening online and simply can't be tracked; other times conversions are happening through other channels and similarly cannot be tracked.

Lost Cookies

Cookies are small data files, passed from a web server to a browser, that reside on the user's hard drive. Online publishers use them for purposes related to making it easier for users to access their sites; for example, the ability of a site to "remember" users, saving them from the chore of entering their usernames and passwords each time they go to the site. Marketers use cookies to track users' behavior. Cookies are also used heavily by advertisers and marketers within web analytics and campaign management software to "close the loop" in respect to understanding which ad banner impressions (when a banner is served on a specific page that is being read by a visitor) and subsequent clicks resulted in sales, registrations, or other positive actions. However, due to cookie loss (which happens when users delete cookies, often at the end of a browsing session, daily, weekly, or monthly due to a software program installed to do so), no tracking system that uses them is perfect, nor does it need to be. As long as the majority of cookies are active and usable, these cookies act as a representative (you hope) sample of the overall visitors received. However, in order to continue to use the systems that rely on cookies as data sources, you need to accurately predict what percentage of cookies you are missing.

A recent Jupiter Research report found that "as many as 39 percent of online users may be deleting cookies from their primary computers every month, undermining the usefulness of cookie-based measurement and leaving many site operators flying blind." Similarly a June 2007 report from comScore stated "approximately 31 percent of U.S. computer users clear their first-party cookies in a month (or have them cleared by automated software), with an average of 4.7 different cookies being observed for the same site within this user segment."

The client data my team has observed indicates that the cookie loss problem may not be quite as dire as all that... yet. But the trend toward blocked or deleted cookies is clearly increasing. Although Microsoft's recent browser releases and Google's Chrome browser all treat cookies differently, it is clear that the general trend is in the direction of making cookie deletion easier for users to accomplish.

The proliferation of spyware and unwanted adware has resulted in a surge in popularity of spyware removal programs. Many of these programs also remove third-party cookies. Additionally, many Internet security software packages include cookie blocking, cookie removal, or cookie management features that are turned on by default.

Without third-party cookies, many industry technologies would have to rely on alternative means to measure ad performance. Cookies, like an email or a postal address, or a customer phone number, can be used by marketers wisely or poorly. Instead of using cookies to enhance the user experience with highly targeted advertising, some have instead focused on short-term gains by collecting personally identifiable information in a cookie, which has caused some to cross the line between justifiable tracking and privacy-intrusive monitoring.

One more word on cookies: When you look at data on measured conversions, be sure to factor in the reality that cookies may have been blocked or deleted, making the true reckoning of ROI and conversions much more difficult than your cookie-based data would suggest. Also be aware that an apparent loss of cookies may in fact represent another kind of user behavior. For example, cookies reside on specific computers and even in specific browsers (IE, Firefox, Chrome, and so on). Therefore a searcher moving from a work computer to a home computer in the midst of researching a purchase manifests itself like a deleted cookie if this searcher converts to a sale at home (on a different computer) after having interacted with your PPC search listings while at work.

Long Lag Times

A related issue to the loss or deletion of cookies is the phenomenon of long lag times occurring between the search visit and the conversion. The standard cookie expiration length is typically 30 days. When combined with random timing of cookie deletion, longer lag times between search and conversion also result in less accurate data.

Consequently, some of the positive impact of your search campaign may occur so far out in the time domain as to make it unlikely that you'll be able to see any conversion data at all. Plus, the data you do see will represent only a fraction of the true value of the true impact of your campaign due not only to data leakage, but also the less measureable influence on a consumer to increase the likelihood of an eventual sale.

Offline Conversions

As mentioned in Chapter 3, "Essential Pre-Planning," online and offline marketers often make decisions in a silo, failing to look at the possibility that some data isn't in front of them. But more and more CMOs (chief marketing officers) and marketing vice presidents are beginning to see the folly of separating business units that are perceived or advertised under the same brand. Clearly, consumers see the brand as one entity, even if profit and loss statements and marketing budgets are maintained separately within the organization.

Being able to look beyond traditional "silos" is vital because consumers are influenced by a wide array of different marketing channels. Study after study shows consumers use the Internet for research when making buying decisions. comScore has conducted studies for Yahoo, Google, and Performics/DoubleClick, which track the relationship between search and buying behavior. comScore's March 2006 study, conducted for Google, shows that 63 percent of those who purchased an item directly related to their search query completed the purchase offline, with just 37 percent making that purchase online.

It becomes even more fascinating when studies look at offline sales and estimate the importance of online site resources and information. A Shop.org study conducted by Forrester found that 22 percent of offline sales are influenced by the web. This figure represents nearly a quarter of total offline sales, and it will undoubtedly go up due to generational effects (as more and more young consumers emerge who have never known a world in which information wasn't instantly available at their fingertips) and the improved quality and availability of online information.

Clearly, the percentage of your customers who rely on online information before making offline purchase decisions will vary by industry geography and demographic target market. Multichannel merchants, which market goods and services to consumers through a multitude of channels that may include both online and offline stores or catalogs, must pay particular attention to the interaction of online information consumption and offline purchasing behavior. Each multichannel merchant must make its own decisions on how to treat these interaction effects. The most important question for most marketers is whether the information consumers find online influences them to select one product over another, choose one brand over another, or select the retail store to purchase from as a result of such exposure.

If the level of influence on these kinds of decisions is high, the web, and search in particular, becomes critical for not only the retailer but also the manufacturer. The manufacturer may not be able to rely on the retailers to do their selling for it and may need to dramatically increase its online presence while dealing with channel conflict issues, such as those that may occur when an identical good or service is offered at a variety of different distribution outlets with different terms of purchase.

Of course, data may show that even though consumers spend time online researching products and purchases, they don't change their behavior based on these interactions. In effect, the web may just remove friction from the product-researching process, allowing consumers to replace store visits by discussions with friends, magazine reviews, and library visits. I'm willing to bet, however, that brand, product, and store decisions are influenced by online behavior.

There are even more critical, immediate reasons why you should care if your business unit measures success based purely on measurable online conversions. You may have a problem, regardless of whether your online-only focus is because the business has siloed you into a separate unit or because your firm is currently an Internet "pure play" whose distribution of goods and services occurs exclusively online. If your competitors aren't siloed and have determined how to better measure or estimate the true impact of search on offline conversions, you'll get your you-know-what kicked, because your competitors' overall conversion rate may be dramatically higher than yours, enabling them to outbid you on key business-driving terms. If this is the case, your only recourse is to either bid irrationally, which may get you fired (or at least get you into trouble), or become such a brilliant merchandiser that your landing pages convert better online than those of your competitors do.

If you don't have serious conversion, operational cost savings, and margin advantages over your competitors, and they use a holistic view of online and offline conversion, as opposed to your myopic view that online-only conversions are the only thing that matters, you may be completely priced out of the positions that generate real volume for your business.

If you're a multichannel marketer and are either active at the corporate level or have been empowered by C-level executives (those with "C" in their title, indicating "chief-level") to manage search based on its true value to the business (net search profit), several options are available to strengthen your case that a more holistic view of media interaction effects is warranted. One commercially available option is comScore. Its new product, qSearch Retail, extends conversion tracking among comScore panelists (of which there are approximately 2 million people who have consented to have their online behavior monitored as part of a panel) to offline purchase behavior. With comScore data, you can gain a powerful understanding of how search and online behavior translates into offline purchases. comScore won't use its full online panel size for offline purchase tracking; instead, it's building smaller panels, based on specific recruited panel member behavior, particularly for the qSearch Retail product. Panelists will then be categorized by industry vertically (in cases in which they searched for keywords that relate to a category), making it easy for marketers to gain additional insight into their offline purchase behaviors.

You don't necessarily need comScore, however, to answer some key questions about the link between online search behavior and offline purchases. Multichannel merchants with catalogs have faced similar issues for years. Some of the catalog industry's best practices can be adapted for use in the online world, including:

- Customer tagging: Look at purchases, then marry the online cookie with the offline customer number or credit card data. Being able to make such a correlation provides positive proof of the influence of your online marketing campaign. The same consumer may shop through several channels.

- Offer codes: Unique offer codes can be provided for searchers to redeem via phone or in stores. Doing so will allow you to measure your online campaign's effectiveness beyond the online checkout process. Armed with that information you can focus on the keywords and engines that deliver phone sales as well as online sales.

- Unique pricing: Unique online pricing can also become a tracking code of its own, so when a person requests that price, it will be obvious that they must have seen the search landing page.

- Trackable phone numbers: Phone sales can be routed through a tracking system similar to the VoiceXML systems built specifically for the tracking of phone calls without use of coupon codes and often deployed as part of pay-per-call systems. This method is expensive but may be suitable for expensive or complex purchases where the cost of tracking can be high due to the high value of the sale and the high cost of the search clicks.

- In-store surveys: Survey your customers to gain better insight into how they use online media whether they searched for information on the products they are buying in-store and how online media influences their offline purchasing behavior.

- Anecdotal data: Ask your sales associates if people show up with printouts from the website or newspaper or other sources.

In the future, lines between online and offline purchasing behavior will blur even more. The closer that your search campaign strategy reflects your true search profit, the more confident you can be about that campaign driving maximum organizational profit.

Passionistas, Influencers, and Buzz

Who is your office geek considered most knowledgeable on technology products? My guess is that the office geek is an *influencer*—someone whose expert opinion is valued by his peers, especially in regard to purchasing recommendations—to many people in the office making technology purchase decisions (both corporate and personal). Search advertising reaches that influencer, and clearly no cookies set on his or her computer will be triggered in a shopping cart tracking model. The influencer's word of mouth may influence more than one purchase, and search results and the resulting time spent on your site may have influenced the influencer.

Sometimes the influencer is also highly passionate about a specific subject. In that case, many marketers prefer to call those people *passionistas*, who consume more content than the rest but also create content on sites that allow for contributions and comments.

It's highly likely that search and your site can influence influencers who create buzz among their friends, associates, and relatives. As a matter of fact, similar metrics (some call them micro conversions, I think of them as engagement factors) may identify both likely direct purchasers as well as influencers. For example, I'd be willing to bet that influencers have a higher than average thirst for information. So, an engagement metric (watching how many pages visitors see or how long they stay on the site) combined with your standard conversion metrics may be just perfect. If you get an influencer to read a lot about your product and stay on-site engaged with your brand and your message, you may have positively influenced the influencer.

Duncan Watts, a Columbia University sociology professor on sabbatical to work at Yahoo, takes the opposite approach and suggests that, "A rare bunch of cool people just don't have that power. And when you test the way marketers say the world works, it falls apart. There's no *there* there." Instead, he argues that the most important factor is to make your content easy to share to create a buzz about it. He debunks all the influencer research saying that on any particular topic anyone can be an influencer—you just need to get your message right. The irony of course is that Duncan's new employer, Yahoo, was the co-sponsor of the research regarding passionistas.

Either way, a lousy, uninteresting message isn't going viral, even between best friends. That brings us back to testing and perhaps creativity, something search marketers don't like to think about. However if you are paying thousands of dollars to get visitors to your site, including potential influencers, you may as well engage them.

Regardless of whether you are going to try to influence either a random influencer (as Duncan Watts would have you believe the buzz created by word of mouth spreads) or you believe that there are magic influencers and passionistas out there, you need to get everyone you can excited about your message.

PART II

Planning a Successful PPC Campaign Strategy

Introduction

No campaign succeeds without a plan. Part 2 of this book covers the planning and setup of campaigns, using Google as the foundation because of its dominant market share and because its creative and structural specifications have become the de facto industry standards in most cases. Once you launch your campaign, you'll be bidding for position in the search results for every one of your keyword and keyword phrase combinations. Getting the strategy and campaign setup as close to optimal before spending the first dollar on clicks can mean the difference between immediate success and significant retooling of a campaign after launch.

Chapter 5

Direct Response and Branding Metrics

You can't manage and optimize a campaign unless you measure the results. Over the years, the advertising community has split itself into two camps, each with their own set of metrics. Direct response marketers measure sales and leads that turn into sales (or those that don't). Rarely will you hear die-hard direct marketers use the words *branding* or *brand lift*. Similarly, although "awareness" is something a direct marketing campaign generates, direct marketers don't generally use the measure of awareness as a metric. The direct response marketer has a laser focus on measurable results and the media driving those results. Branders, on the other hand, have a whole set of metrics designed as proxies for success, which attempt to quantify the influence that marketing, PR, and advertising have on eventual purchase behavior. When conversions to leads, sales, or other positive behaviors can be tracked, direct marketers scoff at branding metrics, and branders fire back that direct marketers are too myopic, focusing only on obviously traceable behaviors.

ROI Is in the Eye of the Beholder

As online marketers, it's easy to get spoiled with the impression, click, and conversion data available at our fingertips. Search marketers are perhaps even more prone to get spoiled because clicks from searches tend to have the highest observable conversion rates. Search campaign reports let you watch those conversions occurring in almost realtime, plus we also have a bunch of additional post-click behaviors you can watch that may or may not be correlated with eventual conversion to leads or sales. You can watch not only every click into your sites from your search engine advertising but also every click thereafter until the visitor leaves your sites.

Every marketer wants to manage search marketing campaigns to maximize profit. Early in a campaign's lifecycle, this process starts out as a goal of achieving positive return on investment (ROI), which then evolves into a profit metric. Profit is not nearly as easy to measure as observable ROI. This is one reason why it's hard to imagine that your competitors, who may have locked in top SERP positions using the tactic of bidding significantly higher than you do for clicks, are running profitable campaigns. Instead, you might assume they are spending money on clicks providing a negative return. Your competitors might indeed be crazy, wasting their money on unprofitable clicks, or they might be measuring profitability and ROI differently than you do. In effect, ROI is in the eye of the beholder.

Imagine all the different ways you might choose to measure ROI or attempt to close the data loop to evaluate positive behaviors that correlate to sales, in order to more accurately measure profit from a campaign. For example, you might look at predictors of lifetime customer value, profit per order, offline conversion percentages, and so on.

ROI is this decade's buzzword. Yet the highest-ROI strategy is rarely a profit-maximizing strategy when it comes to paid search. Bidding less for keywords often improves the ROI at the sacrifice of customer volume. To run a business profitably, you must balance ROI and sales volume. This is called *profit maximization/optimization*.

Profit Maximization

The concepts underlying profit maximization go beyond SEM, into the realm of business and marketing best practices. Yet the more clients I talk with, the more I realize success metrics and strategies used for search are sometimes arbitrary and shortsighted. Worse, they may not be aligned with nonsearch marketing strategy and objectives. Admittedly, execution of search campaign optimization can be complex and daunting. As a marketer, your responsibility is to use metrics and objectives that drive profit. The marketing and profit objectives you select should be consistent across media, online and off.

Warning: The following can hurt your brain! But please don't be intimidated. MBAs need semesters of schooling to absorb the concepts underlying this analysis (it's been over 10 years since I first absorbed them at Yale). Luckily, I liked economics and use these concepts every day in my business and for clients. My objective is to explain and illustrate marginal profit and elasticity. If I confuse you, please let me know.

High ROI campaigns and ROI maximization sound wonderful. But in reality, they're hard to achieve. For example, you may know you can't really achieve volume maximizing ROI, because you run lots of listings in multiple engines. The highest ROI campaign possible is one in which you can have your best-converting listing at a minimum price (cost per click [CPC]). The cost per order/lead/action for this listing is the lowest you can go in the search marketplace; in other words, it is ROI *maximized*.

Let's assume that to acquire this very best listing, you spend $25 per month and drive $3,000 in sales at a 50 percent profit. Don't start celebrating yet. Where's the conversion volume? There may not be any at all. So you need more traffic, and you may be willing to accept lower ROI on broader, higher volume listings that—while they may not share the same ROI as your very best listings—provide marginal ROI that is still positive.

ROI Optimization and Profit Maximization Balance

Sophisticated search marketers balance ROI optimization and profit maximization. Imagine you have the perfect balance between traffic volume and ROI. In this scenario, you get high conversion volume (sales/leads/actions) and positive profit. On a listing-by-listing basis, you're lowering per-unit profit in exchange for additional click-through/sales volume delivering an increase in total profit.

Raise your media price (CPC or CPM) too high on a particular listing, given a particular conversion rate, and you'll get negative profit. Drop it too low and you'll miss out on the additional total gross profit produced by additional sales/leads/actions (*opportunity cost*). Economists would recommend you continue to spend more on traffic until the incremental (marginal) profit you earn by spending more drops to zero.

That's a theoretical solution. The real world is rarely that simple. Without complex marketing automation systems, a manageable way to move to a profit-maximizing campaign management strategy is to know your cost per order/lead/action across all marketing media, as well as where your target price for such media needs to be to make a reasonable profit.

How do you do this? Start by setting a specific goal, in terms of cost per order/cost per action (CPO/CPA) for your campaign (or by individual listing, if listings result in different products being purchased or address different profiles of the purchaser). Manage campaign listings around this CPO/CPA goal. You'll see almost immediately which listings deliver conversions at a rate close to your CPO/CPA goal, while simultaneously driving a high volume of conversions and traffic.

Your campaign management is probably based on some post-click conversion cost objective. Based on your CPO/CPA objectives and targets, you must (manually or automatically) move your bids up and down, causing some of your listings to oscillate in positions. The search engines generally place the top 1, 2, or 3 ads at the top of the screen and often syndicate those same listings to other search engines. Often the dynamic change in positions of your ad occurs right at the edge of the premium high position/heavily syndicated levels. For some of these listings, a small price increase may result in large click volume changes as your listing elbows its way above those of your competitors. This volatile and dynamic situation presents a profit-maximization opportunity. Consider the following scenario:

- Revenue per sale is $200 with a wholesale product cost (to you the merchant) of $130.

- The maximum CPO for your campaign (or group of listings) is set to $50, meaning you are targeting an order costing you no more than $50.

- Net profit per sale (after subtracting the $50 CPO) is $20.

- Given a specific conversion rate to sale for inbound clicks (let's assume a 4 percent rate), you are limited in the price you can bid for each click to $2 ($50 × .04).

- At $2 (all you can afford to pay), your ad listing's search results position tends to be 4 to 6 on average, is not heavily syndicated, and is low in visibility on the search results page, resulting in only 1 percent of searchers who see your ad clicking it.

- At 1 percent of the clicks, you currently get 50 orders per week.

- Total profit is $1,000 (50 × $20).

If you were to raise the allowable target CPO for your listing to $60, based on your conversion percentage, you would be able to raise your bid per click significantly to $2.40, which would likely raise your average position a couple of notches, perhaps to the top position. Because of the higher visibility of the top positions and the inclusion of your listing in more syndicated search engine partners such as AOL (which has a syndication relationship with Google), traffic and orders would increase significantly to 150 orders a week, with a new profit per sale of $10 and a total profit of $1,500 on that specific ad listing. In this scenario, advertising spending rises dramatically, but so does overall profit, even as the presale profit drops. This is an example of using the concept of profit maximization to control bidding for a single listing.

But wait. You don't have just one listing; you have lots of them, in many engines, plus other media opportunities. Assuming you have all the information you need to make decisions (by using killer web analytics) and an ability to execute campaign changes smoothly and efficiently (by not expending too much time and money on processes and analysis), you can profit-maximize your entire campaign at once, raising and lowering CPO targets to find the best trade-off between volume and profit.

Deciding where to put every additional (marginal) marketing dollar involves looking for the best deals all the time by knowing what's working best and at what price. Essentially, you're doing an efficiency and trade-off analysis, not only between listings and engines (comparing them to each other) but also across media types.

This approach is powerful and flexible. If you need to cut your budget, cut the least efficient media placements (the ones with the lowest ROI). Similarly, if you want to increase profitable revenues with more marketing spend, select listings with the highest ROI (preferably where the ROI drop is not large when you raise the CPC or position).

No one has perfect information about all their media buys at the most granular level. But the Internet (and some offline direct marketing media) lets you execute a media allocation method where you can

- Reduce spending on the least efficient element when trimming the budget.

- Add dollars to the most efficient media vehicle to get the biggest bang per buck.

- Generate a media spending analysis based on overall profit.

- Take all actions based on the marginal changes in profit (by going to the highest ROI campaign elements first when seeking volume plus efficiency).

Finding the "right ROI" and the "right profit-maximizing campaign" is where the fun begins. Where marketing, business, accounting, technology, and economics work together to optimize profit, the term *convergence* has a new meaning.

You may not have the tools and technologies to facilitate marketing automation and campaign effectiveness across, as well as within, media. But you can still use these concepts to implement a combination of analytics and automation to maximize profit within your search campaigns.

CPO, ROAS, CPA, Blended Metrics

Campaign metrics don't exist in a vacuum. The last section touched on how an allowable target CPO or CPA can be adjusted to find the right balance between those metrics, sales volume, and measured profitability. However, post-click success metrics can be much more complex. As you're working on an online marketing campaign with the objective of reaching certain post-click objectives, you need to be prepared for these complexities. Some combination of blended metrics, or perhaps a single metric, will become the relative benchmark by which you judge your campaign's effectiveness at the keyword, listing, and Ad Group level, as well as those of your overall campaign. You need to set ranges of allowable numbers for these metrics or at least understand how your campaign is faring in comparison with your objectives. Similarly, you need to be able to compare the performance of different ad listings and keyword combinations in your campaign to determine which ones are performing and which ones are lagging.

Instead of CPO or CPA, many marketers choose ROAS (return on ad spend) as their success objective, calculating their return based on revenue (not immediate profit or net contribution margin). ROAS percentage targets may need to be translated into target CPO targets using average order sizes. If the average order size changes over time, the CPO target changes to maintain the same delivered ROAS.

Not everyone is an e-commerce marketer with a shopping cart that can tally up the kind of income/revenue data used in the preceding analysis. In fact, most online marketers are not running shopping carts because the shopping cart concept is not appropriate for their business. These non-shopping-cart businesses include service businesses, B2B firms, local retailers, and even some high-ticket online retailers preferring a phone call to an online order. Therefore, your objectives might need to be broadened beyond CPO to cost per lead (CPL) or other CPA metric.

Given the diversity of possible metrics, the question then becomes, "what quantifiable value should you set for your post-click objectives?" Perhaps you are undertaking a search marketing campaign, an online marketing effort involving banners or pop-ups, or a combination of the two. Each will deliver against the objectives differently. Should you set the same objectives for all segments of your campaign or use different target objectives for each campaign segment?

By the way, if you haven't gone through an exercise to determine your CPO or CPA, nor thought about setting the objectives differently by campaign segment, don't despair. Nearly 50 percent of marketers I talk to are unsure of what to say when I ask them about their current CPO or CPA objectives. This is why such a large portion of this book covers metrics, measurement, and objectives setting. The payoff will be rewarding for you, because setting your CPO, CPA, or ROAS intelligently can result in huge gains in campaign efficiency.

If you haven't measured your actual CPOs or other metrics yet, now is a good time to start. You should begin by tagging all your listings uniquely with code from a web analytics or campaign management system in order to keep track of the CPCs, and then track your conversions by the individual listing producing them. The cost per action or order is the cost of the traffic divided by the number of actions. Each keyword listing with a significant volume of clicks and conversions will soon be giving you individual data. This data becomes your baseline that you'll subsequently "tweak" in the process of optimization. Of course, some listings will generate actions or orders less expensively than others. Even if you haven't yet set your CPO targets based on your business strategy, you can use your baseline as a guide and set CPO targets to immediately eliminate inefficient listings (those with unreasonably high CPOs).

Now back to the strategy of setting allowable CPO or CPA action metrics. The *allowable* is the target CPO or CPA metric by which the campaign is managed. Let's cover an example from e-commerce first. In e-commerce, marketers most often use the CPO as their primary objective (although they may use secondary objectives as well). If we look at CPO the way many catalog merchants do, we will set a CPO (or cost of customer acquisition) target allowable based on the average profit earned over the lifetime of an average customer. These averages provide some measure of assurance that the marketer will make money on the campaign.

When renting traditional direct marketing mailing lists, catalog marketers are stuck with averages, even if they examine conversion behaviors by list. Such direct marketers do not have the luxury of setting CPOs or costs of customer acquisition separately for different products in their catalogs. As search marketers, however, we enjoy such opportunities and should exploit them. Some items you sell provide high revenue and high margin, delivering a significant profit. So one way you can set a CPO target is to look at the profit derived from the sale of the item we are advertising with a given search listing. If the listing delivers the searcher to a category results page containing many items, you can calculate the typical profit you make on orders from this category and find an allowable target CPO that maintains a per-sale profit. Of course, not all products within your campaign will have the same profit or, for that matter, revenue, so using an average CPO target may be shortsighted. By moving from a fixed campaign-wide CPO to one set by sub-campaign based on profitability, you can put your budget to better use.

Since we have been discussing catalogers, let's use an example from a different hot e-commerce category: travel. (The following numbers are for illustration only and do not represent those from any of my clients.) A travel marketer might initially set a CPO target to $18 for an overall campaign, because the average booking earns $30 in revenue, a figure which should include a reasonable profit. However, the following types of bookings may have significantly higher revenue: cruise vacations, resort bookings, golf vacations, and first-class travel. Each of these booking categories may have revenues from $60 to $100 and have keywords associated with them. While coach airline tickets alone may only earn $21 in revenue, resulting in a wide variation of profitability within the campaign, this marketer should not fail to bid aggressively for the clicks that really have an opportunity to drive big revenues.

Look what happens when we set the CPO targets higher for the more valuable bookings (and perhaps even drop the CPO target for campaign segments that don't drive as much revenue). Listings with higher allowable CPO targets can be bid higher or, in the case of fixed-price listings, kept in the campaign (for example, a listing that would have had an $18 CPO at position 6 can now compete at premium positions and still come in at an acceptable profit).

In B2B marketing, you're often trying to generate leads or registrations. As with e-commerce marketing, not all leads are created equal. Tag your leads and see which ones actually convert to sales. For example, our payroll services client knows the keyword and engine combination driving every lead. If a particular keyword or engine delivers traffic resulting in a better-than-average conversion-to-sale rate, the allowable CPA (or CPL) for this listing should be raised. This will result in more of the valuable leads that convert into sales.

If you have a sophisticated business analytics platform and tag each new customer by the source of its acquisition, you can even factor in lifetime value in both e-commerce and B2B situations. In addition, not everyone is always ready to buy, and some listings may have a greater percentage of attracting potential customers in the early research stages of the buying cycle. Studies of your prospects' behavior may help you map additional positive behaviors to your search campaigns. By using blended success metrics instead of just one, you will find yourself optimizing the campaign around a set of metrics that more accurately reflects the value of each click. Each of the metrics you use has a value. By counting all the positive things that can be measured after the click and summing their values, your campaign will evolve towards one that really does deliver against total measurable value.

Branding Metrics and Measurement

Each year SEMPO (the Search Engine Marketing Professional Organization) does what it calls a "state of the market" survey. As with prior years, the 2007 survey reported that advertisers consistently indicated that building brand awareness is the top objective of their paid placement search campaigns. This is particularly true for larger firms. When asked, "what is your company using search engine marketing (SEM) to accomplish?," 71 percent of advertisers with more than 500 employees answered, "to increase/enhance brand awareness of our products/services." Smaller advertisers shared this enthusiasm for branding, with 56 percent of those advertisers with fewer than 500 employees selecting brand awareness as one of the chief purposes of their paid search efforts.

Yet when asked, "what metrics do you track/measure/generally pay attention [to] to gauge the success of search engine marketing programs?," brand impact was the lowest of 13 different metrics, with only 16 percent of advertisers measuring it. Instead, the top metrics reported as tracked and measured were traffic, conversion rate, CTR, ROI, and CPC, which were all selected by 50 percent or more of 338 advertiser respondents. The gap between the most important reason for doing search and the willingness or ability to measure those branding metrics is a testament to the difficulties of measuring brand impact. Measuring those factors is extremely expensive, and for many marketers the cost of measurement would exceed the cost of the PPC search media.

Branding metrics used by larger marketers (with the budgets to measure attitudinal metrics) are typically brand and ad awareness (aided and unaided), message association, brand favorability, and purchase intent.

My hypothesis is this: When managing a lean-forward media such as search, one in which consumers look to become engaged in links from the SERP to the rich content available on marketers' sites, you can achieve tremendous branding on the post-click engagement while selecting clicks based on predictive DR (direct response) metrics. In other words, *branding metrics can be considered a by-product of a best-practices DR search campaign*. Such correlative metrics include:

- **Brand and ad awareness:** What generates the maximum lift in brand awareness: the ad or the engagement occurring after the click? When allocating dollars across a campaign, should engagement metrics (page views or time on site) be used? Should DR metrics also be included to make a campaign holistic? The research team at my firm, Didit, is testing the hypothesis that branding and direct response metrics are in fact highly correlated.

- **Message association:** Associating your brand with a keyword is powerful. Consumers expect to see a brand in the SERP when that brand relates to the keyword. Failure to be in the results listings, be they organic, paid, or both, can erode the consumer's association of that brand as a leader in its category. After a consumer clicks, it's up to the landing page to reinforce the association between keyword and brand.

- **Brand favorability:** Consumers go through a buying cycle from awareness through consideration to final purchase. Depending on the product category, the Internet—and search in particular—may play a critical role in shaping favorable opinions of the brand, moving that brand into the consideration set. Both appearance in a SERP and the subsequent site visit are important when a click occurs. Marketers must think beyond pure DR mode when crafting their landing pages and text link copy, but DR copy generally has a higher quality score, reducing CPC costs in Google and the other engines. In PPC (pay per click) search, messages and copy should build brand favorability and stimulate CTR.

- **Purchase intent:** This is where branding and direct marketing intersect. When you can find keywords, engines, geographies, and times of day that already index high in terms of purchase intent, it's the search marketer's objective to guide, nudge, or coerce the consumer over the hump. If the consumer isn't quite ready to make a purchase commitment to your brand (or, for that matter, your competitor's brand) but does have an interest in purchasing at a later point in time, there is clearly a huge opportunity. Generally, if marketers don't see purchase intent brand metrics rising, then they will change messages, add promotions, and generally use all the tools at their disposal to build that purchase intent to critical mass.

Therefore, for those of you who believe in branding and branding metrics, there may be brand-lift correlation to all the easy-to-measure direct response metrics we've been talking so much about. If you can optimize on direct response metrics and get branding as a by-product, then perhaps you don't really need to obsess about lifting branding metrics and can instead focus your paid search efforts on the direct response metrics that can be directly tied to sales and revenue.

BEI: Turning Branding into Direct Response

Not every marketer has sufficient direct response metrics to apply the hypothesis put forth in the last section. But creating proxy variables (measurable variables correlating with the results you really want) lets you track behavior that may correlate highly with branding metrics.

Brand marketers have an advantage over unknown brands in terms of their ability to maximize the volume of clicks they receive from search engines. Brands benefit from the well-observed phenomenon that consumers often select an ad with a branded URL over an ad displaying a nonbranded URL. But it's not all roses for brand marketers, because they have great difficulty attempting to use metrics to measure effectiveness and to adjust search engine campaigns. Sure, search text listings have some branding impact. Yet it's far more likely that a brand advertiser will want to create a brand experience on its site, not on a search results page. Being able to measure this kind of post-click engagement requires using metrics to match back the kinds of clicks and keywords resulting in visitors spending time on the site (and thusly getting a big dose of brand exposure) versus visitors who leave immediately without receiving any positive influence.

This situation poses a dilemma for marketing pros with branding objectives who want to use SEM efficiently. In an e-commerce or B2B SEM campaign, not all clicks are created equal. Metrics are used to differentiate between the best and least valuable traffic. Most marketers are forced to "do a study" to compare media effectiveness or the comparative performance of different paid search ad copy. Many studies have been co-sponsored by industry organizations such as the Interactive Advertising Bureau, which coordinates research to examine online media as part of effective overall campaigns, or Dynamic Logic, which employs metrics that compare the ad copy and media.

We need easily measurable data that correlate with branding metrics to make necessary, ongoing adjustments in search engine campaigns. And yet none of the available metrics is particularly appropriate to the process of effectively measuring the differential between keyword/position/engine/time of day/ad creative combinations that search engine marketers typically use. A new metric, based on a behavior mapping strategy, is called the Branding Effectiveness Index, or BEI (pronounced "buy"). BEI is a work in progress, but it's already proven useful in comparing campaign results, which is the objective when optimizing search. If we can determine which clicks are most likely to deliver the kinds of behaviors that lift branding metrics, we will be way ahead.

Of course, each marketer's branding needs are unique. Each determines which measurable actions and metrics combine to create his or her own BEI. The result is a flexible metric that measures branding impact. BEI doesn't measure ad effectiveness; instead it measures the effectiveness of a given site on a visitor driven by such an ad. Visitors interact with the brand on the site and ideally, this process positively changes the way they feel about that brand. If results aren't positive, there may be serious problems. Obviously, you probably shouldn't spend on media providing site traffic until your site provides a good user experience.

When a visitor arrives at your site from a paid search click, your site does the majority of the heavy lifting delivering branding (and raising branding metrics if you were to measure them at this time). So instead of using metrics designed to measure advertising brand effectiveness, use the following proxies, based on user behavior, to build your own BEI:

- Registering for access to content
- Subscribing to a newsletter
- Request for information
- Views of pages (may be scored based on the value of the page)
- Involvement with content
- Downloading a white paper or view of an online webinar

BEI is a flexible, relative metric that is used to compare campaign elements to achieve optimized results. To generate your own BEI, set a weighting factor for the most valuable measurable action on your site to a value of 1. Other significant actions may be assigned a percentage value of this variable, based on importance. For example, if a brochure request is 70 percent as important as a newsletter registration, assign it a weighting value of 0.7 and assign the newsletter registration a value of 1. All actions are added up and multiplied by their factors. These are totaled and divided by spending to determine BEI.

Any campaign or campaign segment (even a single keyword listing) can be measured by how well it did in terms of achieving BEI. Using the current example, 20 newsletter registrations and 10 brochure requests for a $1,000 spend results in a BEI of $((20 \times 1)+(10 \times 0.7))/1,000$, or 0.027. If the number of newsletter registrations rises to 40 for a different campaign segment, BEI becomes 0.047. This value is useful in comparing campaign segments when using the same formula. Keep in mind that if a second campaign with a different set of measurable actions exists, results won't be directly comparable.

A simpler way to think of BEI is as a variable, like a weighted average CPA metric incorporating a range of post-click actions. I'm working with statisticians on how BEI might be normalized to allow comparison across various sites. Doing this requires a more complex formula to set "factors" for actions.

Let's look at some top brands to see the metrics they might use to build BEI:

- **AT&T:** Though AT&T is a brand marketer, customers can buy online from its site. If customer acquisition is the highest valued action (1), a loyalty program signup might be weighted at 0.4, and interaction with a plans and services page might be weighted at 0.15. The company might also include a variety of other metrics in a BEI campaign index.

- **Ford:** Ford might use some combination of brochure request, use of a dealer locator, and filling out a "Contact Us" form. These could be combined with content consumption (page views) or a visit to the "Build Your Ford" section.

- **McDonald's:** McDonald's has a restaurant locator and may assign this the factor of 1, whereas purchase of merchandise might be weighted at 0.9, and visits to the "Treasure Planet Happy Meal" site given a 0.2.

Whether you think BEI is a wonderful new way of combining existing metrics to capture a site's branding impact or the nonsensical ravings of a guy who's looked at too much data, the fact remains that websites impact brands, and marketers should plan and adjust campaigns based on brand awareness measurements. My branding clients are glad to have an empirical way to effectively manage their paid search campaigns.

Engagement, the New Brand Metric

You may have heard the term *engagement* for the last several years. Engagement is an attempt to create a metric that can be used to measure the effectiveness of both media purchases and the actual ads (advertising creative elements) based on how "engaged" the consumer becomes with an ad, content, or any brand-associated activity.

We already know that on a long-term basis, brand marketers must look at search and other online media in new ways, based on how consumers have changed their media consumption behavior. Traditional media metrics don't always fit a brand marketing strategy for a search campaign. Given some recent data from Nielsen/NetRatings, traditional media metrics may be losing their applicability across all media. Brand marketers are accustomed to using metrics that reflect not only campaign objectives but also the way media are sold. Both evolved hand in hand, but this linkage has become decoupled in a world in which digital media suddenly lets marketers get at real-time data that may be far better at describing the impact of advertising than branding metrics collected in a more lab-like environment.

The tide of new users to search engines has virtually dried up in the U.S., according to a Nielsen report, which states that the unique visitor growth rate is nearing zero. Yet the number of pages viewed per person is growing rapidly in certain verticals, indicating a shift in online media consumption. Clearly, as the percentage of time spent online grows and the percentage of time spent with other media drops, traditional marketers will follow direct marketers online (including to search marketing).

Which metric is right for search once a marketer extends a campaign beyond obvious keywords relating to the brand? Let's take a look back before discussing how brand marketers should approach search.

When sellers understood the way marketers wanted to buy advertising, they bucketed media together to make it look good to media buyers. Media targeting levels were usually keyed to lifestyle, psychographic, or demographic buckets. Only direct marketing used micro-targeting media models. All buyers knew there would be some waste in a media plan, in terms of there being people who saw the ad but weren't in the target audience. But if the media price was cheap enough, waste was OK. The true CPM (cost per thousand ad impressions) against a given target audience (a subset of all those exposed) could still be in range and all other impressions were regarded as "free."

You've been a victim of this kind of media targeting if you're under 65 and have been exposed to TV ads for denture cream or seen other ads for products and services you'll never be in-market for. The true cost (CPM) to reach in-market or in-segment consumers is a ratio based on the percentage of the viewing audience that is within the target group. If nearly 100 percent of those watching an ad are in the target market, the true CPM against the target market and the CPM paid are nearly the same. On the other hand, if only ten percent of those exposed to the ad are in the target market, the true CPM against that ten percent is ten times the CPM paid against the overall viewership.

Online advertising initially positioned itself as media sold the same way as offline media: demographically, psychographically, even contextually. Essentially marketers were offered a newer way to buy media, targeted by site or network, using the same old method used to buy TV, radio, or print.

One reason brand marketers have been slow to move into search marketing is their unfamiliarity with search's primary methods of targeting: keywords. Moreover, keywords such as brand names and searches associated with a brand marketer's specific product category are in short supply.

In today's world, brand marketers need to think of search as part of an integrated media plan. Offline and online media purchases drive brand awareness and even drive search behavior on core keywords. But the true value to keyword advertisers may come from promotional tie-ins and product placement sponsorships, because offline media exposure drives search behavior.

The key to effective search engine advertising is knowing that the search ad isn't the complete ad message. It's only the beginning of the ad experience, even if the ad isn't clicked. When the ad is clicked, the experience continues at the marketer's site. If you're a brand or integrated marketer building media models measuring the true value of advertising and even predicting the success of ads used in such conjunction, consider using metrics measuring brand engagement. Audiences and consumers often regard advertising as content—your content.

This holistic view takes the idea of media beyond ad delivery to ad and branding message consumption. Consumption of marketing messages over time is more likely to generate emotional response. As marketers, that's what we want. When messages are re-stimulated in a favorable content environment (or in any environment where messaging exists that can influence the purchase), we want emotional triggers in place that cause consumers to favor our brand. The whole idea of branding is that through a combination of repeated exposure to the brand through advertising, marketing, public relations, promotion, and possibly purchase/consumption, you communicate the idea that your brand is a better fit than your competitor's. Search engine marketing is just one of the ways to lead consumers to interact with branding messages or to simply engage with the brand in a content-rich website.

Even direct marketers can learn how to apply holistic media models to their campaigns and look beyond immediate conversion to a more realistic picture. The fact is that consumers build purchase preferences over time for many products and services, not merely at the last search touch point before purchase.

Chapter 6

Campaign Setup: Structuring Your Listings

Having the right campaign structure can make the difference between success and failure. Often, search marketers set up PPC accounts in the search engines when they are just learning about search engine marketing and never revisit their original campaign setup or structure. This is a mistake, because the engines are constantly tuning their algorithms and adding new features. Unless you regularly revisit your campaign structure, you'll find yourself falling behind, losing money, and missing opportunities. Therefore, although this chapter is primarily for first-time campaign setup, it's just as valuable to those with existing campaigns. Later chapters dig deeper into some of the areas covered in this chapter, but this chapter serves as both a primer and refresher, regardless of skill level.

Considering the Search Engines

The temptation in planning any search marketing campaign is to start with the keywords. However, you need to understand the choices you have in pay-per-click advertising systems and search engines. Nearly everyone starts with Google, for a variety of reasons. The primary reason is Google's dominant market share of overall search queries. Regardless which search engine traffic ratings you believe are most accurate, Google has a commanding lead on Yahoo and Microsoft when it comes to the number of searches or the percentage of use. **Figure 6.1** illustrates the data in February, 2009 from several data providers.

Figure 6.1

Each of the data providers measure search market share differently, however it's easy to tell the leaders.

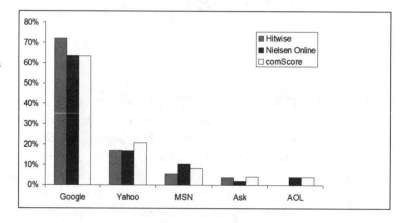

When setting up a search marketing campaign, always start with Google. Successfully deploy a Google campaign and then use the Google campaign structure, keywords, and ad creative specifications as a baseline for any export/imports you do into Yahoo, Microsoft, or other engines. This is not only possible but also optimal, because the majority of search engine advertising, ad creative specifications, and settings of other search engines are compatible with Google. The search engines didn't all start out that way, but once Google gathered a commanding lead in share of searches, it made no sense to have vastly different creative standards. When importing campaigns from Google into the other search engines, you need to watch out for a few differences, but many of the importing processes make adjustments so that they import perfectly or at least acceptably.

Another reason to start with Google, even if the click prices might be higher, is that you can learn very quickly what is working and what isn't, or whether a campaign is completely off track.

Structuring Your Campaigns

The largest structural grouping unit within each engine is the campaign, which provides a way of organizing your keywords and advertising messages in particular groups for both reporting and control. In all the engines, as you go through the setup process, you can name each and every campaign to make it easier to remember the types of keywords and ads that campaign contains. The general idea of setting up campaigns is to match some logical business or financial structure or to make reporting match reporting used in other kinds of marketing or media. Here are some options you might consider for campaign-level structures, and the reasons for those structures:

- **Business unit campaign structures:** If your business has several divisions, each with its own budget, a campaign per business can make managing budgets easier while allowing for a centralized dashboard. Business units often have different budgets and campaign objectives making campaigns based on business units a logical choice for many search marketers.

- **Product or services clusters:** You may have sections of your business that have different profit margins, different objectives, or different managers. If so, consider a campaign structure that reflects those distinctions, allowing you to more easily control spending and view reports logically.

- **Brand keywords versus nonbranded keywords:** Often the highest ROI and most profitable keywords are your brand terms (your company name, product and service names, and trademarks). Even when you rank highly in the unpaid (organic or natural) search results, it still makes sense to bid on your brand and control the user experience in ways you couldn't in an unpaid search result.

- **Seasonal campaigns:** Because campaigns can be turned on and off, controlling a very large number of ads and keywords, advertisers often set up campaigns that are in use only at certain times of the year. By pausing these campaigns and having them ready for the next seasonal use, such campaigns need only be reviewed for relevance and freshness.

- **Promotional or *sale*-driven campaigns:** Sometimes you'll need to run sales that aren't seasonal in nature but are instead related to a reduction in price or a special offer that increases sales volume, sometimes at a lower margin.

- **Temporary campaigns:** If you are testing a new idea or creative concept, it may be easier to control and monitor the experiment when it resides it its own campaign.

Depending on the engine, the level of control you have at the campaign level differs. Google allows for up to 25 campaigns per account, and most businesses can fit into that structure easily given that there is an option within each Ad Group for clustering keywords and creative standards. (Ad Groups, a critical campaign component, will be covered in detail later in this chapter.) However, because budget caps in Google are controlled at the campaign level, sometimes 25 is not enough. In that situation, Google has a feature called My Client Center that was originally designed for ad and search engine marketing agencies. My Client Center is a way of tying several accounts to the same login, therefore multiplying the number of campaigns available to a single user. **Figure 6.2** shows the screen to start a new campaign.

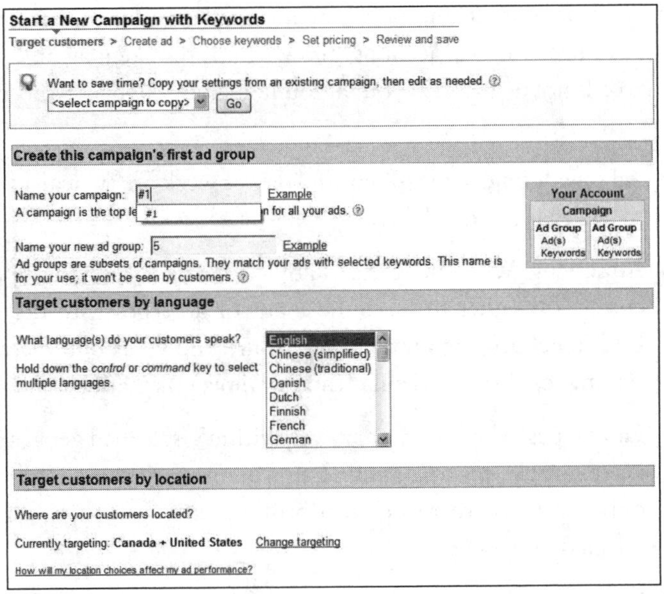

Figure 6.2
Starting a new campaign with keywords.

When setting up campaigns, the best first step is to think about a logical structure that works for your business. Because budget caps are set at the campaign level, budgeting often drives the campaign structure. However, in addition to being able to set budget caps at the campaign level, the search engines provide a variety of options that let marketers target specific segments of their audience. The targeting options in the campaign group for each engine are slightly different, and they tend to change from time to time. Following are the set of targeting options in the "big three" engines at the time of this book's writing:

- **Delivery method:** Specifies how to space out your ads in relation to your budget.

- **Syndication networks:** Includes site and category exclusion when using contextual ad placements, meaning your ad won't show on certain sites or categories of sites. Each engine defines these settings differently, and they change over time, so check the options available to you at the time of account setup.

- **Bidding strategy:** Some search engines have some form of auto-bidding or position preference that automates bid changes for you.

- **Automatic matching or automatic account adjustments:** Adds keywords to your account, allowing ads to match against keywords not included in your account, making changes to account structure or ad copy.

- **Ad scheduling:** Time of day and day of week are typical adjustments that are available.

- **Ad serving:** When there are multiple ads or ad types, this option controls whether to serve those ads or ad types with the best CTR (click-through rate), a procedure known as *optimized* ad serving, or through regular (non-optimized) rotation.

- **Languages:** These may vary even within a specified geography. For example, picking Spanish in Miami versus Fargo will still only serve ads to those with browser settings at the default selected language.

- **Geography/location:** You can specify the customer location or geography at the country level all the way to city and Zip.

- **Campaign-wide negative keywords:** These are keywords you prefer not to show up against if they occur in conjunction with a word that is in your campaign on phrase or broad match type (more on match types later).

The geography option is really important. When setting up a new campaign in Google, make sure you deselect Canada from the USA + Canada option if you don't want both to serve as the default geography.

Similarly, there are several highly recommended default settings that you adjust during the preliminary launch stage. For example, match types (which control exactly how your keywords interact with search queries) for keywords are set to broad match unless you specify otherwise.

To reiterate, you should start your campaign organization and structure in Google, given that Google is the most important search engine for reaching the largest audience (although clicks may not have the same profitability in Google). Because Google is the industry standard, the campaign structure you create is generally transportable to the other engines.

Organizing with Ad Groups

It's hard to talk about Ad Groups without talking about keywords, but keywords will be covered in the next section, and then keyword research will be covered in-depth in Chapter 7, "Campaign Setup: Keywords." Ad Groups are the units within the campaign that cluster keywords together to share a similar ad creative (ad copy). When structuring Ad Groups, the shared ad element becomes central to deciding how to set up your groups because when a search is performed by a searcher, the search engines apply boldfacing to the search terms (**Figure 6.3**) within the displayed ads. Consequently, if your ads are well written and contain the search keyword, they are more likely to catch the searcher's eye. The simplest way to do this is to structure your Ad Groups in such a way that keywords and phrases in the Ad Group are also in the ad copy you write for that Ad Group.

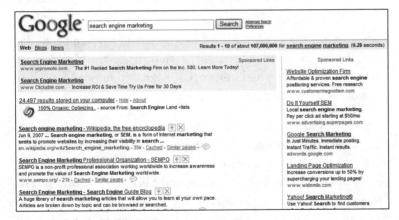

Figure 6.3
Search keywords are
boldfaced in the results.

Be careful when simply following Google's wizard-based campaign setup (**Figure 6.4** on the next page). The setup process using the wizard may result in too many keywords in one Ad Group, which will cause the loss of the boldface feature for your ads.

Instead of using Google's wizard-based system, I recommend that
you do your keyword research separately, using the Google keyword research system and others. The next section takes a look at
keyword selection and generation.

The best way to structure Ad Groups is to look for common keywords
and phrases that can share the same ad creative. Later in this chapter
we'll talk about the specifics of ad copy and ad creative. However,
you've probably seen Google, Yahoo, and Microsoft text ads in your
favorite search engines. Those lines of copy are your opportunity to
entice and communicate with the searcher who moments earlier entered
the keywords in your Ad Group into a search box. Therefore, your ad
copy should match up to the keywords in the Ad Group and, similarly,
your keywords within that Ad Group should be limited to ones that
make sense with the ad copy you provide.

Another factor to consider when deciding whether to group keywords together or separate them is reporting. You'll likely be doing
a lot of reporting within the search engine interfaces unless you are
using a bid management solution to manage your campaigns via an
automated technology and maintain separate reporting. So, if there
are keywords that you'd like reported separately (even if they could

have shared the same ad creative), the best solution may be to separate the keywords into Ad Groups that will result in aggregated data shown in a structure you prefer.

Selecting Keywords

On the first go-round of setting up your keywords, you don't have to select all the keywords you'll ever need or make sure that your Ad Groups are perfectly structured. However, you should start by selecting some strong foundational keywords and using those keyword listings as a baseline, adding more later as you find out how well they perform. Chapter 7, "Campaign Setup: Keywords," is all about the keyword research process. Here, you'll learn how to do a comprehensive, initial identification of your keyword lists and then use the resulting data to tune and tweak your campaigns on an ongoing basis.

Note

We use the term *keyword* interchangeably with *keyword phrase* when discussing setup, research, and management of the campaign. The industry (and occasionally this book) refers to keywords as *terms*.

The high level of trackability provided in the wonderful world of online marketing means you never have to say you are finished with your campaign. A campaign including keywords has the capacity to grow and evolve over time.

You need to recognize that all the major engines afford you an option to assign a different landing page URL (destination URL) to each keyword within an Ad Group during the keyword setup process. This is important for several reasons:

- You may want to be able to track the post-click (onsite) behavior of visitors at the keyword level. This tracking could be part of a web analytics package, campaign management solution, or other mode of tracking.

- You may decide that there are differences in the purchase intent or desires of searchers who have used one keyword versus another, even when those keywords seem very similar. For example, *discount Alaskan cruises* and *luxury Alaskan cruises* would generally be keywords in the same Ad Group. Therefore, if the same default settings were used, all keywords in the same Ad Group would have the same destination URL. Singulars and plurals may also have sufficiently different meanings to warrant sending searchers to different landing pages.

- There may be times when you want to reconcile the keyword searched on (the actual keyword or phrase) with the keyword you have bid for. They sometimes differ for a variety of reasons, including match type (more about match type in Chapter 7).

Writing Ad Creatives (Your Ad Copy)

Chapter 8, "Campaign Setup: Titles and Descriptions," goes into significant detail regarding the development of your ad copy. However, since this chapter discusses the structural elements of campaign setup, it makes sense to cover the basics first here. It is useful to understand how and why the search engines arrived at the somewhat arbitrary ad copy length restrictions that follow. In essence, the search engines wanted the text ads to somewhat mimic the non-advertising results on the page, but they also wanted to squeeze as many ads on that page as possible to serve the searcher (more choices) as well as to make more money (more ads means more clicks overall, assuming those ads are relevant).

Your paid search ad is made up of several lines of ad copy, not all of which may end up being shown to a searcher. These lines include:

- **Title:** Your ad's title is your headline; you have 25 characters for it.

- **Description:** The description portion (the sub-headline) may be displayed on one or two lines, depending on the search engine and the placement obtained within it. It can be two lines of 35 characters or 70 characters in one or two lines.

- **Display URL:** This tells searchers where they will land after clicking.

Because the key to deciding how many Ad Groups you need depends largely on where to put the keywords that you want to include in your campaign, let's cover the basics of ad copy development, or more specifically, the lack of ad copy standards next.

At first glance, it would seem the search engines could at least be made to work together using a common creative of 25/70 characters. At 25 characters, titles are shorter than Yahoo's previous title maximum of 40. The fact that title character counts are not standardized has important consequences for marketers attempting to port campaigns from one engine to another. For example, you could use Google creative in your Yahoo campaign, ignoring the extra 15 characters (even though having them might be handy). Microsoft's adCenter shares the 25-character title limit, so all's well there. But going from Yahoo to Google used to pose a problem when campaigns were longer. Yahoo has since adopted the Google standard for title length and even auto-truncates the advertising text from ads that were never edited by advertisers during the switch.

The differences between the search engine specifications become annoying as you move to the ad's description. In this case, Google is the odd man out. All three engines allow 70-character descriptions. But Google forces them into two lines of 35 characters each, whereas Yahoo and Microsoft allow for 70 characters, regardless of how the characters break. This means you can't confidently port a Microsoft or Yahoo campaign to Google, but you can port a Google campaign to Microsoft and Yahoo. Argh!

The one thing you need to keep in mind is that you and your competition all (should) know that the search term will be displayed in bold in the title and/or description, making those ads that include the keyword generally "pop" more for the searcher. Unfortunately, this tends to result in ads that all look the same. In order to differentiate yourself and your ad, you need to find a way to appear relevant (due to the inclusion of the search term in the ad) without blending into the pack.

Resist the temptation to have your ad copy be cute or clever. Searchers only give your ad a very cursory glance (if you are lucky), and they don't have time to decipher your clever play on words or marketing message.

Creating the Right Landing Pages

The *landing page* for a search engine advertising campaign is exactly what you'd expect it to be: the page of your website where the searcher lands after clicking the ad you placed in the search engine results page (SERP). Your ad was triggered based on your keyword, CPC (cost per click) bid, and targeting choices. The right landing page is the one that meets both your needs as a marketer and the needs of the searcher, who has expressed a desire through a search engine and then selected your ad link from a mixture of paid and unpaid results.

There is a magic multiplicative power of landing pages when they are done right, and failing to take advantage of the power of an optimal landing page is a missed opportunity every time a visitor arrives at your site. Clients often ask me how their competition can place such amazingly high bids in the CPC search engine marketplaces. Some of the main reasons why your competitors may be able to afford high CPCs that result in high positions are:

- Competitors are not paying prices based on rational business rules but on emotions. For example, some marketers insist on being "#1 on the SERPs" without regard to how much this is costing them.

- Competitors have determined that getting visitors to interact with their brands and sites is of high worth; hence a high CPC is warranted.

- Competitors with similar site conversion processes have determined that customers acquired from these sites have a high immediate or lifetime value, so they will invest more in acquisition.

- Competitors are working with similar cost-per-order (CPO), cost-per-action (CPA), and return-on-investment (ROI) objectives and financial constraints, but their website landing pages have higher conversion rates.

As a marketer, you may not have the ability to change your lifetime value formulas or your organization's willingness to pay for experiential branding. However, you have a great level of control over the landing pages you designate for each listing in your paid search campaign.

The first thing the searcher sees after clicking your paid or unpaid search engine link is your landing page. How that landing page performs is one of the keys to a positive ROI from search marketing.

High ROI on an SEM campaign hinges on achieving the right mix of pre-click variables and post-click conversion behavior. Pre-click variables such as search venue, position, and offer/creative have an impact on post-click behavior. But even with those variables optimized, there is often huge room for campaign ROI improvement.

The next place to look for ROI improvement is the landing page and the site. For example, if your existing conversion-to-sale ratio is 3 percent and your allowable CPO is $30, then you can afford to pay only $0.90 CPC in the venue that provides that conversion rate (conversion rates on the same keyword change by venue). The $0.90 maximum bid may not give you the volume you want, leaving you in a poor position at Google, Yahoo, or Microsoft. Now imagine that a change to your landing page, site structure, or shopping cart/lead generation process changes conversion positively. At a 4 percent conversion rate, your campaign can now be adjusted to pay as much as $1.20 CPC and still be at your target CPO. At 5 percent, you can afford up to a $1.50 CPC. The multiplicative power of a more effective landing page can make the difference between a successful campaign and one that fails to live up to expectations.

Imagine all the campaign flexibility an increased conversion rate delivers. How can this landing page magic be accomplished? What variables on a landing page and site will influence your particular type of visitor? The places to start looking include copy, product images, merchandising, color, visual use of brands, site navigation, shopping cart ease of use, pricing, alternative conversion paths (for example, collecting a name in case the buyer is not ready to buy, or leading the buyer through testimonials or continued selling/education), and a host of other things.

Most marketers want to get the most out of both organic (unpaid natural results) and paid search. Existing sites are getting more attention as marketers make sites search engine–friendly (or even search engine–maximized) as well as user-friendly. Any search engine marketer can tell you SEO (search engine optimization) requires compromise in areas such as layout and copy length, style, and flow.

Yet, marketers recognize such a compromise can result in a great experience for spiders and users alike. After taking into account a site's search engine–friendliness and adapting copy and design, you may have made compromises in user-friendliness and conversion. These compromises may yield thousands of new, targeted visitors to your site. The navigational structure helps both search engine spiders and human visitors understand the breadth of your site's offerings. A bit of conversion loss as part of SEO efforts is generally OK.

Paid search campaigns provide something SEO doesn't: complete control over the user experience. When you pay for clicks, your ability to afford high positions is directly related to your ability to meet marketing objectives with each and every inbound click. Those objectives usually include several conversion behaviors, which may include lead generation, purchase, and site immersion (to indicate early-stage, research-related buying behavior). Of course, the least desirable site-side behavior is clicking the Back button.

The control that PPC search gives you is a precious asset that you might almost think of as a gift, because unlike unpaid organic search traffic you can take full control of searchers from the time they see your ad until they reach your site, and sometimes beyond. By not exercising this asset, you hand it to your competition, who may be taking the same searchers though a rich and relevant experience different than that of a casual visitor to their site via organic search or direct navigation. Following are 10 reasons why your existing website may be completely wrong for your PPC search landing pages:

- **Call to action:** Landing pages for visitors with specific needs (as articulated by their search queries) require specific calls to action. Regular site pages don't carry strong call-to-action messages because this kind of messaging is often inappropriate for general visitors.

- **Copy:** Regular site pages often have more copy than you want to show to paid search visitors. You need a tight correlation between the specific search and the landing page copy to engage potential customers arriving from search engines.

- **Navigation:** Regular site pages generally have full-site navigation, which can distract paid search visitors. Less is often more when it comes to navigational clutter. You already know exactly what every paid search visitor seeks; additional navigation can distract the visitor from your message and his or her mission.

- **Animation:** Flash, illustrations, and other animation are a significant part of the user experience for paid search visitors. These elements may not be present on your general site.

- **Personalization:** The rich data you generate from PPC search means that you likely know more about your paid search visitors than you do about visitors arriving via different means, because in many cases you chose the targeting parameters far beyond the keywords alone, including geography and origination site. Personalize their experience! Many automated personalization engines and methods don't play well with search engine spiders and may be disabled as part of organic SEO efforts. In paid search, personalization takes on a whole new meaning, including treating returning customers differently from new prospects.

- **Merchandising:** A retail store is merchandised based on geography, neighborhood, and season. Route paid search traffic to pages designed to take advantage of different merchandising.

- **Offer testing:** It's much easier to test an offer when you know what makes the traffic unique. You need a control to test, and paid search provides it.

- **Microsites:** Sometimes you need an entirely new look, structure, and flow for paid search visitors. A *microsite* (a custom website designed for the specific purpose of catering to a specific audience segment) may be your best route to strong conversions. Microsites live outside your traditional site and can take on a life of their own or can be very similar to your primary site with only subtle differences in navigation and content.

- **Domain name:** If you don't have a branded domain, a new keyword-packed domain coupled with a microsite may provide far better impression-to-click conversion at the ad level. Particularly in Google, this results in a higher score for the efficiency of your campaign. (Google's metric for judging this efficiency is called AdRank.) When you don't have a brand, a descriptive URL may more readily catch searchers' attention.

- **Ambiguity:** Some keywords fit your target market but not your landing pages. A new landing page, separate from your current site, can help test your results, improve efficiency, and offer new opportunities. For example, your ad may show for the phrase *Kate Spade white sandal* because you are bidding on *white sandal* as a phrase match, but you may have a special Kate Spade section that would be more appropriate as a destination.

I highly recommend that you set aside a separate budget or additional internal resources to take your site beyond what's necessary for organic SEO and a regular navigable site. Look closer and imagine the characteristics of the perfect landing page for each power keyword (one that can deliver both volume and ROI) in your campaign. If optimal landing pages don't exist for those important keywords, create them.

Google's Quality Score

One thing to keep in mind as you decide how to build either great compromise landing pages (those that exist within your existing site structure and will be used for SEO and as landing pages for PPC search) is that the search engines increasingly care what content is on your landing pages. Google, for example, uses a *Quality Score* that is made up of dozens of variables, including the relevance of a landing page to the search keyword. So, while you can be much briefer with ad copy on a paid search landing page, it can be risky to shorten copy length radically. Some copy should be available in the HTML for the Google search spiders to find, so that it can serve to validate that the landing page is in fact relevant and deserves a good Quality Score.

I talk more about the Quality Score and landing pages in Chapter 9, "Conversion Pages, Bids, and Budgets."

Landing Page Testing

The challenge is often to determine which landing page works best for a given keyword, set of keywords, or a particular geography. There are two basic forms of landing page testing: A/B testing and multivariate testing. Unless your monthly paid search budget exceeds $10,000 and you receive the bulk of clicks from a highly concentrated set of keywords, you'll probably stick to A/B testing, at least in the early stages of your campaign. *A/B testing is a process of pitting one landing page against another to see which one outperforms.* The winner is then subjected to tests against new challengers.

Multivariate landing page testing endeavors to find the perfect mix of variables on your landing page. This statistical method (which has several flavors) requires that your campaign receives a sufficient amount of traffic to generate statistically valid results. If you have a large campaign, multivariate testing can often dramatically outperform A/B testing. However, when poorly executed, it can still leave opportunities untapped, most often because the statistician failed to take into account the segments or clusters within the inbound traffic stream. For example, you really don't simply want the best converting page for the average visitor; you want to identify targeting segments within your stream of visitors and treat them differently if they respond differently. For example, when testing landing pages against the keyword phrase *cruise vacation*, it's easy to imagine that the optimal page design (copy, images, layout, and colors) might vary for searchers who happen to live in Miami versus those who live in Chicago.

Chapter 7

Campaign Setup: Keywords

Keywords (and phrases) are the foundation of any search engine advertising campaign because they are proxies for the needs and desires of the searcher. Each search is the searcher's best attempt at converting those immediate desires into something the search engine can understand. Within the millions of daily searches performed are concepts that represent requests for information about the products and services of specific advertisers' businesses. The keywords and phrases marketers select and bid upon define the conditions specifying when a particular ad is eligible to be served. Regardless of whether we as advertisers chose to include specific keywords or phrases in our campaign in order to trigger ads that may bring the searcher to our site, the searchers are out there asking Google, Yahoo, Microsoft, and other search engines for help solving a problem. Searchers lack information.

Keyword terms and keyword phrases are more than simply the foundation of any paid search engine advertising campaign. They are also a bridge to the other form of search engine marketing, organic (or natural) search engine optimization (SEO). Whether your site shows up in the paid advertising listings, the unpaid results, or both is all dependent on search engine keywords. Another common theme shared by organic SEO and paid search is that in both instances, for the keywords to perform optimally, pages of your site must in fact be relevant to those keywords, or you'll lose search visitors seconds after they arrive.

Consider Using Brand Keywords

Keywords can be broadly defined as brand and nonbranded keywords, but different marketers define these two segments differently. So perhaps it is best to allow you to make your own definitional decisions of brand versus nonbranded keywords based on your business. Obviously, if a searcher is seeking information on a brand or brand name, they have a preconceived notation about that brand (most likely positive), and that makes the brand owner quite protective of its use as a trigger for a paid search ad.

The primary reason many marketers choose to put keywords into brand versus nonbranded buckets is that they often assign different success objectives to each group of words. Doing so may include setting different ROI parameters that translate into different SERP position preferences.

To illustrate the diversity of keywords that can be defined as "branded," let's again use the example site www.We-Care.com, which creates online marketplaces or malls for nonprofit causes where each cause gets its own URL. In this instance, you could define brand keywords very narrowly and therefore only have the terms *we-care*, *we-care.com*, and *wecare* because these are the only brand names specifically tied to the corporate name and permutations thereof.

A broader definition of brand keywords for We-Care.com would include the names of all the nonprofit causes for which we have built malls/marketplaces. Those might include single keywords in some cases (where the cause name is one word) or phrases (where the full nonprofit is also a phrase or where portions of the domain name or broader phrases include the nonprofit's name). For example:

- *save the children*

- *savethechildren*

- *support save the children*

- *donate to save the children*

Another way to look at brand keywords in a paid search advertising campaign for We-Care.com would be to consider bidding within the search results for the names of the merchant stores within the marketplace. For example:

- *Best Buy*

- *David's Cookies*

- *Brooks Brothers Coupons*

- *Expedia deals*

- *Target.com*

Keep in mind that in many instances the owner of the trademark prohibits brand bidding, and this may be the case with your business as well, even if you have the right to sell the product in question. For example, at the time of this book's writing, Marriott prohibited the online travel agency brands such as Expedia, Hotels.com, Orbitz, and Travelocity from bidding on Marriott trademarks. Trademark-based restrictions are discussed more fully in the "Consider Trademarks and Search" section later in this chapter. However, the preceding examples provide a perfect segue into the next set of keywords that might be classified as brand keywords for the We-Care.com campaign.

The next set of keywords that might be classified as brand keywords go one layer beyond the merchants. It is quite possible that someone might want to bid on the names of products sold by the 800 merchants participating in the We-Care.com marketplaces. As you might imagine, that list of products and services is huge. Unless someone thought it possible to provide a better shopping experience with regard to landing pages than the merchant site itself (or a similar experience with a higher conversion rate to sales), it would be unlikely that such a bidding strategy would be successful. This is because that same someone would then be competing in the search advertising auctions with all merchants eligible to sell the brands in question.

Finally, some marketers include the brand names of their competitors as brand keywords. Those brand names might include the name of the competition as well as the *mid-portion* (between the *www* and the *.com* or *.net*) of that competitor's domain name. Again, using We-Care.com as an example, you might include the following competitors' keywords in a campaign:

- *I Give*
- *Igive*
- *One Cause*
- *Onecause*
- *Good search*
- *goodsearch*

Another reason that so much time is taken in defining and obsessing over brand keywords is that searcher behavior is different when it comes to brands. All other things being equal, search result listings for branded URLs get a higher click-through (percentage of clicked ad listings) than for nonbranded URLs. Similarly, when searching for a brand, consumers are usually very close to making a buying decision (most often for a product or service associated with that brand), but they may be open to persuasion in the last stages of their purchase decisions. Brand search clicks are therefore coveted by the brand owner, the marketing channels for those brands, and of course by competitors (who can pull a double whammy if they capture a competitor's customer just before that customer is about to buy).

Deciding how to define brands in your campaign is important because it can fundamentally change the strategy of your campaign. In the mid-1990s, the Internet was publicized as "the great equalizer." Finally, it was said, small and midsized businesses could have a web presence right up there with Fortune 500 companies. With the implosion of many web ventures in 2000 to 2002, many lost hope of achieving this equality until search marketing appeared, apparently leveling the playing field once again. Any marketer who wanted a listing for any appropriate keyword needed only to buy the clicks resulting from a paid listing. Now, however, it's looking like the marketplace is once again shifting to favor the established deep-pocketed brands, particularly in some sectors, forcing the smaller marketer to be even smarter and better prepared. Here's why:

- **Organic search algorithms favor larger brands on average.** The organic (unpaid) search engine results algorithms tend to favor sites with links from trusted sources. Larger sites with larger advertising and marketing budgets end up with more visibility and press—both online and off—driving link popularity and enhancing position in organic results.

- **Limited inventory drives search click-through pricing.** When it comes to search, one fact is immutable: There is a limited inventory of every search term. What will be the result of the heavy competition for this traffic? Let's look at the landscape to help us answer the question. The portals "own" the traffic, and therefore want to find the perfect balance between the maximization of revenue and the provision of a great user experience that brings back searchers time after time. Look at Google. A single-minded focus on the quality of organic results brings searchers back, and that same quality helped to close some major syndication deals further broadening Google's reach. Google's AdWords program is designed in a way that allows searchers to "vote" for ads that are better and more enticing. Ad results are rotated and tested, and the ads that deliver the highest click-through rate and greatest income (scoring highest according to a metric that Google calls "effective CPM") are rotated to the top more often. Searchers' votes count heavily in the position and traffic levels for an ad.

- **Brands have a distinct advantage.** Brands in titles and descriptions tend to generate higher CTRs than those listings without a brand, on average. Similarly, branded website URLs tend to have an advantage when shown or indicated in the listings' copy. This would seem to give brands a leg up in the search engine marketing war for position and traffic. Of course, any marketer who carries brands in its inventory can capitalize on the *brand effect* in its listings when advertising products or items that are branded, leveling the playing field again.

Between the advantage of listings that include brands and branded URLs and the economic advantages that come with being a branded larger site, it would seem that smaller sites have little chance to win the search engine marketing war. However, many of the benefits that the larger sites have also can be used against them. Specifically, larger sites have higher overhead and don't benefit from the emotional investment that an entrepreneurial venture does.

Select Product and Service Keywords

Keywords denoting products and services are equally appropriate for search engine marketing campaigns. Services marketers such as my wife, who runs a referral network for psychologists and social workers in New York City specializing in cognitive-behavioral therapy, have a challenging task. Unlike products, her services-related keywords group the professionals that the searcher is seeking by the profession (such as psychologist, therapist, counselor) as well as by the modality of therapy (CBT, cognitive therapy, behavioral therapy, couples counseling) and by the problems or diagnosis that the searcher is trying to solve with therapy (stress, depression, anxiety, PTSD, OCD). If you have a services business, you likely have some of the same categorization types. The challenge for many service providers is that the keyword set is very limited in comparison to sets used by product marketers.

The product marketer, on the other hand, often has it easier than the services marketer. Often the same product database used to track inventory and run the online store already includes all the product names and model numbers. This gives product marketers a great place to start to develop campaigns around these products. Although the existence of this database doesn't obviate the need to perform keyword research, in conjunction with the keyword research tools available for the search engines and other sources (covered in the "Use Keyword Research Tools" section later in this chapter), a well-formed exported product database can speed the process of campaign development.

When you generate large keyword lists for a campaign, remember that you may need to keep them in separate Ad Groups to have relevant ad copy. One way to keep campaign structures manageable (by avoiding having too many Ad Groups) is to take advantage of the fact that each keyword can have its own landing page specified within an Ad Group and then use an advanced technique called Dynamic Keyword Insertion (DKI), which Chapter 8, "Campaign Setup: Titles and Description," covers in more detail.

Understand the Head and Tail of the Search Curve

Clearly there is life beyond brand and product keywords. It is important for every campaign to include nonbranded keywords. Are you always ready to buy, ready to register, ready to call, ready to subscribe? I didn't think so. Neither is your target audience. Remember Marketing 101 or those sales books that talk about the buying cycle? They have a point well worth considering when it comes to search marketing: Not every visitor is ready to buy all the time, and that doesn't mean they are worthless to you; quite the contrary, they may be close to becoming a valuable customer.

A strategy for choosing the best, most profitable nonbranded keywords for your search campaign should be informed by an understanding of search curves. A *search curve* is a graphical representation of the number of times a given query is searched within a given period. While the *head* of such a curve consists of just a handful of terms that are searched millions of times a month, the curve's *tail* is amazingly long and flat, consisting of hundreds or even thousands of keywords and phrases that may only be searched on a few times a month. These latter terms may not provide much volume or scale, but they may offer you healthy conversion rates, because these low-volume queries may represent consumers performing very specific queries (such as *Nikon D80 with 300mm zoom lens best price*) associated with the final stages of the buy funnel. They are, in other words, very close to making a purchasing decision, making them highly desirable targets for your campaign.

When selecting nonbranded keywords for search engine marketing campaigns, marketers often pick the top 20 or 40 keywords they think will be important for their businesses and set up those words as the core of their campaigns. These keywords tend to be the obvious ones that are located within the search curve's head and have a high volume of searches. Consequently, there is often heavy competition for these terms, driving up the prices within the auction marketplaces. Even worse, the more generic the keyword search, the less sure you can be of the intention of the searcher and how best to convert that searcher to a lead or sale. So how does a marketer put together a campaign where prices are reasonable and volumes are sufficient? The answer for many marketers is to "go broad" into the tail of the search curve with any and all keywords that might be deemed relevant, but do this strategically.

Going broad is a way of capturing the rather large tail of the search curve. Once you decide to go broad to capture that highly targeted traffic, the real work begins. Broad campaigns are worth the effort. In many engines, the broader terms are cheaper and equally or better targeted, and if you add them all up you'll get one powerful campaign.

In addition to brands or product or service-related keywords, you should do keyword research from a problem-solution mindset. For example, the following searches represent a consumer in need of a solution, but the searches contain no brands and no products and are sometimes ambiguous as to whether a product or a service is the appropriate solution:

- *Grass stain removal*

- *Diaper rash*

- *Achieve top Google rank*

- *Measure marketing effectiveness*

- *Highest rated summer getaways*

- *Discomfort after drinking milk*

These problem-driven searches represent a great opportunity for product or service providers to capture the attention of searchers in their time of need. However, before considering the use of these types of keywords, make sure you have supporting content on your site and landing pages. The reason is that not only do the search engines now look at landing pages when deciding your ad's relevance, but you never want to pay for clicks and then have searchers quickly abandon your site when they don't find what they are looking for on your landing pages.

Use Plurals and Stemming

Sometimes the intent of a searcher changes dramatically between the singular and the plural form of a search. When evaluating the keywords to include in your campaign, you need to place yourself in the shoes of the searcher. This will somewhat simplify your campaign setup. *Stemming* (use of plurals and other forms of the word) is often automatically taken care of by the search engine. However, there are some important reasons to create a campaign structure that proactively includes whatever keyword versions you might have an interest in, with each covered separately within an Ad Group or in some cases in a separate Ad Group (when the ad creative for the root and keyword permutations must differ by more than just the keyword). Generally the closest match is considered most relevant, and only the exact match is bolded by the engine. As you know, bolded keywords in titles and descriptions increase visibility and CTR, which is becoming increasingly important in all engines.

Chapter 8 covers how to use Dynamic Keyword Insertion (DKI). This fairly advanced feature allows you to keep several permutations of a keyword in the same Ad Group and yet still benefit from the bolded text that Google and the other engines provide when the searched keywords(s) are present in the ad copy or URL.

Use Keyword Research Tools

In the early days of paid search, keyword research was a task filled with real drudgery. The search engines were of some help, but the tools were limited and advertisers ended up missing many really important keywords. The tools provided by the search engines were so poor that an entire industry of third-party keyword search tool providers sprang up. Some of these third-party tool providers still provide incremental value, but as a general matter you can launch a complete campaign relying purely on tools supplied by the engines.

Google Tools

As you might expect, Google has a great keyword research tool, but only fairly recently has its data set of research information grown large enough (Google has the most searchers) to empower Google to provide search engine marketers with a rich mix of keyword information.

Google Keyword Tool

If you use the main Google Keyword Tool (**Figure 7.1**) from within your AdWords account, you can easily add any keywords that Google has found directly to your account. The Google Keyword Tool basically has two modes. One is keyword-driven, and the other is URL/site-centric. Each has its place, but my preference is for those new to starting a campaign to use the URL version.

Figure 7.1

Google Keyword Tool

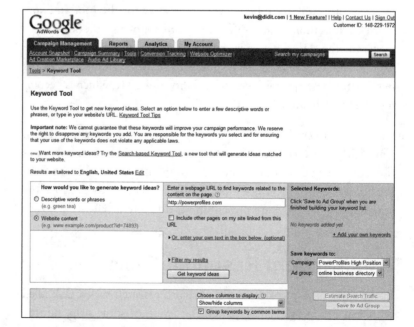

When using the tool in URL mode, leave the checkbox (which includes all the pages on your site linked from the URL you entered) deselected to keep your process more focused. Just take the URLs for those site pages for which you'd like to buy keyword traffic and enter them one by one into the Google tool. The tool will provide you with a list of keywords found on each page. It's important to know that Google includes navigational keywords (keywords in links to other pages) in the results for any page. So, it requires human oversight to determine if the page you are researching is the most relevant for the suggested keyword or if there is another page on the site that is better suited.

When you find keywords you want to add to the campaign, simply click Add to save those selected keywords to any existing campaign/ Ad Group combination. For this reason, I find it useful to pre-create as many campaigns as I'll need prior to using this tool. Otherwise you may find yourself putting keywords into a sub-optimal Ad Group (perhaps temporarily) while you complete your research.

The Google tool supplies a statistical report for the keywords you have specified for a particular page (**Figure 7.2**). Statistics include degree of advertiser competition (expressed as a horizontal bar), search volume for the past month, and average search volume.

Keywords	Advertiser Competition ⑦	Approx Search Volume: January ⑦	▼Approx Avg Search Volume ⑦	Broad ▾
Keywords related to mining equipment - sort by relevance ⑦				
mining equipment	▰▰	74,000	40,500	Add ⌄
gold mining equipment	▰▰	2,400	2,400	Add ⌄
coal mining equipment	▰▰	1,600	1,300	Add ⌄
used mining equipment	▰▰	1,300	1,300	Add ⌄
underground mining equipment	▰▰	1,300	1,000	Add ⌄
construction mining equipment	▱	590	480	Add ⌄
joy mining equipment	▱	480	390	Add ⌄
mining equipment for sale	▰▰	480	390	Add ⌄

Figure 7.2
Google Keyword Tool report

You can sort the keywords the Google tool returns by recent (past month) volume or total search volume. Recent volume is handy if you have a seasonally- or news-driven set of keywords; the Approx Avg Search Volume smoothes out the monthly spikes to give you the overall available search impression data. Knowing the available search volume is important because you can't build your business on keywords that don't get enough search volume. Another great sortable field (column) in the results is called Advertiser Competition. In graphical form it shows whether or not you have many or a few advertisers targeting the same keywords you might be interested in. Because the volume for each keyword shown in the report may vary widely due to your selection of Match Type (Broad, Phrase, or Exact), you probably want to toggle through each type to see these match types' effect on volume.

Regardless of whether you find keywords based on a site analysis with the Google tool, you must add the keywords to the best campaign and Ad Group combinations. You can always move them around later and perhaps even duplicate them (across campaigns with different targeting settings, for example), but finding a home for your newly minted keywords is critical. It's not just about getting a huge list; it's about knowing where to send searchers so that their queries can convert into revenue for you.

Google Search-Based Keyword Tool

The Google Search-Based Keyword Tool is also site-driven, but it extracts keywords based on actual Google search queries, which are also matched to specific pages of your website with your ad and search share, and are new to your AdWords account (typically excluding keywords matching those already in your account). **Figure 7.3** illustrates the way this report combines keywords extracted for specific pages with the common phrases used on Google. You may get similar keywords and phrases using both tools, but using them together is the most comprehensive way to use the Google toolset.

Figure 7.3
Google Search-Based
Keyword Tool

Keyword ideas						About this data ⑦
Save to draft Export ▾						1-20 of 165 ◀ ▶
☐ Keyword		Monthly searches ↓	Competition	Sugg. bid	Ad/Search share	Extracted from webpage
New keywords related to powerprofiles.com (165) Keywords not already in your account						
☐ promotional companies	🔍	8,200	▬▬	$2.27	0% / 0%	4TH GENERATION PROMOTIONAL PR
☐ car body repair	🔍	3,500	▬▬	$2.05	0% / 0%	Find a Company	Delaware	Middletov
☐ promotional products companies	🔍	1,500	▬▬	$4.69	0% / 0%	A & R PROMOTIONAL PRODUCTS D&i
☐ auto body repair shop	🔍	1,200	▬▬	$2.12	0% / 0%	Find a Company	Delaware	Middletov
☐ rent a car in nj	🔍	660	▬▬	$1.61	0% / 0%	ABLE RENT A CAR D&B Profile Bayville
☐ auto glass company	🔍	660	▬▬	$2.86	0% / 0%	Find a Company	Delaware	Middletov
☐ rent a car in new jersey	🔍	540	▬▬	$1.65	0% / 0%	ABLE RENT A CAR D&B Profile Bayville
☐ car wash companies	🔍	540	▬	$1.35	0% / 0%	Find a Company	Delaware	Middletov
☐ automotive glass replacement	🔍	540	▬▬	$2.49	0% / 0%	Find a Company	Delaware	Middletov
☐ automotive body repair	🔍	440	▬	$2.22	0% / 0%	Find a Company	Delaware	Middletov
☐ tractor leasing	🔍	440	▬▬	$2.89	0% / 0%	3KB TRACTOR LEASING INC D&B Pro

Yahoo Search Tools

Yahoo used to have a keyword research tool separate from its ad management interface. That's been shut down. So marketers choosing to do keyword research within Yahoo use tools that are built into the Yahoo campaign setup wizard. The only research option available in the wizard uses base keywords you suggest and has an optional crude URL-based refinement feature (**Figure 7.4**).

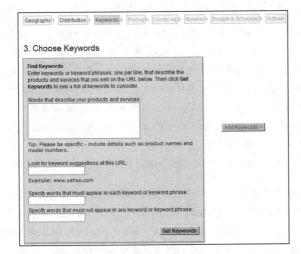

Figure 7.4
Keywords research tool in Yahoo

It's a shame that Yahoo hasn't supported and advanced its own research tools, but on the other hand, because nearly every search marketer on Yahoo also has a Google account, perhaps Yahoo simply made the decision to cede dominance to Google in this area.

Microsoft Keyword Tools

Although the Microsoft adCenter has a research tab and a pretty good keyword research tool built in, the far superior way to use the keyword research data that Microsoft has is through the Keyword Services Platform (KSP).

You have two ways to access that data. First, if you have a recent version of Microsoft Excel (at the time of this writing Microsoft had released support for Excel version 2003), there's an adCenter add-in for Excel that directly accesses the data center at Microsoft from your version of Excel. Since many marketers prefer to manage their keywords in Excel anyway, this tool is a great way to access the research and immediately have it at your fingertips. Although for small niche marketers the Microsoft data tends to overinflate the popularity of some phrases occasionally, in general the data is sound and is a great validation source for whatever you are using as a foundation, plus it may uncover some new ideas.

Your Log Files and Internal Search

Your site may have an internal search engine (a search box/form). If you have a search box and visitors don't immediately see a direct link to what they are looking for, chances are they will use the search box. Often, the types of things that visitors search for within your site are the same kinds of keyword searches that belong in your paid search and unpaid SEO campaigns as well. For this reason, the log files from an internal search engine can be a great source of keyword additions, particularly when new words or longer phrases show up repeatedly.

The other source of keyword information is your site log files (or reports provided by your web analytics). Nearly every log file analysis program or web analytics solution has a report of the keywords that were searched on by visitors arriving at your site from search engines.

Those visits are often (if you are lucky) the result of clicks coming from unpaid organic search results links, and in this case you may discover keywords for which you rank moderately well with an existing page of your site in a particular search engine for which you'd be willing to pay. You might decide on a second listing with a different title, description, and landing page that might serve your needs as an advertiser as well as or even better than the current set of links being used to navigate to your site.

The Others

There are dozens of other third-party keyword research tools. Some of them are stand-alone tools, and others are bundled with other search engine marketing competitive reporting. These offerings change on a monthly basis, and because these services are both numerous and their offerings so fluid, I'll provide an overview of selected keyword research and competitive intelligence-gathering resources for those of you who register this book at my website (www.kevinlee.net). The website will have a link for book buyers looking for these online resources.

Consider Keyword Clustering

The process of *keyword clustering* is one in which you attempt to find keywords that are semantically related and group them together in a way that approximates similar intentions in the searcher's mind. For example, the keywords *Jack Bauer, special agent*, and *24* are all semantically related. Similarly, there may be many keyword phrases that either share the same root word or root words that are synonyms of each other.

There are several reasons you might consider clustering keywords, including doing so for purposes of campaign simplicity or reporting. In general, you will likely be clustering keywords already within Ad Groups. However, when making bid decisions on extremely long-tail groups of keywords, some statisticians recommend that various forms of matching be used in an attempt to gain useful conversion data earlier (taking into consideration that such individual keyword phrases alone have very low traffic and see too few conversions to base statistical decisions upon). In rare cases, such analysis is appropriate. However, given all the other variables regarding a searcher (beyond the keyword) that also correlate with the likelihood to buy (including the profitability of the click or the favorability of the conversion rate), such an analysis must be performed very carefully. I mention it here only because some of you may venture into the areas of statistical analysis without thinking through the various targeting levers (including daypart, geo, and demographic) that we as search marketers have at our disposal, many of which go far beyond keyword phrases.

Understand the Traditional Match Types

Google and Microsoft have somewhat standardized the *match types* in paid search engine advertising to three types:

- **Broad match:** In a broad match, an ad can be triggered or is eligible to be shown if the search performed by the searcher contains the keyword anywhere in the query. So, if you advertise on the keyword *workboot*, someone could type in *men's size 12 extra wide steel-toe leather timberland workboots* and your ad will be eligible for display.

- **Phrase match:** If you enter in a keyword phrase and select phrase match, the method in most search engines is to enclose the keyword phrase in quotation marks within the tool or interface. Using the workboot example, your ad would be eligible to show if you specified phrase match and the search was *leather workboots* since those keywords appear in the search.

- **Exact match:** An exact match is, as you might guess, a request by the advertiser to have an ad shown only if the searcher enters the exact word or phrase in the same order.

There are flavors of the match types, particularly when it comes to defining just how broad one can go. Extensions to the core three match types are covered later in this chapter.

Yahoo chooses to define its match types differently, using standard match to denote its form of exact match (with some notable exceptions) and advanced match denoting its form of broad match.

When establishing campaigns in all the major search engines, the default match type setting is broad match. Accepting this default can be dangerous, and although broad match has a place in nearly every search marketing campaign, it needs to be used with caution. With broad matches, if you enter in the keyword *travel*, your ad will be displayed for the following phrases: *air travel, travel map, discount travel, travel agency, adventure travel, travel agent, travel accessory*, and even *travel medical insurance*, plus every other phrase containing *travel*. But wait—some of those key phrases don't fit your target market or are a poor fit for your landing page. Therefore, using the default broad match setting may not be the best way to go broad in your Google campaign. Title and description creative is particularly important, because in Google, your creative needs to *pull* (get you high CTR). Honing your Google creative to get a good CTR means separating out your keywords and phrases into different Ad Groups. That's where Google's matching options of phrase match and exact match come in.

What if multiple AdWords ads in your account could be shown based on the logic selected? Google has a specific logic in this case; exact match generally takes precedence. When there is no exact match, and more than one keyword set might be triggered in a phrase environment, the longer keyword phrase that matches is selected. An exact match within an Ad Group takes precedence over the broad match of another Ad Group.

While the search engines will generally include plurals, even with exact matching, it's often useful to add both singular and plural forms to an Ad Group if you want both forms and use the advanced feature DKI (Dynamic Keyword Insertion) to make sure the ad copy matches the form of the word that the searcher selected.

Use Negative Keywords

As you might expect, the search engines have evolved to allow you to tune your broad and phrase match listings with a negative match option. Different engines allow negative matches to be applied at different control levels (campaign versus Ad Group) and those options may change again. Conceptually, negative keywords are designed to allow you to suppress your ads from showing, even if the conditions ordinarily triggering them are present.

Broad and phrase match options have their positive sides and provide you with additional inventory that otherwise would be missed. But not every broad match is a good fit for your ad and your business. That's why you have to "think negative." With negative matches, you can specify keywords that will result in your ad not being shown.

When a searcher enters a query, they are expressing an interest in a specific topic. Often, the longer the query, the more targeted their intent. To serve targeted ads against these targeted searches, Google looks in the AdWords system to find the most appropriate broad, phrase, and exact match ads. Of course, any advertiser who happened to select an exact match to the search query would appear to be an excellent match. A broad match on a portion of the query may also be good. That's why Google pulls what its system considers to be the best ads from a pool of exact, phrase, and broad match ads.

For example, you may not be a retailer that competes on price. The keyword *discount* in conjunction with your product or category keyword can result in the wrong kind of clicks. Luckily, you can use a powerful negative match keyword. In Google, specify them in the Edit Keywords option. Enter negative match keywords preceded by a minus sign (–). By eliminating clicks that don't fit your preferred profile, overall conversion percentage increases, and budget is spent more efficiently.

A full campaign often merges keyword matching and breadth as well as use of negative keywords. **Table 7.1** shows how another hypothetical campaign might look:

Table 7.1 Hypothetical Campaign Keywords

Ad Group	Keywords	Negative Matches
1	*travel*	*accessory, insurance, channel, time, nurse, space, magazine, job*
2	*air travel, airline ticket, plane ticket, air ticket*	*pet, animal, insurance, free*
3	*adventure travel*	*job, employment, magazine*

The negative keyword option might better be employed at a campaign level if the engine supports campaign-level negative matches.

Compensate for Advanced Match, Extended Broad Match, and Other Surprises

Buying traffic based on keywords is simple. You pick the keywords you're interested in, and that's the traffic you get to your site. But if you think that you only get traffic on the keywords you buy, you're in for a rude awakening.

Unless you specify otherwise, most engines use broad match as a default when you set up a campaign. You might think you know what broad match is and the kinds of keywords that will trigger your ad being shown (and, therefore, cost you money) when searchers select your ad. But you could be in for a broad match surprise that might include misspellings, synonyms that are not as similar as you might prefer, and even typographical errors on domain names (both your own and those of the competition).

Google's match type extender has been called both expanded broad match or extended broad match, and in each case the way it operates results in an ever-widening definition of what queries can trigger display of a broad match ad by Google (resulting in a click that you, the advertiser, pays for). Google has updated its definition of broad match (at the time of this book) to say, "with broad match, the Google AdWords system automatically runs your ads on relevant variations of your keywords, *even if these terms aren't in your keyword lists* [italics added]. Keyword variations can include synonyms, singular/plural forms, relevant variants of your keywords, and phrases containing your keywords." The catch-all here is "relevant variants," and those variants have been known to stray quite far from the expected keywords you might purposefully include.

The only way to monitor this activity is to use your own web analytics and campaign management software as well as running a Google Search Query Performance Report. Use negative keywords if you'd like to prevent your ads from showing on certain keyword variations. Usually you'll have to wait until you've paid for traffic you didn't want before you can adjust your negative keyword list to address the problem. This situation provides one more reason to use broad match settings carefully in Google campaigns.

Yahoo used to call its match type extender *match driver* for the U.S. but now calls its matching system *enhanced matching* for standard match (Yahoo's version of exact match). According to support documents available at the time of this book's writing, "the enhanced matching feature of standard match allows you to receive traffic from user queries where the intent of the user is to find your product or service, even though they have not typed in the exact keywords you've bid on." Matching occurs when all the keywords in the query can be found in the terms you have bid on, or in your ad's title and description.

For example, let's say a user searches on *engagement ring diamond solitaire*. However, there are no advertisers bidding on this search term. The enhanced matching feature will then match (based on term, title, and description) selected listings from advertisers that have bid on search terms like *solitaire engagement ring* and *solitaire diamond ring*.

At least Google provided negative keyword control to all advertisers with its broadest matches. At the time of this book's writing, Yahoo provides no negative match overrides to enhanced matching or match driver (their older system) for most advertisers.

Consider Trademarks and Search

According to *The American Heritage Dictionary*, a trademark is "a name, symbol, or other device identifying a product, officially registered and legally restricted to the use of the owner or manufacturer." This definition is a bit simplistic. The phrase I've often heard lawyers and the legal press use is "likelihood of confusion." Keep that in mind as we probe trademark issues. The search engines' trademark enforcement and advertising policies (trademarks as keywords) differ and are changing regularly by country due to court cases and the regulatory environment. So rather than document a snapshot in time that is likely to be out of date before you read it, I'd like to cover the concepts of trademarks in search so that you can approach the issue as either a trademark holder or as an advertiser considering bidding on the trademarks of your competition.

Often a trademark is shared by several players in different industries, business categories, or classes. Sometimes several firms or organizations hold a trademark on the same term for different classes. For example, there are many trademarks on the term *Yale*, including locks, education, meat, material handling (forklifts), and clothing. A search of the U.S. Patent & Trademark Office's Trademark Electronic Search System (TESS) shows over 100 broad trademark registrations for Yale. The same holds true for many brands, including Delta, Continental, and many more. If you and fellow holders of the same trademark are bidding for SEM traffic and position, you have to live with this situation. Regardless of what the engine rules are with regard to trademark enforcement, it is likely that you and several other trademark holders have an equal right to show up.

The retail distribution channel sells a brand/trademark. It's your channel, and you may think you have given your wholesalers, distributors, and retailers the right to sell your products and services you might think they have the right to bid. However, there have been notable instances where that right has been taken away by the trademark holder.

Suppose your retail channel sends traffic on your keyword to a landing page where 50 percent of the content cross-sells to your competition, including low-priced competition. Your trademark may be used to route a searcher to the competition. Or, you may be competing against your own gray-market product or used/refurbished product (*gray-market* goods are those sold without the formal approval of manufacturers).

In the online marketing world, there are affiliates that act like retailers or distribution channels, but they are really just performance-based sales channels. However, unless you regulate keyword bidding, your affiliate network may bid on your trademark/brand. Many retailers' affiliate networks use SEM heavily to arbitrage the difference in their traffic costs and their earnings from you. When testing my clients' trademarks as keywords, these keywords tend to have the best conversion rates, and therefore a high return on investment (ROI), particularly at reasonable bid prices. That's why many trademark holders, in some cases, have started barring their affiliates from bidding on trademarked terms. Restricting affiliate use of trademarks often leaves the trademark holder free to bid on traffic unperturbed.

You'll have to look at the strategic, ethical, legal, and perhaps even moral ramifications of a trademark bidding strategy (assuming you want to move beyond your own). With respect to competing trademarks, do your research first, particularly in the legal and regulatory areas.

Campaign Setup: Titles and Descriptions

You don't have a lot of space and time to accomplish your paid search engine advertising objectives. The first stage of a consumer's impression of your ad occurs just milliseconds after the rendering of a SERP (search engine results page). And all you have to work with are three or four lines of extremely brief ad copy. So your ad copy had better hum, convince, and in every way work better than that of your competitors. Because no matter what the keyword is, there are only a limited number of searches per day, and the search engines prefer to show the titles and descriptions that are most relevant and compelling (all other things equal). For this reason, those few characters you write for a title and description can make a huge difference in your campaign's success.

Maximizing Search Scent

What exactly is search scent, and how do you use it to improve ROI (return on investment) and campaign profitability?

Search scent is an extension of the concept of information scent, initially developed by scientists at the Xerox Palo Alto Research Center (PARC). The most relevant of the PARC papers to search engine marketing was titled "The effects of information scent on visual search in the hyperbolic tree browser." Information scent is concerned with how users navigate the web, both within sites and from one site to the next, while pursuing information on a specific topic. The research illustrates that humans forage for information on the Internet in much the same way animals follow scent and visual cues to find food. Conceptually, scent is an application of user interface optimization best practices, and search scent is a specific niche based on the fact that searchers are even more wedded to a particular information-gathering mission than surfers or casual browsers.

This may be old news, but it's critical to note that the PARC team illustrated and proved that landing page testing and optimization must take a searcher's mission and needs into account. In PARC's research, the team was able to speed up surfing behavior by as much as 50 percent. And while you might not care much about navigational speed, you certainly care about *stickiness* (the degree to which the content on your site engages users and attracts them to return to the site) and being able to induce a set of positive visitor behaviors. If your paid placement landing pages don't reinforce the search scent, you will lose too many visitors to the Back button. Moreover, because Google has incorporated landing page relevance into its Quality Score, failing to reinforce search scent means that you will overpay for clicks (or miss out on higher positions for listings priced at the same CPC [cost per click]).

Ad Creative and Search Scent

They don't call ads "creative" for nothing. The best PPC (pay per click) ads contain at least one element of a multi-keyword search query. In the case of a single keyword search, it's also often a good practice to include that keyword in the title or description. DKI (Dynamic Keyword Insertion) provides an easy way to do this, but you need to use this technique with discretion because of an interesting phenomenon: The overuse of DKI (which automatically inserts the searcher's exact query in the ad title) can result in ad homogeneity within the SERP's PPC portion if all your competing advertisers are also using the DKI within their ads in a similar way. This makes the DKI a double-edged sword that you need to use with caution.

So to stand out, it may make sense to skip the DKI to use the full search term in the title and use it creatively in the description instead.

In **Figure 8.1**, note how many of the ads for *Elton John tickets* look nearly identical. Users (who often spend less than a second scanning search engine results pages) will consequently have a hard time deciding which ad provides the most compelling offer.

Figure 8.1

An example of unwanted ad homogeneity caused by marketers' overuse of DKI.

One thing to test, then, is the performance of a scent-heavy ad against a lightly scented ad. In cases where all the ads are heavily scented, try testing something else entirely. In my experience, scented ads usually win, but there are cases when a completely unscented ad may outperform amidst the clutter of look-alike listings.

Creating the All-Powerful Title

Twenty-five characters is all you get for a paid search advertising title. Your potential customer has just asked Google, Yahoo, MSN, or another search engine to satisfy an informational or commercial desire. So your headline, like a newspaper headline, has only a few fractions of a second to make a good impression before the searcher moves on.

In most engines, if the keyword searched upon is in the ad's title or description, the keyword will appear in bold type. Look at how **Figures 8.2** and **8.3** show SERPs with the words from the query *online marketing* in bold type.

Figure 8.2

Google's results page for the query *online marketing*

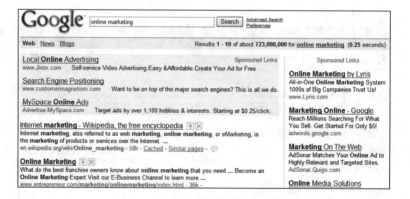

Figure 8.3

Live Search's results page for the query *online marketing*

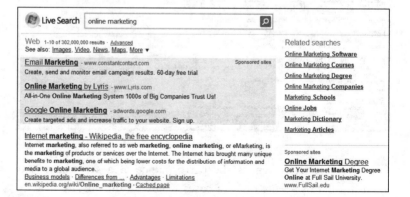

According to a Yahoo study (at the time of the study the company was still Overture, which was acquired by Yahoo) conducted by Nielsen, "users were nearly 50 percent more likely to click on listings in which the keyword was included in both the title and description." Clearly, the title is shorter but in a larger font size in the search engine results page. So when the search query is short (25 characters or less), one option you have is to exactly replicate the search query in the title. Figures 8.2 and 8.3 illustrate the pros and cons of using the search term in the title. Again, if too many competing advertisers use identical search terms in their listings' titles, your title may no longer "pop." On the other hand, if you are the only search marketer using the query in your listing title, you will dominate the paid listings section of the SERP. DKI use must be evaluated on a case-by-case basis because it is both a powerful tool and a crutch for lazy advertisers.

You may feel you have to give up too much space to use the keyword in the title, especially if the keyword is a lengthy phrase. If it's a long phrase and you don't have room, or if you want to include more in the title, at least distill the phrase's essence and include it in the title. If you have room for the full search phrase, trade off a portion of that phrase to get across a marketing message. For example, if your search term is *Olympus stylus 720 sw digital camera*, the title could include key search term elements that help the ad pop for searchers.

Some title choices might be:

- *Stylus 720 digital camera* (25 characters)

- *Olympus digital camera* (22 characters)

- *Buy Olympus 720 camera* (22 characters)

But not:

- *Olympus 720 digital camera* (at 26 characters, too long a title to fit, and would be rejected)

Creating Descriptions That Work

Description copy length, at two lines of 35 characters each, seems almost spacious compared to the length available in the title. If you use the search keywords in the title, you have the option of reusing them again in the description. However, even if you choose to re-include the search terms in the description, you may not want to have those search terms lead the description because doing so will result in the ad seeming awkward, unnatural, or manufactured, dissuading searchers from clicking.

A description works well when it contains one or more of the following characteristics:

- It reads like a sentence.

- It has an embedded benefit statement.

- It differentiates you or your offer.

- It includes additional information.

- It isn't too "sales-y" to the point where it seems unbelievable or less than genuine.

The best title/description combinations follow the time-honored journalistic format of writing called the *inverted pyramid*, and landing pages often incorporate some aspects of this style as well. In journalistic writing, you start with the conclusion or a bold statement, capturing the attention of the reader, and then use the strongest follow-up statements supporting that conclusion. If editors must cut, they can cut from the bottom without losing much impact. Similarly, a reader can come away with a solid idea of the story thesis from the first paragraph. PPC search ads should be similarly top-loaded for immediate effect. Just be aware that some venues that display PPC search results (search engines' syndication partner sites, for example) truncate listings, which means you may lose part of the title and description you just perfected.

Making an Offer

The title and the description combine with your site landing page(s) to form an offer. You may not think of your ad as an offer, but in reality you are offering to solve the searcher's problem. By articulating why they should select your ad and click through to your website, you are making an offer that they either accept or refuse (assuming they saw the ad). If your competition does a better job of promising to solve the searcher's problem in the ad and makes a more compelling case on the landing page as well, then you've lost that customer, perhaps forever.

Your ad's position on the SERP is the single largest predictor of a high click-through rate (CTR—the percentage of those who are exposed to your ad who click on it). However, you do have a chance, even if your ad is lower down on the page, and that's where the combination of keyword inclusion and the offer become relevant. My firm, Didit, collaborated with another search marketing firm, Enquiro, to conduct the search marketing industry's first eye tracking study (see **Figure 8.4**).

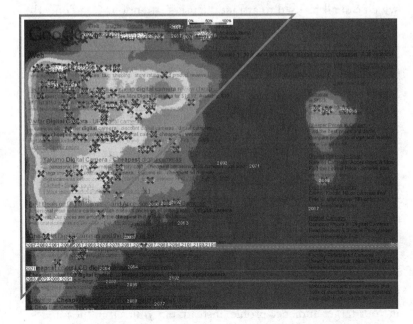

Figure 8.4
Didit, Enquiro & EyeTools Golden Triangle

The eye tracking study resulted in a "heat map" showing where users' eyes were drawn on a Google SERP. The most frequently scanned areas of the SERP are coded in red, followed by orange, yellow, green, and blue. As you can see, the most frequently scanned area occurs in an F-shaped or roughly triangular-shaped region in the top-left portion of the SERP. This region has since been called "the golden triangle" because marketers seeking the highest click volumes must all compete to place their listings there.

This study clearly validated the click-through data we already had based on position. It wasn't just that the ads at the top were the best performers in terms of CTR; it was that they were often the only ones that received significant attention.

In both traditional online advertising and offline advertising, most ad space is sold by the impression. With online display advertising, this means that marketers with objectives beyond immediate branding must write compelling copy. However, marketers often won't spend as much time on the copy or message as they should, because the graphical nature of display media means they have several crutches, including images, animation, rich media, and even audio, which can all be used to attract the users' attention. Consequently, marketers and agencies sometimes get so caught up in imagery that they forget to consider how an ad could be improved with a compelling textual message.

With text advertising, you're forced to focus on your actual message. What do you have that your competition doesn't? Can you fit your unique, relevant, targeted benefit into 70 characters? If you want to drive sales or lead volume, even a slightly more compelling offer may raise the CTR on your ad significantly, while maintaining click-stream quality. Every click to a relevant landing page reduces the chance your competition will get the click and make the sale or get the lead.

When thinking about which offers might be attractive or how best to describe what you have to satisfy the searcher, don't think about what you would like to see personally. After all, you probably aren't in your target audience profile. Instead, put yourself in the mindset of your best prospective customer. What gets them excited?

Some of my clients have had dramatic success changing their copy to be more enticing. However, not every tactic is best for every marketer. That's why a testing regimen is critical. Don't start changing things without understanding your baseline. Always compare any new creative against current ads. Compare the CTR and watch for changes in conversion (percent conversion for the clicks you pay for). That said, consider the following tactics to make your ad copy more compelling:

- If you sell on price, put the price in the title.

- Put the price in the description; lead with it if it's important.

- Consider using a percentage-off or percentage-savings message if you sell on price.

- Add *free shipping*, but make sure your free shipping doesn't have strings.

- Use hot, power words such as the ones in the following list. Make sure not to use superlatives because engines regulate the use of many superlatives and even some of the keywords listed.

great	*now*	*rebate*
save	*wholesale*	*coupon*
savings	*special*	*wonderful*
shop	*on sale*	*search*
huge	*compare*	*stunning*
latest	*massive*	*detailed*
excellent	*experienced*	*easy*
selection	*specializing*	*guaranteed*
low	*deals*	*quality*
discount	*leading*	
cheap	*VIP*	
choose	*outstanding*	

fabulous (works better on some demographics than on others)

■ Use brands in the copy if you carry them. If you're a brand, use that. A ton of money was spent building the brand. Use brand equity to improve the copy.

Let's talk about the importance of relevance. In ads, keywords, combined with powerful, compelling copy, are a killer combination. However, if the landing page doesn't follow through on the key points made in the ad, chances increase that visitors will hit the dreaded Back button. You'll pay for a click but get very little, if any, value from it. If the ad promotes low pricing or free shipping, meet this expectation on the landing page. You may need to shift around copy or layout on the landing page to improve the stickiness of that page for the searcher.

Making Your Benefits Resonate

If you aren't conveying benefits with your ad copy, and your competitors are, you are cutting your odds of success. What benefits does your product or service deliver that are unique? I'm not talking about special prices or other promotional incentives. There is often a place for these in your ad copy, and we'll cover that in the next section. However, you can't rely on promotional incentives as a crutch.

Consider making your ad copy benefits-driven. What will searchers receive if they chose your ad? What promise will you make in your ad and then fulfill on the site (and afterwards, when the customer buys)? Searchers, regardless of economic climate, are looking to solve needs, but they weigh factors other than price and promotion. If you can find a way to do it in the few short characters you have available, your best bet may be to emphasize emotional benefits. Benefits must resonate with the heart, not just the mind.

To determine what benefits may end up resonating with your audience, you have to remove yourself from your role as a search marketer who knows everything about your product. Instead, put yourself in the place of a searcher who has just revealed his soul to Google about a problem he has (OK, so that's a bit over the top) and is scanning the results looking for a perfect solution. The searcher had a motive for the search that occurred seconds before, and the more you can intuit his motives, the better you can write an ad containing benefits that resonate.

The biggest problem in moving beyond the searched keyword while staying away from simple promotions is the fact that searchers seeing your ad are not homogeneous. They aren't the same in every way and so therefore may have different emotional hot buttons. Some marketers describe and assign these different audience clusters using demographic differentiators, assuming that age, gender, wealth, or geography are the appropriate ways to think of different audience groups. Other marketers have recently begun to think of groups with different needs, desires, motives, and behaviors as having different personas.

If, in fact, there are personas, these personas must be identified using one or more of the targeting variables over which we have control, otherwise they become a moot point. Chapter 6, "Campaign Setup: Structuring Your Listings," discussed some of the additional targeting options available to you, and Chapter 9, "Campaign Setup: Conversion Pages, Bids, and Budgets," will discuss more about targeting beyond the keyword. For now, if there are ways to pinpoint large groups of customers sharing a similar mindset through additional targeting options, consider splitting up your campaign in order to market to these different segments with different messages. In the meantime, look for a message that will resonate with the largest percentage of your target audience.

Considering Incentives (Pros and Cons)

The obvious incentives are those that will increase the likelihood of a click but don't degrade post-click quality (conversion to a lead or a sale, or meeting whatever other success metrics you desire). You can't actually ask (or tell) searchers to click or take action. That's prohibited by the search engines. So let's look at the types of incentives and promotional language that may improve your click-through rate. Many of the tactics that follow are more appropriate for online retail businesses, but even services businesses or local businesses looking to drive in-store activity, phone calls, registrations, or inbound email should think about the psychology of incentives.

Price may seem like the obvious choice as an incentive to click, but price is a dangerous area for many marketers. Before embarking on including pricing in your ads, consider the following factors:

- Your brand position may not be as a price player in the market, so touting an aggressive price may actually convince people to look elsewhere. If you compete on other variables, price can be a dangerous incentive.

- Sometimes people prefer to pay a bit more if they believe there are additional service benefits. Buyers may have been burned in the past by lowest-price providers, and the simple mention of a price may cheapen your image.

- If you can't win the price war, why start it?

- Do you want a price shopper as a customer? Some studies (and some evidence I've seen with clients) show that price shoppers have the lowest predicted lifetime customer value because they are always shopping on the basis of price. You cannot count on price shoppers to be loyal customers.

There are other ways to communicate value besides price. Another favorite is free shipping, which is just a pricing message in disguise but may seem less aggressive.

Sweepstakes and contests messaging can be woven into ads. However, if you choose to explore this promotional area, be aware that the legal/regulatory environment can be a burden. Check with your legal team before doing even the simplest contest or sweepstakes. Another thing to remember is that if a searcher is really looking to solve a problem and is in the late stages of the buying cycle, a contest or sweepstakes may be more of a distraction and add little perceived benefit, yet for a shopper still in browse mode the incentive of winning something may be enticing. This means you'll be paying for clicks with a lower conversion rate to sale and instead are simply registrations, which, depending on your business, may be either highly valuable or nearly worthless.

Free trials work well for some online or offline services where trust is required before a long-term business relationship ensues. Not everyone perceives a free trial as a benefit, so the result may be a cheapening effect similar to that suffered when offering low prices.

Great return policies have taken some online retailers to the point of no longer having to compete on price. Their customers will pay a premium to have a liberal return policy. If there is something unique about your policies, and you can express this in a few short characters, consider weaving it into one of your ads to be tested.

Bundles (buy one thing or a particular level of purchase and receive something else free) can also be interesting, but rarely can you pre-identify a bundle that will be of interest to the majority of searchers. Unless you can increase your click-through rate, your efforts in bundling products or services should be focused instead on the landing page.

Adhering to Editorial Guidelines and Policies

Each of the search engines has its own editorial guidelines, and although some of the guidelines have existed for more than 10 years, other changes and adjustments have happened fairly recently, and such modifications happen on a continual basis. So your best bet is to read the editorial guidelines at the time you are crafting your ads. The guidelines can be quite in-depth and onerous, and until you become familiar with them, it's best to have them at your fingertips. Rather than discuss them in full detail here, I'll cover the most important areas and focus on Google's guidelines because it tends to be the biggest stickler on most issues.

The biggest divergences in editorial policies revolve around bidding for trademarked keywords. In this area, Google tends to be a bit more permissive than the other search engines, so that's one area where you may not be able to use your Google account as a master to export into Yahoo and Microsoft. The rest of the editorial policies and guidelines at Google tend to be similar to those of the other engines. Here are Google's editorial and format guidelines:

- **Accurate ad text:** This is perhaps the fuzziest and most subjective of policies and focuses on Google's mantra of relevance over all. Google never wants ads showing that aren't relevant to the searcher, just as it disdains the use of SEO (search engine optimization) to alter the unpaid results to the point of reduced relevance.

- **Capitalization:** Only standard capitalization is allowed. See Table 8.1 in the following section for a complete itemization of these standards.

- **Character limits:** These are obvious with the 25/35/35 maximums.

- **Competitive claims:** If you make a competitive claim such as *better than*, it must be supported. See the following entry for "Superlatives" on why *best* is disallowed.

- **Grammar and spelling:** It's tough to have your ad be a sentence with so few available characters, but sentences and phrases are the standard.

- **Implied affiliation:** Don't imply that you are somehow endorsed by or affiliated with Google (or one of its brands).

- **Inappropriate language:** No offensive or inappropriate language is allowed, including obvious misspellings.

- **Prices, discounts, and free offers:** According to Google, "If your ad includes a price, special discount, or 'free' offer, it must be clearly and accurately displayed on your website within one to two clicks of your ad's landing page." This may seem obvious, but it is more difficult to keep ads and landing pages synchronized than you might think.

- **Proper names:** Don't advertise on proper names.

- **Punctuation and symbols:** Use standard punctuation and symbols.

- **Repetition:** Don't use unnecessary repetition.

- **Superlatives:** This is an important one. We often find ourselves drawn to superlatives. According to Google, "If your ad contains the comparative or subjective phrases *best* or *#1*, verification by a third party must be clearly displayed on your website. Third-party verification must come from someone or some group unrelated to your site; customer testimonials do not constitute third-party verification."

- **Target specific keywords:** This may seem obvious, but then again, marketers who aren't used to a new form of advertising may miss the obvious.

- **Trademarks:** Google's trademark policies tend to restrict use of a trademark in the ad copy even though Google allows bidding for trademarked keywords. Become aware of Google's policies at the time you are placing your ads as there tend to be ongoing court cases that may result in policy changes. For example, the policies at Google vary by country. See Chapter 7, "Campaign Setup: Keywords," for more information on trademarks as keywords.

- **Unacceptable phrases:** This is the second catchall category and is designed to prohibit the use of call-to-action phrases such as *click here* or *click now*. Even *see this site* is considered too strong a call to action.

Using the Fancy Stuff

For many marketers, the task of customizing ad copy for each Ad Group, each of which contains similar keywords, is too onerous. The two options are to try to use some automated tools to pre-generate the different ad creative elements. An Excel spreadsheet with fancy macros can accomplish this purpose as can some pre-packaged software tools designed for this purpose.

The search engines also have a solution that works particularly well in cases where a generic ad container can still provide a relevant-looking ad. The search engines call this solution Dynamic Keyword Insertion (DKI). DKI is a fully automated method that inserts the searcher's keywords into your ad (assuming the keyword string isn't too long to fit). The DKI system uses a creative template and keeps all the other ad copy the same.

Here is an example of Google's DKI formatting:

Title: {*keyword*: cruise} sale

In this example, *keyword* is replaced by the actual search phrase or term. If the actual search is too long to fit in the title or description, the default is displayed in its place. In this example, *cruise* is what would be displayed. If the default text was *cruise vacation*, and the actual search was too long to display without running out of space, the system would use *cruise vacation* instead. Anything outside the curly braces ({}) is always displayed. Putting something outside the braces is not required, but it often results in a better ad. The downside is that you are more likely to run out of room. So, in all cases in this example, the word *sale* is in the title. So, if a user searched *Alaskan cruise*, the title result would be *Alaskan cruise sale*. Say the user searched for *Alaskan cruise vacation for singles*. The phrase is too long to be dynamically replaced, so the title would read *cruise sale*.

The Google DKI can be used in the title, description, and even in the landing page URL (to track the exact phrases searched). Generally, CTR increases with DKI over many other creative executions when it isn't overused by your competitors.

For the most advanced implementations of DKI, you can even take control over capitalization, automatically (see **Table 8.1**). However, be warned that excessive capitalization (even if triggered by the automated DKI) can result in ads being disabled. Also, the other major search engines don't necessarily support Google's capitalization rules. This can result in problems if you choose to export the campaign without addressing the inconsistencies in DKI implementation.

For your most important Google keywords, using templates may not suffice to make creative as compelling and relevant as possible. Therefore, instead of using DKI, put your important keywords in specific custom Ad Groups, where the message can be tuned to the specific offer or landing page.

Table 8.1   DKI Capitalization Rules

Keyword Capitalization	Example	Rule
keyword	google ads	None
Keyword	Google ads	Sentence (first letter of first word)
KeyWord	Google Ads	Initial or title case (first letter of each word)
KEYWord	GOOGLE Ads	Entire first word and first letter of each remaining word
KeyWORD	Google ADS	First letter of first word and all letters of each remaining word
KEYWORD	GOOGLE ADS	All letters of all words*

* AdWords ads cannot include excessive ad text capitalization (for example, BUY DVD BURNERS HERE). Capitalization may only be used where the natural spelling of a word requires full capitalization, such as in acronyms, technical terms, and trade-marked terms.

In Microsoft's adCenter, not only do you get an opportunity to use DKI, but you can use a feature called parameters to dynamically change landing page URLs as well as ad text. This highly complex feature, when implemented incorrectly, can do as much harm as good, so use it only if you are a sophisticated search engine advertiser. The features are well documented in adCenter as well as on the adCenter blog.

Starting with Two

No matter how well I've explained best practices in writing ad creative, and no matter how brilliant you are in coming up with amazing ads, you must test your ads against each other in order to establish which one gets a higher click-through rate while still maintaining a good conversion rate to sales or leads. Start with a second ad within an Ad Group to compare performance to the original ad. When testing new creative, use Ad Groups that contain power keywords first. Power keywords are high-volume keywords, brand keywords, or keyword combinations designed to match generic searches (shorter keyword phrases that represent early buying-cycle phrases). To give new creative a chance to outperform the old, boost price/position at least a bit (except if you boost from position 2 to 1). Unless you conduct a multivariate test, you'll often get an answer to your creative "survivor challenge" in a short period. If you test many variables simultaneously, however, the amount of required traffic will rise dramatically. This scenario often requires more time and investment.

To get a statistically valid sample for one keyword/engine/creative combination, expect to pay at least twice your CPO (cost per order) allowable. Assume you want leads at $75 each or to bring in orders at a given ROI that translates into $75 (based on a cost-per-order or a return-on-ad-spend percentage and average order size). The test requires a sufficient number of clicks to know if the new creative combination will work. If the clicks are inexpensive and the conversion rates are low, expect to use lots of clicks to get an order. If your clicks are more expensive, you'll need a high conversion rate to hit targets. You can use existing data to help model the test.

A good rule of thumb is you must spend 110 to 130 percent of your target allowable to reasonably conclude that the media pricing and creative aren't working. Even when you overspend the target by 20 percent (here, $90) without getting a lead or an order, it still may not be enough data to deem the test a complete failure.

Nothing hurts your business more than giving up on a potentially important keyword that can deliver enough click volume to make a difference, assuming you can find a way to hit your media objectives with that keyword. By giving up on a keyword, you give visibility, leads and, potentially, customers to your competitors.

That said, some competitors may use much more aggressive ROI targets than your own, factoring in data that supports lagged or offline conversions or using branding metrics or buy-cycle data. Or they could just be lunatics bidding for keywords at crazy prices. Regardless of a competitor's motives, you're stuck with them in an auction environment.

When a keyword tested at a particular price/position with specific ad creative and landing page selection doesn't deliver, you may be tempted to give up on it. Here are some reasons you shouldn't give up on a keyword with only a small data set on the first go-around:

- If you can get the keyword to work, the upside will potentially be very high.

- At a lower position, the same listing will be distributed to a different set of search engines.

- As position changes, page placement often will change radically, resulting in a different type of searcher seeing and reacting to your ad. A top position may attract the attention of "compulsive clickers" with low or nonexistent purchase intent.

Creative, keyword, and price/position work together for success. If one or more isn't optimal, the combination fails. Therefore, before condemning a keyword or ad creative to the garbage heap, consider ways you could test a different ad, landing page, or even set of targeting criteria (geography, time of day, syndication network and so on). Continuous testing is a requirement for a PPC search campaign, or, for that matter, any marketing campaign. Clearly, top marketers, including your competitors, likely reserve a portion of their budgets for testing, knowing that some of that money will be spent learning what does and doesn't work. To succeed in this marketplace, you too must continually allocate some percentage of your budget toward testing. I prefer to allocate 15 to 20 percent of the budget to exploring efficiency improvement and testing. Half goes toward new media (keywords and engines), the rest toward trying existing media with different creative elements (landing pages and ads). A well-constructed test is never a waste, even if all you learn is which ads actually outperform and which ones can't pull their weight.

Again, it's best to focus on high opportunity experiments and work your way down through your keywords and Ad Groups based on total inventory (popularity of the term), keeping in mind your typical conversion rates. For example, if two keywords are equally popular, and one already has a higher conversion rate, test new creative elements on the high-converting keyword first. Any gains will be multiplied by the high conversion rate. This multiplier is almost like compound interest. If your test results in a gain, this gain can result in dramatic increases in click volume due to the engine's preference for high click-through rate ads.

Chapter 9

Campaign Setup: Conversion Pages, Bids, and Budgets

Once your campaign goes live, you are paying for search clicks, so you should be well on your way to a well structured and tightly integrated campaign that hums along. Getting the click, however, is only half the battle. If you don't get the person behind each click to stay, look around, be influenced positively toward your company, make a purchase, or register (if you're doing lead generation), then you've wasted your money on most of the clicks. The solution is to have a system in place to measure the results of every click so that you can buy clicks (either manually or automatically through technology) more intelligently as the data guides the changes you make to your campaign. Most search engine marketers rely heavily on data gathered at the "thank you" page, the page after either an order is taken or a lead form has been filled out. Those pages are indicative of the highest levels of success. However, conversion pages are any pages that represent a positive outcome of the search marketing campaign and can extend across a website.

Picking a Landing Page

Now is a good time to revisit the topic of landing pages (discussed in Chapter 6, "Campaign Setup: Structuring Your Listings") because before talking about conversion, we need to determine the entry points for searchers visiting your site. The *landing page* is where the searcher ends up milliseconds after you paid for that click. Everyone wants the clicks to turn into revenue, but exactly how you measure revenue differs based on your business or industry. For example, a publisher might be out there buying clicks for multiple purposes and may be thinking about paid print subscriptions, newsletter subscriptions (which turn into ongoing ad revenue), or immediate page views. The search engine publisher may even consider those who sign up to buy advertising on the site to represent a positive outcome. An e-commerce merchant, a professional services provider with a local website, and a brand marketer will all have different objectives. However, what they share in common is that they must either pick an existing landing page on a keyword-by-keyword basis or create an entirely new one. The search engines all have policies in place that police and enforce some form of relevance standard.

Most marketers have more than enough existing pages to choose from, so the idea of creating custom landing pages or even fully self-contained microsites is not usually a priority. There are some good reasons to consider creating custom landing pages or microsites, but if this is your first campaign, or your anticipated paid search spend level is low, it's more difficult to justify investing in them because the payback period is likely to be long.

When you're selecting a landing page, think about the concept of search scent (discussed in Chapter 8, "Campaign Setup: Titles and Descriptions"). Some content management systems (or add-on technologies) allow for the creation of dynamic and personalized copy based on the source of the visitor, treating each searcher a bit differently. Such systems and technologies can execute advanced strategies and tactics designed to ensure the landing pages have some element of search scent and to merchandise the site correctly.

If you don't have the ability to dynamically enhance scent on your landing pages based on core keywords in a search query, you may want to consider implementing such a system. Alternatively, make sure your landing pages have sufficient scent to keep visitors moving forward rather than backward. The most common action on landing pages is clicking the Back button. You paid for that visitor, and the last thing you want expensive site visitors to do is head back to the SERP to click a competitor's listing. When this happens, you potentially lose that customer forever.

Information scent research seems to recommend fairly significant measures to increase search scent. This research generally measures and values the speed of information retrieval, not site stickiness. But highlighting words with color or enlarging buttons can often help searchers and site visitors find the content they're looking for, therefore increasing stickiness. Instead of highlighting, you may want to consider bolding keywords or otherwise making them stand out in the copy.

One example of real-time landing page customization is at CNET News. When you arrive from an organic Google link, the landing page says: "Welcome Google User! More headlines related to [your search topic]." CNET wouldn't do this if it didn't increase site stickiness. For publishers, it's all about page views and site stickiness, and we can learn from this example.

In research testing client landing pages, the results found search scent to be an important element. The jury's still out on exactly how "in your face" the scent should be. But the principle of search scent is clear: You need to put yourself in the searcher's shoes when selecting landing pages.

Determining Mission Accomplished: Conversion

You may be lucky and have a simple and straightforward online-only, measurable, conversion event such as a shopping cart "thank you" page. Or you might have a lead-generation form for a service or highly complex or expensive product where a purchase can't be or isn't typically added to a shopping cart. E-commerce sites generally have it easy with their online purchase processes. More often than not, they define success as a visitor arriving via search (or other measurable click source) and making it to the "thank you" page within a certain time frame.

Many marketers don't even bother to look at the conversion and success data they have. In paid search, however, the success metric data drives your decisions (or that of your technology), so the more data you have, the more options you have for managing your campaign. You can elect to use this data, or you might determine that its value is insufficient to warrant analysis. Or you may not be able to feed it into the decision-making process you use for bidding, segmentation, and campaign structure or keyword refinement.

If you are lost about how much data to use, you aren't alone. The online ad industry can't even decide how many marketers use data and analytics. Studies and surveys of marketers differ on exactly how many of them use analytics to measure the results of their marketing campaigns. The audience polled by these surveys has a huge impact on the estimates of level of analytics use. One 2009 survey by Alterian reported that "less than half (47%) actually use analytics to measure their campaigns...." Yet, if you ask a different audience and phrase the question differently, you'll get vastly different results. The CMO Council asked a similar question in 2008 and reported that "when asked how they tracked and measured return on marketing spend, nearly 20 percent of marketers said they did not...."

The question you need to ask is whether you have data you can use to improve your campaign through manual or automatic means. Larger data sets in the hands of sophisticated analysts with powerful software can give rise to some great epiphanies. But most marketers don't have large enough data sets, even when they choose to capture a lot of information about every visitor. It takes a lot of data to build an accurate predictive model that isn't out-of-date by the time you want to use it. Both large and small marketers can benefit from at least evaluating whether additional data fields in their conversion data might be useful for building better models and, in the case of the largest marketers, influencing real-time bidding.

On most e-commerce and lead-generation platforms, you capture a lot of data during the sales process. Perhaps you even have pre-existing data from prior orders from the same individual. Of course, you already know all the details about the current order or lead-generation session as well. Because all this data is accessible to your systems, with the right coding your "thank you" page can pass a variety of data into a third-party campaign management, analytics, or business intelligence package. Often the importance of some of this data is overlooked. So let's highlight why you may want to consider looking at data you might have overlooked before.

The obvious data point that you collect on the "thank you" page is just that someone made it there, that is, accomplished a yes/no binary conversion. This fact alone is valuable in tying this event back to all the targeting variables at your control, particularly:

- Keyword and listing ID (exact searched query and therefore match type)

- Time of day

- Geography

- Engine (not just the account, but the specific search engine or site source)

- Ad creative (some engines)

- Landing page (assuming you are doing comparative landing page testing)

The real value accrues when you start to move beyond the convert/don't convert data and look into variable data. For example, the following variables give you more options on how to manage and optimize your campaigns. These variables and data types are used differently depending on whether you have an e-commerce business, are a service provider, B2B, or some other types of marketer. Collection and analysis can be done in campaign management, web analytics, or e-commerce software and then used to create key performance metrics.

- **Revenue:** With revenue data, you can manage your campaign based on a ROAS (return on ad spend), also often called revenue per dollar spent.

- **Net immediate profit:** On either a dollar basis or as a percentage of revenue, many e-commerce systems can calculate the profit (or profit margin) of a sale. This ties in more to the bottom line than to the top line, and many ROI-driven marketers will prefer to manage to an ROI ratio (where return is defined as profit).

- **Number of items in shopping cart:** The breadth of the shopping cart may be indicative of or a predictor for lifetime customer value (LTV).

- **Use of coupon code and coupon-code type:** May also predict LTV or whether the customer is sensitive to price (additionally, this data could be regressed against promotional or nonpromotional creative elements).

- **Repeat customer:** Is the customer a repeat purchaser or a new one? This may be interesting if you want to know the different keywords used by new versus returning customers, or it could be regressed against any of the targeting variables in the previous list.

- **ZIP Code:** Does the stated ZIP code match the ZIP code derived from the IP address? Knowing this will allow you to gauge the resolution and accuracy of your web analytics software.

- **Lead score data:** For lead generation, were there variables that you can use to construct a lead-quality score? For example:

    - Company size

    - Time to purchase

    - Title (for a pull-down list)

Each business has its own data set, too many to cover in this chapter or, for that matter, in this book. Imagining the diversity of those data points and how powerful they will be in honing your campaign to deliver increased profitability is often a daunting task. Yet if you fail to take advantage of the extra data available at your conversion pages, you definitely will have a sub-optimal campaign running.

Using Binary Events and Scored Conversions

As shown in the prior section, even simple lead generation can represent a far more sophisticated process than a simple conversion to lead. Lead-generation campaigns are often managed on a binary basis (either the click resulted in a lead, or it didn't). Campaigns managed purely on a binary basis tend to be oversimplified. What's worse, in addition to oversimplifying, the data leaves out conversions that should be counted. The result can be a search marketing manager or even a technology solution making the wrong bid choices. "Garbage in, garbage out." This saying, from the early days of data processing, illustrates the fact that even the most brilliant computer program can't deliver when poor data are fed into the system. Well, the problem hasn't gone away; it's a serious issue today because many search marketing campaigns are based on garbage data or insufficient data.

A huge segment of marketers bases their entire bid strategy (assuming they even have one) on bad or insufficient data. Sometimes, reasonably accurate or actionable data is incorrectly interpreted with respect to bid intelligence (for example, how much to bid for particular keywords at certain times of day and in certain geographies). Marketers and agencies seem to focus heavily on the bidding process when it comes to managing paid-placement search campaigns. Often the data used to make these bidding decisions is assumed to be the right kind when in fact it's only surface data. It therefore doesn't accurately reflect business and marketing objectives. Hopefully this isn't happening to you.

For example, within business sectors where the only option is collecting information on leads generated, often only binary data is collected, when numerical data would be far more valuable. This is the case when a generated order or lead is recorded in a vacuum with no additional information allowing you to judge the value of the lead. Sure, you may be managing around an average cost-per-lead/acquisition (CPA) target, but chances are your business is driven by more than averages. All leads are clearly not equally valuable.

By treating all leads as equally valuable to your business, you are missing opportunities to obtain richer, more informative data and passing this data back to your other analytics systems. Better campaign management and web analytics systems benefit from additional data relating to marketing objectives. For example, passing back ZIP Code, customer score, new versus returning customer, or gender data can be important, particularly now that MSN allows for bid boost and targeting by demographics, and Google's Site Targeting network allows site selection based on visitors' demographic profiles. These additional targeting levers let you cherry pick the clicks that are more likely to lead to more and better-quality conversions.

When you determine what to bid for a keyword, you may be neglecting to include offline conversions. Study after study shows that a high percentage of retail conversions occur offline (the percentages vary by industry, price point, and shipping costs). Those conversions occur when customers use search engines to finalize a product or vendor selection. The offline conversion percentages may be even higher for B2B and services markets. Certainly for my wife's business (running a network of psychologists and social workers in the New York City region), a lead form or email contact link isn't the preferred mode of communication for an interested client. They call, and like in other professional services, it's not easy to interrupt a health conversation to inquire which keyword/engine combination the person seeking help used. In cases like this, page views and visits to the "contact us" page must act as success proxies for conversion events.

Optimizing with Shopping Carts and Revenue

Online retailers and all those who collect their revenue online would seem to have it easy. Their online shopping carts are the primary way that customers order, so those shopping cart pages and the resulting revenue are the means by which campaigns are optimized. The most common way that a shopping cart–based campaign is optimized is based on a ROAS ratio. This optimization metric and ratio works well if the marketer

- Has a consistent profit margin across products
- Prefers to focus purely on the immediate measurable results of the campaign while ignoring:

  - **Lost cookies:** Tracking is generally accomplished via a piece of code called a *cookie*. A significant percentage of cookies are lost due to cookie blocking programs and cookie deletion. So conversions may be occurring that are not tracked. Estimates range from 10 to 30 percent or more lost cookies over a month.

  - **Lagged conversions:** Cookies have expiration periods, and conversion sometimes occurs after the expiration of a cookie.

  - **Cross-computer use:** Some buyers research on one computer and then consummate the purchase on a different computer, for example, using work and home computers.

  - **Influencers and designated searchers:** Some households or workplaces have a designated searcher. Sometimes this designated searcher uses his or her computer to locate a particular product. After searching and finding the requested product, the link to that product can be emailed or instant-messaged to the requestor who subsequently makes the purchase. Clearly no cookie tracking is possible in this type of situation.

  - **Brand lift or influence:** Not every customer is ready to buy today or even this week. Some marketers prefer to include lift in branding metrics as a success factor.

Other forms of optimization take these issues into account either through a fudge factor or through the results of some kind of test or research. When information is available within your e-commerce platform at the time of the purchase, you have several choices as to where to collect the data for analysis and optimization:

- Collect the data in your e-commerce platform and attempt to reconcile or integrate the data from the search engines (for example, click price data).

- Use the tracking systems provided by the search engines to transmit the sales and related conversion data to the search engines so that you can see the ROI or ROAS in their standard reporting formats.

- Collect the data in your web analytics platform using tracking codes similar to those used by the search engines. Some web analytics packages are owned by the search engines; others are independent. In both cases, there are instances where the analytics packages can import click cost data directly into the reporting facility provided by the search engines. This data is important for generating the ROI or ROAS ratios.

- Send and collect the data in a campaign management system that will not only report the revenue and sales data in relation to the search campaign (by keyword and other metrics) but also make the appropriate bid changes to your keywords and adjust campaign settings to optimize your campaign. These campaign management systems typically let you optimize based either on a target ROAS, ROI, or CPA, or they let you provide a budget so that the system can maximize revenue, profit, or registrations based on that budget.

The campaign management process starts once the revenue, profit, conversion, and cost data have been combined to generate ROAS, ROI, or CPA information. One core element of campaign management is bid management, which Chapter 11, "Campaign Management, Bids, Technology, Agencies, In-House or Blended," covers.

Tracking conversions drives bid decisions, but many marketers prefer to at least estimate the conversions they can't perfectly track. Many will even provide some process or mechanism to factor in gains in influence brought about by a search engine marketing campaign. Direct marketers are more likely to ignore these fuzzier metrics and focus exclusively on those metrics that can be reasonably tied to an eventual sale.

Using Blended Conversions

Blended conversions are the direct marketer's answer to a holistic campaign that takes conversions that have a quantifiable value into account. A marketer with brand-related intentions will accept the fuzzier brand-lift metrics. Either way, the concept is one of blended conversions. The idea is to rank in order all the positive measurable outcomes occurring as a result of an inbound search click.

A holistic marketer will evaluate any post-click behavior and assign what are called *micro-conversion* events to the process. Micro-conversion factors may identify both influencers and likely direct purchasers. Alternatively, marketers can consider the use of a Branding Effectiveness Index (BEI), as described in Chapter 4, "Marketing Campaign Foundation." This index can be used to attribute value to nearly every conceivable positive behavior based on our understanding of branding metrics.

You might even make the argument that because micro-conversion or BEI metrics are an attempt to measure influence, even behavior from site visitors who are never tracked definitively to a sale should count positively. Search marketing is all about influence. Search marketers try to influence consumers or business prospects to take an action that will eventually lead to a sale, increase the value of a sale, or, at the very least, increase the chance that a sale is made. Micro-conversion or BEI blended metrics are an attempt to capture the lift in influence that is delivered throughout a site visit.

Many practitioners of micro-conversions would prefer to stick to measurements specifically tied to the online buy-flow, not taking into account the lift in influence or brand metrics that is bound to exist as a result of a visitor's extended time and engagement on a site. It's really a matter of preference. You may choose to be as direct response–focused as possible, attributing only the countable conversion to revenue (assuming you can measure those), or you can combine fuzzy branding, influence, and engagement metrics.

Blended Conversions Measure Influence

We've established why blended conversions were designed to reckon with the subtle problem of measuring influence. Interestingly, some evidence indicates that the buyer isn't necessarily the one influencing the purchase most heavily. Those influencing the buyer go by various names, and their descriptions are similar with some nuances. They are called the *influentials*, *influencers*, *mavens*, *passionistas*, perhaps *early adopters*, or, in the world of technology, perhaps just *geeks*.

Who's your office geek? The one considered most knowledgeable on technology products? My guess is that your office geek influences many people's decisions on technology purchases in corporate and personal spheres.

Search advertising reaches this influencer, even though no cookies set on his or her computer are ever triggered by a shopping cart tracking system. This influencer's word of mouth may influence more than one purchase decision. You need to reach these types of people with your paid search campaign, moving them to destinations where they'll spend time and absorb your message. The metrics associated with influencer behavior may be much more like engagement metrics (is the visitor engaged in the content?) and less like direct response conversion metrics.

Because influencers are located at the buying cycle's early stages, you must think beyond the measurable online conversion behaviors we know and love (such as filling out lead forms, shopping cart conversions, and visits to "contact us" pages) when designing search campaigns for them. Even tracking offline behavior, like phone calls, won't properly account for the influence they may wield over an eventual sale.

How to Identify an Influencer

It's highly likely that search and your site can influence influencers. For example, influencers probably have a higher-than-average thirst for information. So, using an engagement metric combined with your standard conversion metrics may be an appropriate means to identify them. If you get an influencer to read a lot about your product, remain on site, and otherwise engage with your brand, your message may positively influence this person.

Making Exit Clicks Count

No search visitor stays around forever. One way or another, they'll eventually leave your site. There are a limited number of ways a search visitor leaves your site, and (depending on your business) one or more of those exit paths may be a positive one worthy not only of measurement but as an objective of your paid search campaign. Exit-click percentages on particular pages can also tell a story of the relative merit to a visitor of staying versus leaving. So what happens to search visitors (or other visitors for that matter) when they exit your site?

- Searchers click the Back button. The dreaded Back button is the worst way to lose a search visitor to your site, even if you are a publisher whose sole revenue source is display advertising. Whether you paid for a visitor or they arrived as a result of organic SEO, PR, buzz, serendipity, or other marketing, it's a shame to lose an opportunity to engage that visitor unless your business is truly irrelevant to them. For search marketers, the most aggravating thing about a Back-click is that in many cases the search engine results page waiting for the searcher when they back-click is loaded with listings from competitors. These site abandonments are not to be confused with the next option.

- Exit clicks occur when searchers move forward through links you've provided to other sites. These links to other sites are there for a reason, although the reason will vary based on the industry, site type, or even where the page resides within a site. Not all exit clicks need to be measured, but if there are exit paths for which you'd like to gather data, it makes sense to use some form of measurement. The two most common are a redirect (typically something called a temporary redirect, or a 302 redirect, which routes the click through a click-counting system) or a JavaScript implementation that works on most browsers and reports the click simultaneously with the click action without redirecting the click. In both instances, an exit click could hypothetically leave your site behind, because many link types allow for the spawning of a new browser window.

- Searchers transact with you either by placing an order or registering (converting to a lead). Once they reach your "thank you" page, they may navigate out via an exit click.

- Searchers simply close the browser (or browser window) with your site loaded whether they have transacted, registered, or not. They may navigate away using the URL bar, a search toolbar, bookmarks, or other means. Google Analytics calls this exit behavior the *exit percentage* or *exit rate*.

Because exit clicks are clicks from your site to some external site or landing page that you have selected, an exit click can often be included as a success metric for a campaign. Measuring exit clicks therefore becomes important, and they might even be defined as the primary or secondary success objectives of your paid search campaign.

For example, some publishers sell advertising on a per-click basis. There are situations where a publisher may be buying paid search clicks (or image ad banner–based clicks), as well as selling search clicks to other marketers. This is called *arbitrage* or *click-arbitrage*, and publishers profit from it by pocketing the difference in cost between the clicks they buy to gain traffic and the clicks they sell when this traffic clicks on ads they host. Click-arbitrage is actually quite challenging to do because if the landing page is relevant to a keyword, you would need an exit click rate of nearly 100% assuming you were charging a bit more than you were paying for clicks. (Several years ago, there was a wave of "made for AdSense" sites that used the large price difference between CPCs for top positions and bottom positions to make arbitrage work, but most of those sites got caught in the Google Quality Score changes). Google sought to punish sites that gave a less-than-optimal user experience by recycling search listings as the only way out of a landing page. Therefore, they instituted a set of formulas that reduced an advertiser's Quality Score if the landing page was seen as being typical of a click arbitrageur. That doesn't mean all publishers selling clicks have been punished, but Google is certainly careful to see that a publisher adds value to a click before passing it on. Many publishers are either selling clicks or using clicks to justify their media's effectiveness.

Publishers, however, aren't the only paid search advertisers seeking to measure and optimize around exit clicks. Manufacturers often list their retail partners on a "how to buy" or "where to buy" section of their sites. Similarly, distributors and financial services companies supporting a distribution channel may send clicks to trading partners as part of their natural mode of doing business. There are often reasons why you might want to count or measure these kinds of exit clicks in much the same way that a publishing site charging for clicks does. You might want to show evidence to your distribution or sales channel that you are sending over clicks that should turn into leads and sales for both of you. You might be interested to see clicks to a parent company, a subsidiary, a press release, investor relations site, or even to an industry association.

If positive exit clicks are a success metric that you should be including in your campaign, put a method for tracking them in place at the individual session level.

Avoiding the Dreaded Back Button

When paid-search visitors click the Back button (which happens a lot), you've just paid for visitors who got nothing out of their visit. They may have clicked the Back button because you gave them a poor branding experience, which is something you never want to do. Recently web analytics programs have started reporting Back-click behavior as *bounce rate*. Google recently defined bounce rate as "the percentage of single-page visits or visits in which the person left your site from the entrance (landing) page." To effectively maximize the return on your campaign, you have to figure out how to minimize bounce rate while you are simultaneously managing bids and all other marketing initiatives.

Site stickiness or page views per visit is sometimes used as a metric that measures the opposite of the bounce rate. You will benefit from looking at both bounce rate and page views because more page views per visit isn't necessarily a good thing for many sites and marketers, especially if they can achieve the desired result either on the landing page (via registration form) or within a couple of clicks. More page views per visit could mean that your site is confusing.

You'll have to determine if site stickiness and engagement through page views are positive or negative behaviors based on your business and the flow of your site.

In a nutshell, the bounce rate is a proxy for relevance. The more relevant your site, landing page, and offer, the more likely the searcher is to move forward rather than backward.

Here are some things to look at when trying to bring down the bounce rate and improve the relevance for a keyword/ad/landing page combination:

- **Match types within each ad group:** Do you run the right mix of broad match, phrase match, and exact match? By taking some phrases and breaking them into separate ad groups with separate creative elements, you'll likely improve your Google Quality Score, which is another measure of relevance. That's very good.

- **Landing pages:** Review keywords in an ad group to determine whether to give them a unique landing page or move them to a new ad group. Some phrases within an ad group, even those you break into separate ad groups, might benefit from a different landing page—one that better addresses the searcher's needs. You'll therefore reduce the bounce rate and increase conversion, ROI, and net search profit.

- **Negative keyword use in ad groups:** Phrase search brings up advertisers with dubious relevance due to broad match being used without appropriate negative keywords to limit irrelevant results. Those searchers don't realize that the advertiser is a nonrelevant click and then return to the SERP after you paid for them.

- **Keywords by ad group:** Do your ad groups contain keywords and keyword phrases that aren't highly similar in meaning? By grouping similar keywords, you can tune your ad creative and reduce bounce rate, and as an added benefit, Google can assign Quality Scores more accurately.

- **Engine syndication settings:** Do you really want all your keywords running on all engines? If Google traffic converts better than AOL, Ask, EarthLink, and others, consider running separate campaigns. For example, create one campaign that opts in to Google's network with one set of bids and a second, Google-only campaign you're willing to bid more for. Unfortunately, you can't run this trick backwards. If AOL and other search engine traffic convert better than Google, you're forced to opt in equally for all search sources, Google, and the network. There's no way to bid more for AOL traffic alone. Yet pay attention to average position if this is the case, because lower average positions are less likely to be syndicated to AOL, Ask, and to the other network partners.

- **Contextual distribution settings at campaign level:** Do you have *contextual syndication* (listings active in the content network) turned on or off? The default in many search engines is to have contextual traffic turned on. Contextual clickers are not as ready to buy and more likely to abandon a page.

- **Geographical distribution settings at campaign level:** Some marketers achieve objectives more efficiently by using ad geotargeting. Think about your target audience and whether geo-optimization makes sense for you. Someone arriving from a region you don't serve is much more likely to leave unhappy.

The mantra, at Google in particular, is relevance above all else. Relevance for the searcher nearly always improves conversion rate. However, keep in mind that sometimes you may have to stretch the boundaries of relevance as well as the boundaries of measurable ROI in order to educate your target market on the existence and benefit of your product or service.

Setting CPC Bids by Ad Group and/or Keyword

The search engines will let you set default CPC bids at different levels depending on the engine, but all the major search engines (Google, Yahoo, and Microsoft) have one thing in common. They all let you set bids at the ad group and keyword level (because ad groups often contain several keywords that may have a different value to you or may be more or less competitive for position in the online auction). In **Figure 9.1**, for example, you can see that you can set the ad group bid. To set bids by keyword (to override the ad group default), you can select the Keywords tab. Also, notice that in this case the content network (keyword targeted ads displayed based on the content on a page, not a search result) is turned off in the section called "Content." Within each major section, there is a row illustrating additional information on the source of traffic. The best way to become familiar with all these settings and data fields is to open a Google AdWords account and delve right in.

Figure 9.1
Google's Ad Group settings.

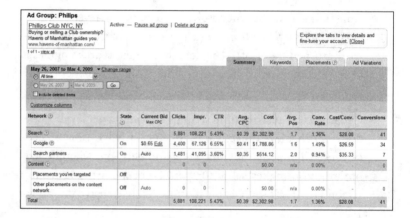

You can also see in Figure 9.1 that the search partners are turned on because there is both a status column and there are impressions and clicks showing up in the row called "Search partners." Often the click-through rate (CTR) for the search partners is much lower than for the Google portion of the campaign. Many postulate that even though you can't presently set current bids (max CPCs) separately in the search partner network, there might be good reason to do so. The cost per conversion at the current bid prices is higher than Google's CPA. There may be a reason to lower bids in the search partner network specifically to get CPAs in line. However, lowering bids will likely cause the ads to lose position. Therein lies the tradeoff analysis that every search engine marketer must make (manually or through some automated campaign management system).

If you're working on an online marketing campaign with the objective of reaching certain post-click objectives, you need to set CPCs (bids) at the right level based on the value of each click to you in near real time. There are two basic ways of managing a search campaign and a third hybrid of the two. The first is a pure direct marketing approach with no set budget. The second is a fixed budget approach that seeks to maximize the metrics being optimized (revenue, net profit, leads, and so on). The hybrid is a fixed budget with an allowable range of acceptable ROI or CPA metrics that can't be exceeded. For example, you might set a $30,000 budget to get leads for a law firm with no lead costing more than $50. If you can't get leads for less than $50 beyond a certain volume, often a portion of the budget remains unspent. In the vast majority of cases, marketers set their search campaigns to be "self funding" regardless of the budgeting method.

Running Self-Funding Campaigns

Self-funding marketing campaigns aren't a new concept. Yet they're particularly appropriate for paid search engine marketing (SEM). Campaigns are an investment. Marketers can set budgets and objectives to ensure profit. Profitable campaigns are often self-funding. When a campaign segment's net profit exceeds campaign cost, that segment is self-funding. Marketers understand that being self-funded helps them prove to management that bigger search budgets can pay for themselves.

Most marketers with a self-funding strategy in an overall marketing plan use an *allowable*. That's the cost of an order (or lead) below the net profit and, therefore, a guarantee of a profitable campaign. Allowables can be set using a CPO, CPA, or another ROI metric, such as profit per dollar spent, where return is calculated as net profit per order (instead of revenue alone).

At the end of the day, it doesn't matter which ROI metric you use, as long as the metric calculates the transaction's net profit and compares it to the cost of driving that transaction. When, on an ongoing and predictable basis, the cost of achieving a sale is less than the net profit on that sale, the marketing program is self-funding. The closer net profit is to the cost of marketing, the less actual profit is left for the company.

To get rolling and ensure a reasonable profit, marketers using the self-funding concepts don't factor in lifetime value. If some buyers actually buy more than just one order and generate profits far in excess of the initial net profit, that information isn't taken into account when setting allowables. In reality, some customers are heavy buyers. Over time, including lifetime value data can further improve the accuracy of a self-funded campaign.

Table 9.1 illustrates a travel company selling vacation packages to Orlando. Each package earns $90 in net profit. If a campaign runs the keywords in the table, it's self-funding:

Table 9.1 Self-Funded Campaign Keywords

Keyword or Listing	CPC ($, illustrative)	Conversion (%)	CPO ($)	Net Profit ($)
Orlando vacation (Google)	4.29	5.0	85.80	4.20
Orlando vacation (Yahoo)	3.30	4.5	73.33	16.67
Orlando trip (Google)	1.40	4.1	34.15	55.85
Orlando trip (Yahoo)	0.70	4.3	16.28	73.72
Orlando package (Google)	2.20	3.8	57.89	32.11
Orlando package (Yahoo)	0.40	5.2	7.69	82.31
Orlando (Google)	0.90	1.3	69.23	20.77
Orlando (Yahoo)	3.00	1.5	200.00	−110.00
Orlando package (Microsoft)	0.30	1.2	25.00	65.00
Orlando (Microsoft)	0.50	1.5	33.33	56.67
Orlando trip (Microsoft)	2.00	3.6	55.56	34.44

Net profit across most of these listings is positive, although some deliver a higher net profit than others. The listings with poor conversion rates compared to cost result in revenue, but at a negative net profit per booking. Negative net profit listings aren't acceptable for self-funding campaigns. The marketer should reduce the CPC and/or position in a paid-placement auction to bring the listing into compliance with a self-funding strategy.

Maximizing Profit

Profit maximization is always a consideration, even in a self-funding campaign. That's the process of weighing the trade-offs between net profit per order and total profit. Once you've established a self-funding program, you know every order pays for itself. That still doesn't mean you're making the highest total profit.

To maximize profit, establish a method to calculate whether higher bids for keywords that are making a net profit would deliver sufficient additional order volume to offset, and more than compensate for, reductions in the net profit per sale. In paid placement, dramatic increases in traffic volume can occur with only small changes in price. This is most evident with Yahoo but is also true for Google and other paid-placement engines. Increased click volume generates higher order volume, possibly resulting in higher overall profit.

Your objectives may include a CPO, cost-per-lead (CPL), or other CPA metric, or even a branding metric. The question then becomes: What quantifiable value should you set for your post-click objectives? You may be undertaking a search marketing campaign, another online marketing effort involving banners or pop-ups, or a combination of the two. Each will deliver against the objectives differently.

If you have not gone through an exercise to determine your CPO or CPA nor thought about setting objectives differently by campaign segment, don't despair. Nearly 50 percent of marketers are unsure of what to say when asked about their current CPO or CPA objectives. That's why we are circling back here to the basics of setting your numerical objectives. Setting CPO intelligently can result in huge gains in campaign efficiency.

If you have not measured your actual CPOs or other metrics yet, now is a good time to start. It is preferable to tag all your listings uniquely and keep track of the CPCs and then to watch your conversions by individual listing. The cost per action or order is the cost of the traffic divided by the number of actions. Each listing that has a significant volume of clicks and conversions will give you individual data. This becomes your baseline.

Of course, some listings will generate actions or orders less expensively than others. Even if you have not yet set your CPO targets based on business strategy, you can use your baseline as a guide and set CPO targets to eliminate inefficient listings (those with unreasonably high CPOs). Now back to the strategy of setting allowable action metrics.

Setting Allowable Action Metrics

Let's cover e-commerce first. In e-commerce, marketers most often use the CPO as their primary objective, although they may use secondary objectives as well. If we look at CPO the way many catalog merchants do, we will set a CPO or cost of customer acquisition target "allowable" based on the average profit earned over the lifetime of an average customer. This practice works with averages and ensures that the marketer typically makes money on the campaign.

When renting traditional direct marketing mailing lists, catalog marketers are stuck with the averages even if they examine conversion behaviors by list. They do not have the luxury of setting CPOs or costs of customer acquisition separately for different products in their catalogs. Search marketers have that opportunity. Some items you sell are high revenue and high margin, delivering a significant profit. So one way you can set a CPO is to look at the profit derived from the sale of the item you are advertising with a search listing. If the listing delivers the searcher to a category results page containing many items, we can use the typical profit we make on orders from that category. By setting your CPO objectives proportional to initial profit, you can concentrate your marketing efforts on the areas where you make the most money.

By moving from a fixed campaign CPO to one set by sub-campaign based on profitability, you put your budget to better use. Let's use an example from a hot e-commerce category: travel. (The following numbers are for illustration only and do not represent any particular campaign of any real company.) A travel marketer might initially set a CPO target to $18 for an overall campaign, because the average booking earns $30 in revenue, yielding a decent $12 profit. However, the following types of booking may have significantly higher revenue: cruise vacations, resort bookings, golf vacations, and first-class travel. Each of these booking categories may have revenues from $60 to $100 and have keywords associated with them. Coach airline tickets alone may only earn $21 in revenue.

Look what happens when you set the CPOs higher for the more valuable bookings and perhaps even drop the CPO target for campaign segments that don't drive as much revenue. Listings with higher CPO allowables can be bid higher or, in the case of fixed-price listings, kept in the campaign (for example, a listing that would have had an $18 CPO at position six can now compete at premium positions in Yahoo and still come in at a high profit).

Setting Campaign Budgets

The search engines all have some form of budget capping at the campaign or ad group level. The concept behind budget caps is that the Google, Yahoo, or Microsoft systems will determine what percentage of available daily, weekly, or monthly impressions to allocate to your ad listings in order to deliver the right number of clicks (too many or too few overspends or underspends your budget). The goal is to get very close to that daily budget.

Think about budgeting like a car's cruise control. By setting it at the right level, the campaign won't exceed budget. The engines allocate a lower percentage of available ad listings, not 100 percent of them, so that they can coast in at close to the right spending level.

Assume, based on your historical CTR and predicted impression numbers for tomorrow, there will be 100 clicks available at $0.80

each for the upcoming day. But you don't want to spend $80; you want to spend $40. So, the engine only shows your ad half the time.

Rotating ads is certainly better than only showing your ad during the first half of the day. But let's look at budget caps from a profit-maximizing perspective. Are budget caps for you? Probably not and here's why: Not all clicks from all keywords have the same value. Some keywords have wonderfully high ROI, and some are strong. Some teeter at the edge of unacceptable, but you run them because the ROI is still positive. If you were given the choice to buy only one click, you'd surely buy the click with the highest likelihood to convert to a positive ROI event (sale, lead, and so on) at the best ROI.

When structuring a campaign around a given budget (monthly, daily, and so on), the objective is to buy all the most valuable clicks first with the dollars at your disposal, then move down the click value (click predicted profitability) chain until you've spent your last dollar. If you can execute this mode of buying clicks every day or month, you'll have a highly efficient, perfectly budgeted campaign.

If daily budgeting is turned on at Google (or an insertion order with daily caps is in place), the engine usually randomly decides when to show your listing and when to skip it to stay within budget. That's inefficient. Randomness is never as efficient as a well-executed profit-maximizing strategy.

To strategically manage a campaign to a budget, don't use the engine's random budgeting method. Instead, apply the following manual techniques using conversion and ROI data from your tracking or web analytics system (some automated campaign management solutions dramatically speed up this process):

- Prioritize keywords by ROI.

- Understand the click volume and spending levels of each keyword listing.

- Get an idea or ratio of total click inventory you could get versus what you spend now (or, if you have budgeting turned on, what the maximum budget would be if budgeting were disabled).

- Based on the difference between the potential budget and the amount you want to spend, you have an idea of how much spending you need to strategically remove from your campaign.

- Examine the listings at the lower ROI portion of your campaign, and take one or more of the following actions:

  - Reduce the bid and position, which simultaneously reduces spend and raises ROI.

  - Disable listings that have an unacceptable ROI and already are running at low positions.

  - Consider day-parting some listings that have high volume and so-so ROI. High-converting times of day may deliver good ROI. Cutting spend levels during some day-parts will remove "bad" clicks from your bill.

If you use these manual techniques, chances are your highest value keyword listings, such as your brand name and other very targeted, relevant listings that drive the bottom line, will remain undisturbed. You control spending by reducing or eliminating the inferior clicks.

In Google, the ability to set budget caps by campaign means if you aren't using an automated campaign management solution, you could still group less-than-stellar keywords into a single campaign and budget-cap those keywords as a group.

Daily budgets can also help when you don't use an automated campaign management system that tracks conversions and quickly catches unforeseen changes in volume or conversion. Imagine if the product you sell was suddenly declared as unsafe. The surge in traffic volume and the compulsive clickers will select your paid link despite the low relevance for an information seeker on the dangers of the product. Spending would soar, and ROI would drop.

Don't leave your pay-per-click (PPC) search marketing campaign's success to chance. Take control of the listings. Use a profit and ROI strategy to spend in the most efficient manner. If you employ budget cap settings in the engines, use them as a fail-safe or when testing new campaign segments. They're not the best way to keep spending at the right level.

Chapter 10

Going Live

The moment of truth in a campaign is after the ad groups, keywords, and ad creative are all in place and the time comes to go live. After you've entered your payment information into Google, Yahoo, Microsoft, or another search engine provider, often the Next button pushes those ads live (unless they require editorial review). For most marketers, the scariest thing about going live is not knowing whether the searchers you are paying for are going to become paying customers. There are no guarantees. However, I can tell you that after 15 years experience as an online marketer, the visitors to a website from search have outperformed those from any other source, which is why I've become a huge fan of search engine marketing and made it my profession.

On the flip side, in many industries and for many marketers the bid prices that you must pay to achieve high visibility can be quite steep due to the auction-based nature of the paid search systems. You might think of these systems as Darwinian environments where only the strong survive, and perhaps in the long run that will be the case. However, in the short or intermediate term, it's not unusual to see evidence of irrational bidding. At conferences, I like to joke that there are only two kinds of marketers at the top of the PPC search results: brilliant marketers and total idiots. The brilliant marketers are paying a rational price for clicks, and the idiots are overpaying because they just can't bear the thought of losing the opportunity to have their ad chosen by the searcher.

A Fight You Can't Always Win

You probably haven't read much negative press about search engine marketing. Ever since Google went public, there's been somewhat of a love affair between the press and Google, and in the beginning that love affair extended to nearly every paid search advertiser. Only recently has the press started to report that search engine marketing by its very nature isn't going to work for every marketer and business owner. Business owners, CMOs, and VPs of marketing have also started having mixed feelings about the control Google (in particular) has over customers seeking information or even those who already know they want to find a specific company. A huge percentage of people who use Google, Yahoo, and Microsoft, or another search engine use it to navigate to brands and companies they know well. Use of bookmarks is diminishing. People just search, and they overwhelmingly start their search in Google. Consumers are changing their behavior, and forward-thinking marketers need to reach them where they live.

You also have competition in the offline world, in addition to those bidding against you for visibility in the search results. Although not every one of your competitors bids on the same keywords in the same search engines that you do, many of them do, particularly if you are in a large industry and have a lot of offline competition. If you define winning the search marketing war as having every keyword in a position higher than your competition, all the time on every keyword, you are unlikely to remain profitable. Instead, you may be in for a wild ride, and you'll make Google (et al) very happy with your competitive bidding. For any combination of industries and regions, you and your competitors will often want clicks on the very same keywords. It would be unusual if you were the only bidder on even half your keywords (especially in Google where the number of advertisers is well over one million). Google doesn't publicly share how active its millions of advertisers are and how competitive they are with each other. However, one thing is clear: There is only room for 10 to 15 paid listings in a SERP (search engine results page). According to all available data regarding click density across SERPs, clicks are heavily concentrated in the top four or five positions, particularly if between one and three ads are displayed at the top in the paid results.

By definition, most search engine advertisers are failing to capture the lion's share of the clicks they'd love to have but can't afford. The majority of advertisers have to make do with the scraps (lower volume clicks occurring at lower positions). If you've only recently launched a campaign, you will suffer from several disadvantages, including a poor Google relevance score (Quality Score) and a fresh unoptimized campaign. Consequently, you may end up as one of those search engine marketers forced to live on scraps. After all, your campaign is much newer than that of your competition. If one or more of your competitors is smart (and some of them may be), they've had months or years to experiment with ad copy, landing pages, offers, and keyword match types. Chances are that unless you've got something really special to offer or a very strong brand in your industry to trump their finely honed campaign, you'll have to pay more to get in there and grab clicks away from them.

This brings us to the concept of the *winner's curse*. This concept generally applies to *common value* auctions such as paintings, houses, or cars where the winner is the high bidder who clearly estimated the value of the asset as being greater than all the others. In many cases that estimate differs so much from the other estimates that it is highly likely that the winning bidder overpaid. Wikipedia defines the winner's curse as follows: "...the winner's curse says that in such an auction, the winner will tend to overpay. The winner may overpay or be 'cursed' in one of two ways: 1) the winning bid exceeds the value of the auctioned asset such that the winner is worse off in absolute terms; or 2) the value of the asset is less than the bidder anticipated, so the bidder may still have a net gain but will be worse off than anticipated."

In paid search, every marketer puts a different value on clicks from a specific keyword, engine, time of day, and geography. Because there isn't a common utility (value) of the click to the marketer or advertiser, each advertiser should be bidding rationally based on estimates of a click/visitor's value to them. The "winner" in paid search doesn't even necessarily get the click every time (each time a SERP is displayed it's a new auction); all you control with your bid is your likely position and the odds that your improved visibility will let you get the click. Another interesting factor in paid search makes the winner's curse analogy more fascinating: Sometimes there is more than one winning bidder per search result. In a single SERP, a searcher may navigate to you or your competition and then click the Back button, or if the searcher is like me, open several paid or unpaid pages in quick succession in order to take advantage of background content loading while I peruse the first result to load.

The important thing to take away from the winner's curse when adapted to paid placement billed on a CPC basis is that you or other bidders may overpay if you mis-estimate the value of a click. Also, if you lack enough information about the click, you might be forced to push bids higher than you would given adequate information. For example, because you aren't given an opportunity to re-bid in real time on a SERP-by-SERP basis, you are managing bids based on a variety of targeting and campaign settings. A particular search within the Google network, for example, may be originating from Ask.com, AOL.com, or Google.com. Plus, this search may have been made by a new or a returning customer. Lacking this information, you are generally going to err on the aggressive side, because once you've missed the opportunity to grab this searcher, you may never get that opportunity again. Instead, your competition may close that customer and recognize a significant profit over time.

The better you are at estimating the true value of a click from a particular keyword, engine, and set of targeting parameters, the less often you'll be cursed with a paid click that doesn't convert to a profitable sale or take other positive steps toward a purchase.

Start with Google

You can clearly learn what might work within a paid search campaign much more quickly in Google. The traffic volumes are much higher, and although the clicks may not be cheap, particularly for new advertisers who haven't yet demonstrated relevance to Google (as measured by a Quality Score), the learning process is fast. But before you set that daily budget cap or even set your initial bids in Google, take a step back and think about the role Google plays in the broader marketing ecosystem and how your customers and prospects interact with Google. The consumer has habituated their Google use, and the significant lead that Google has in search query share volume makes it the no-brainer place to launch a campaign. Google owns more eyeballs, and even when it doesn't own them it leases them via syndication deals (AOL, Ask.com, and so on).

That's one of the reasons marketers start with and often never move beyond Google. But others think about the money they pay Google and the constant efforts they have to put into SEO as a tax. Increasingly, I hear an undercurrent of discontent from more and more marketers. They're concerned that search engines and pay-for-performance marketing channels (such as affiliate marketing, where commissioned affiliates build websites specifically designed to rank high in Google, Yahoo, or Microsoft search results for a specific advertiser or brand) have turned into tolls or taxes on their businesses. The claim is that these advertising and sales channels are becoming less about customer acquisition and more about repeatedly paying to maintain share of wallet with existing customers.

Reach Consumers When They Search

The online marketing ecosystem has evolved in an interesting way, creating unexpected pinch-points or conduits through which customers generally pass by choice (even if they don't have to). Search engine SERPs and organic landing pages generated by affiliates well versed in SEO represent a huge segment of inbound traffic to marketers. They have the cancelled checks to prove it. Few would have thought 15 years ago that libraries, newspapers, and the Yellow Pages would all be replaced by a new information and commerce conduit, the search engines.

At first glance, it seems that search engines and affiliates are often in positions to get a free ride, making money by capitalizing on the interest stimulated through a merchant's or brand holder's advertising, marketing, PR, and even sales efforts. Consequently, many might call the search engines and affiliate marketers leeches. After all, a big segment of customers originating through these channels are existing customers, returning with a price tag attached.

Affiliates often use both paid and organic search results to generate revenues, leveraging the content and brand names obtained from the merchants. Are the search engines any different when they sell clicks from the query demand generated through a marketer's advertising, PR, and buzz? Do the engines unfairly appropriate and leverage the copyrighted material on billions of websites, and then charge for clicks from humans who already know they want to access a merchant or site? Do affiliates who use PPC arbitrage or create organic pages that rank highly for brands, trademarks, and model numbers profit unfairly, joining the search engines by sucking the profit out of the marketers' and merchants' pockets without adding value?

The answers clearly depend on your perspective. But the alternative to paying the continued fees to both affiliate and search engines might be even more painful than the ongoing toll marketers pay to gain (and regain) customers through search and affiliate channels. Consumers are changing their behavior, and forward-thinking marketers need to reach them where they live, which is increasingly in the online space. To continue capturing these customers, marketers are necessarily tied to the new ecosystem. To gain some perspective on this issue, let's take a step back, looking at the world of advertising, marketing, and sales outside the Internet.

Advertising and marketing aren't just about getting new customers; they're also about holding onto the customers you already have and maximizing share of wallet for customers you might share with your competition. Coke and Pepsi have, at this point, had nearly every cola drinker as a customer at least once. Yet the two organizations continue to spend hundreds of millions of dollars on advertising, sponsorships ("American Idol," for example), and in-store promotions (including slotting fees, which are fees paid to display goods in high-volume locations).

The truth is that a healthy chunk of revenues for the vast majority of companies are funneled toward marketing to maintain share of wallet and customer loyalty. This practice in the offline media world is longstanding and established, and yet for some reason the Internet is judged by a completely different set of standards. It's easy to accuse Google, Yahoo, Microsoft, and the affiliate networks of being leeches both because they're so visible in the value chain, and because their value seems invisible. Consumers have simply changed their behavior from watching TV and reading newspapers to surfing and searching. TV networks and newspapers that don't have strong online migration plans will suffer as consumers' eyeballs migrate online.

What's difficult for marketers to swallow, however, is the clear evidence that the search engines (and affiliate marketers with good organic rankings on brand terms) have the power to insert themselves between the consumer and the brand, even when consumers clearly have an interest in the brand (as indicated by search queries containing the brand or trademark). Some (including American Airlines) have even resorted to lawsuits against the search engines in an attempt to enjoin competitors from bidding on their brand keywords; so far, these efforts have all been unsuccessful, either failing in court or being settled out of court.

Yes, it does seem unfair that marketers who've spent millions or billions over the years to establish brand equity must now repurchase their own branded terms, and it's understandable that many might be tempted to refuse to pay for brand keywords, sticking instead to the generic keywords clearly aimed at any given target audience. But in every case we've tested (and I have tested many and will likely test many more), doing so would be a mistake, even when the marketer has high organic rankings on its brand terms. The results of every test I've executed indicate that the incremental gain received when paying for traffic on a brand term has a very high net ROI because:

- You gain significant additional screen real estate on the SERP.

- The total control over title and description allows for greater offer control.

- Top positions on your brand usually aren't very expensive due to the engines' relevance algorithms.

- You gain the ability to control and tune the landing page results in a conversion rate percentage, which in many cases is higher for the combined pages than for one alone.

I urge you not to think of Google and its brethren as leeches any more than other media are leeches. Think of search as the net you cast to capture the demand created by all your sales, marketing, PR, and advertising efforts. Fail to cast this net, and your customers will get away. Perhaps a more productive way to think about all of these costs is to regard them as CRM (customer relations management) expenditures.

Model the Launch

Before you launch, you need to set initial bid prices, and to do this you need at least a rudimentary model. Setting your metrics is important before launch because having an ROI target, a CPO, or a CPA at least provides something of a temporary proxy for estimating what CPCs you are likely to tolerate. Setting these targets intelligently at the beginning of the process can result in huge gains in campaign efficiency.

Here's how to go through a prelaunch CPC target range estimation. First, estimate a conversion rate from click to lead or sale. If you have access to benchmarks for your industry, you can use them, but benchmarks can be misleading because brand keywords can convert at ten times the benchmark and less relevant keywords at one quarter the benchmark. It's not unusual for conversion rates to be in the single digits or low single digits. Once you've picked the conversion rate for you model (let's assume an aggressive 5 percent), you back out the CPC you can afford based on your ROI target. If you are using a CPA or CPO, then simply do the math. Assume that your CPO equals $20 and one in 20 (5 percent) of your clicks convert. You can therefore afford a CPC up to $1. If you need to use an ROAS percentage target, you'll need to use the average shopping cart size to convert this number into a CPO and then use the same math we just outlined.

As you go through the campaign setup processes described in this book, many of the search engines, including Google, will estimate prelaunch CPCs and the positions you can expect to achieve given particular bids. By going through this very rough estimation process as to the affordability of clicks beforehand, you can make a judgment call as to how high to bid when you set up the account. If you are optimistic that a keyword will outperform the assumptions you made during your initial calculations, then bidding high during launch may be perfectly OK. As the data flows in after you go live, either yourself, a staff member, or an automated campaign management technology will know fairly quickly how far off your assumptions were (positively or negatively).

E-commerce ROI is often measured in a continuum using revenue or profit per order. Lead generation for both consumer and business-to-business (B2B) should also be measured and optimized on a continuum, and therefore initial bids can be set based on assumptions with regard to lead value. In B2B marketing, you're often trying to generate leads or registrations. As with e-commerce marketing, not all leads are created equal. Tag your leads and see which ones actually convert to sales. For example, our payroll services client knows the keyword and engine driving every lead. If a particular keyword or engine delivers traffic resulting in a better-than-average conversion to sale, the CPL allowable should be raised for that listing. This will result in more of the valuable leads that convert into sales.

If you have a sophisticated business analytics platform and tag each new customer by the source of his acquisition, you can even factor in lifetime value in both e-commerce and B2B situations. In addition, not everyone is always ready to buy, and some listings may attract a greater percentage of potential customers in the early research stages of the buying cycle. Studies of your prospect behavior may help you map additional positive behaviors to your search campaigns. So when you do your calculations of initial bid pricing on a lead generation campaign, any prior data as to what targeting factors might generate a higher quality lead can be factored in. The objective for launch is to set bids in the general vicinity that they will settle down to (on average, since day-parting will of course create intraday volatility, which we'll cover in the next chapter when we talk about bidding). The conservative marketer can estimate low (or round down), and the aggressive marketer can round up and therefore learn more quickly.

Make the Leap to Yahoo and Microsoft

Yahoo and Microsoft know that there is a high likelihood that you started your search advertising campaign in Google and perhaps have done a fair amount of testing, tuning, and adjustments to that campaign. So both engines have provided advertisers with tools to import a Google campaign that has been exported into a spreadsheet. However, the import process doesn't always go perfectly, and a certain amount of human oversight is often necessary. Plus, you may be using an analytics, tracking, or campaign management system requiring that all campaigns be run with new tracking codes. Other systems can go in through the API (application programming interface) and make the appropriate adjustments directly in the search engines.

You should check for the following after a campaign export and re-import process:

- **DKI listings:** Not all the engines treat the dynamic keyword insertion process identically. This requires at least a spot-check or perhaps even a full review.

- **Landing pages:** Do they all still resolve?

- **Tracking URLs:** Have they been implemented, and are they working?

- **Ad creative:** If you had more than one creative ad copy running for an ad group, is it still there?

- **Bids:** Do you want to set bids identically for launch, or as I'd recommend, raise them significantly and let the poor performers prove themselves as such?

Implement Targeting, Beyond Keywords

With more accurate targeting, the industry can move one step closer to a perfect marketplace: one in which people only see ads relevant to them, and preferably at times when that ad is most relevant. When marketers can better target ads, they'll pay higher prices for advertising. This has been a primary driver of increased CPC in the PPC ad markets.

As marketers begin to truly understand the value that impressions and clicks bring to their businesses, they bid more for these opportunities. The pressure to fight for scale (click or impression volume) can be grueling within auctions. For those with strong businesses, strong brands, and compelling offers, auction-based media offer great opportunities.

What opportunities do the evolution of search and contextual targeting create for you and your business?

All three search engines now let you select your audiences using targeting methods extending beyond the keyword. Google hasn't yet implemented such methods for search clicks, but Yahoo and Microsoft now offer demographic bidding for paid placement listings on their content networks. Would you like to target women 18 to 25 with your advertising, because they're more likely to buy your product or they're the kind of profitable customers you dream of? If women or men of any age represent high-value segments of your overall target audience, you can boost your bid per click on any keyword for that segment alone.

The search engines recently have provided a whole new level of targeting by allowing marketers to better select their target audience by age, gender, geography, or day-part (time of day or day of week). This results in more relevant ads. More relevant ads create a win-win scenario for advertisers and consumers. Improved relevancy also drives up prices (monetization and yield). This makes targeting improvements a home run for publishers and ad networks alike. Available segments are typically:

- Age (five demographic segments)

- Gender

- Geography (designated marketing areas [DMAs])

Ad creation, media research, media targeting, real-time bidding, success tracking, ad testing, landing page testing, offer testing, segmentation modeling, strategy adjustment, campaign re-trafficking, and spending reconciliation are all individually complex tasks. When they all must occur on an ongoing basis, it's clear that running search marketing campaigns (as well as other campaigns that run through the search engine auction networks) requires a significant amount of resources. Unlike the early days of paid placement search marketing, this isn't something you can do in your spare time.

The question becomes this: Can these tasks be automated so technology is doing the heavy lifting, or is this a situation where human experts must watch and learn, applying creativity to the challenges an automated solution could never master? For most marketers, the answer is that some combination of technology and people is optimal. The key is to select the right technology and the right team to deploy, manage, and monitor it.

A large team, even a dedicated one, is meaningless if it isn't top notch, up to speed on SEM, and professional in its execution of a project plan. Sure, sometimes humans and technology can both accomplish the same tasks, meaning you can replace technology with additional human resources. Often, though, this is a foolish mistake. I've seen instances where marketing teams have made agency selection choices based to a large extent on dedicated headcount in the hope there might be a superstar or two at the agency who might be redeployed to their account. That's a risky proposition to be sure, particularly given some agencies' turnover rates. I'd also worry about an agency's willingness to dedicate a superstar to win a contract, only to yank that person away when other clients complain or until the next pitch.

An example of humans being almost fully replaced with technology is bid management. The search engines have provided tools for marketers who want to manage campaigns through the standard online interfaces. Much functionality that once was available only in third-party bid management solutions is now showing up in the Yahoo interface, Google's AdWords, and Microsoft's adCenter. Better budget control and bid control are becoming standard, engine-provided features. The engines also offer third-party providers' sophisticated APIs, allowing for the execution of whichever formulaic campaign or bid strategies those third-party providers find appropriate.

Of course, those of us in the business of building technology have taken full advantage of engine-provided APIs and have adapted technology and service offerings to go beyond bid management into full campaign management solutions. As the engines make the black-box formulae controlling the position of listings more opaque, there's a need for more sophisticated, customizable technology for more sophisticated marketers for whom the engine-supplied solutions are insufficient.

Regardless of which technology solution you use—engine-supplied tools, rudimentary third-party bid management tools, or a more sophisticated platform—you can't discount the importance of expertise and the human factor. The keyword and advertising text alone are only part of the overall campaign structure. It is critically important how ad groups (I'm referring to any engine's ad groups) are populated; match types and negative keywords are selected; and creative elements are maximized. All of these still require the human touch. Larger advertisers may get some help from the search engines in these high-touch areas; others must rely on their agencies or do it in house. There's no shortage of tactical to-do items in any campaign at any time, so it's often a matter of prioritization for those running campaigns and strategies.

There are probably a whole bunch of tests that will help improve ad response and relevance. Moreover, each business is different, meaning there are strategic implications to SEM campaigns that militate against cookie-cutter solutions. Someone experienced in business and marketing must look beyond the day-to-day tactical work to explore the campaign's strategy. Objectives used by the technology and tactical teams must always be aligned with the interests of the business as a whole. Business objectives can change based on season, competitive landscape, profitability, and management preference.

Some folks think complexity and the need for technology and smart marketers will dissipate as the engines and ad marketplaces simplify interfaces and add tools. Yet across the online and offline advertising ecosystem, one thing is clear: Consumers control the ads they pay attention to and those they choose to interact with. So targeting and relevance must always improve. Technology can only do so much of the work. Your site and business must be in sync with your marketing campaign and in tune with consumers' willingness to engage. That takes a smart campaign.

Herein lies the challenge. The SEM industry has a shortage of search engine–savvy tacticians and an even greater shortage of search engine strategists. It's simply too new to have created the staff needed by more than 500,000 search advertisers. This shortage can make building an in-house team a daunting task, even if the team's primary function is to supervise external vendors (SEM agencies or technology companies). Clients and prospects regularly request my help in recruiting in-house staff (if you're looking for a position, let me know). Realistically, you can't supervise a vendor if you don't know enough about its tasks and responsibilities to distinguish good decisions from poor ones or superb execution from mediocrity.

Take the time to make sure you know enough to do it yourself, even if you plan to delegate the actual tasks to others (internally or externally). This way, you'll recognize the excuses. In the meantime, use technology to automate as much as possible given your campaign's makeup. Pull together a top-notch team internally and at your SEM agency (if you outsource), then focus on tactics and strategies that can make a difference. If you correctly prioritize tactics, tests, and strategic initiatives, you'll progress. Rally for the internal and external resources you require.

It's not about a body count or a hands-off, set-it-and-forget-it technology. It's about the right team of internal (and/or external) people and the right technology for your business. Everyone's needs are different, so know what you need for your business and keep track of what the engines are rolling out. The arrival of more precise targeting and more ad formats (such as video, rich media, and audio) won't make your life easier.

Weed Out and Manage Failed Listings

Your search engine marketing budget is an investment. The money you spend with Google, Yahoo, Microsoft, and the rest helps you grow your business, meet marketing goals, and deliver revenue and profits, at least if you invest your SEM budget wisely. Although it is true that your entire marketing budget is an investment, most online and offline marketing is not as measurable and controllable in real time as paid placement search is. Only recently has it become possible to buy display banner inventory in real time through a bidding environment similar to the one we use every day in PPC search. Paid search is great, but there are tradeoffs—the real-time auction marketplaces for paid placement can be volatile and unpredictable, just like some stocks in the stock market.

Let's delve into the strategic decision-making process regarding removal of underperforming listings. When do you drop a keyword listing out of the high-volume, premium positions? When is it time to remove it from a campaign altogether, because even at minimum CPCs and positions, the keyword listing still does not meet your objectives? Once again, we will use stock market analogies to illustrate strategies and then delve into tactics.

In the financial markets, traders and professional investors require some minimum level of return in order to even enter into a transaction. Often this is because they have a cost of capital. Professional investors understand that they are making decisions between easy, low returns or a more aggressive strategy that may carry risk and reward. Some traders play the market with other people's money (or borrowed money), and there is an interest rate that they must pay to have access to the capital. Imagine if you were to trade stocks on margin. You would never buy stocks on margin where you were not convinced that your earnings on the stock transaction would exceed your margin interest. Similarly, some keywords deliver revenue, but at a cost higher than you are willing to pay. Poorly managed listings also have a good chance of resulting in a negative profit. These keyword listings don't belong in your overall portfolio.

When managing your PPC paid placement campaign, you want to give every keyword listing a chance to perform and meet your ROI objectives. If a keyword misses your ROI goals at a top position, it might achieve those ROI objectives at a lower position (at a lower cost per click, but unfortunately yielding a lower click volume). PPC campaign management is all about finding and maintaining the sweet spot where the profit, ROI, and volume goals are balanced.

You don't want low-performing keyword listings dragging down overall campaign performance. However, the appropriate tactics to address low performers is different for each marketer. Before deleting any keyword listings, consider the following factors:

- How well targeted is the keyword to your business? Was the keyword listing a good fit?

- What is the upside potential of this keyword if you can get your metrics to work? For example, a keyword getting 20 clicks a month at a premium position has less potential than one that could get 2,000 clicks. Generally, if you have to dump a 20-click-per-month listing, the ramifications of making the "wrong decision" are minor. However, if you cut a listing with thousands of clicks per month when you could have saved the listing, this is a huge opportunity lost. Cutting keywords from a campaign requires human review.

- Did your creative do a good job explaining the benefit the searcher would get from clicking?

- Did you use the keyword in the creative in a clear manner?

- Is the landing page you selected for the listing the best possible fit, or should other landing pages be tested in an A/B or multivariate test?

- What is the competitive landscape for the keyword? If you are a high-end luxury provider of products or services and you are up against a discounter for a commodity product, all your efforts for this keyword may be doomed.

- Are you running the keyword listing in broad match without the inclusion of appropriate negative keywords?

- Is the keyword seasonal? Perhaps the keyword will work for you, but not all year round.

- Is the keyword ambiguous or the intent unclear? *China, windows, apple, bug, virus,* and *lemon* are great examples of ambiguous search terms, but yours may be ambiguous as well, because you can't tell what the searcher really wants from the search terms. Good copy can help to alleviate this problem.

- Is the keyword one that is used by those customers early in the buying cycle who may be ordering much later or through another channel?

If a keyword can't support itself in top-position premium SERP slots, lower positions may still be a viable option. If the keyword listing continues to fail and has been reduced in CPC and position to near an engine's minimum, and you have tried reasonable efforts to get the keyword to work, to no avail, then delete that listing and focus on the high performers. If a keyword listing really looks, acts, and smells like a dog, and there is no obvious way to turn the dog into a star performer (or even a reasonably good performer), then dump it.

Chapter 11

Campaign Management, Bids, Technology, Agencies, In-House or Blended

PPC search is an auction, just like an art auction, car auction, or for that matter the financial auctions at the New York Stock Exchange and elsewhere. The true and perceived value of the auctioned product or asset is different for each buyer in the market. In paid search, the divergence between perceived and true value is even more pronounced, because you and your competitors have different conversion rates, profit margins, and campaign strategies.

Search campaigns that are currently generating a positive ROI are under constant pressure to continually improve their efficiency and effectiveness to offset the inevitable increases in click costs. To remain successful in the search space, clients need the very best search engine campaign management possible from their agency, consultant, or internal staff. This chapter covers the main issues you'll need to know about when choosing a campaign management tool, selecting an SEM agency, or setting the functional requirements for an in-house team.

Automating Your Campaign and Bid Management

It takes brains, brawn, and finesse to run a search campaign. The best results come from a combination of search knowledge and the use of the right management tools. What type of knowledge and experience does it take to design and maintain a successful SE (search engine) campaign? You must know the marketplace and be aware of all the available search media and their nuances. For example, Microsoft offers five different ways to buy search media. Each method has its advantages and disadvantages. Not everyone has the experience to make these types of media placement decisions in an ongoing, ever-changing marketplace. In addition, an effective SEM team must help determine and set an appropriate CPO, CPA, or other success metric for their product or service as well as provide assistance in keyword expansion, listing, and landing page creative elements. These are the types of decisions that only a professional can make, and the quality of these decisions will be based on that professional's knowledge and experience.

What Is the Right Tool?

But knowledge alone is not enough. An effective search campaign must be managed using the right tools to implement and maintain maximum efficiencies. What are the functions that a tool should deliver? The most important function is that of control. When you consider a search campaign that contains thousands of search terms, running across many engines, it's almost impossible to control such a campaign without some sort of consolidated reporting system. An individual, department, or agency can't be burdened by having to look at separate reports from Google, Yahoo, Microsoft, and others to determine how a campaign is going. The tool's reporting features should be both detailed and flexible with an emphasis on the unique needs of a search marketing campaign. Some agencies prefer a tool with features such as agency reporting, which combines reports for multiple clients into one easy-to-read report, allowing the agency to quickly and easily assess how all their clients are doing. This function alone can help identify opportunities with a very broad view that may be easily missed by an individual client reporting system.

Although control of the overall campaign is maintained through the tool's reporting system, an agency should not be burdened with the day-to-day, minute-by-minute keyword bid changes necessary to keep the campaign optimized. Therefore, an effective tool must include automated bid and listing optimization. Many tools let marketers set specific keyword positions and maximum bids, but using the wrong strategy to drive such functionality will inevitably result in overbidding and underbidding, dramatically reducing a campaign's effectiveness.

A professional should only use a tool that is capable of optimization based on post-click behavior, ROI, profit, and traffic quality assessment. Such a tool is said to be capable of *post-click optimization*, which is a methodology that tracks CPO, CPA, or other conversion data and uses this data to make the real-time, ongoing keyword adjustments necessary for maximizing orders, registrations, profit or whatever metric was chosen as a goal. The system continually compares this cost data to a target cost set by the marketing team, and it makes the logical bidding decisions based on this comparison. In essence, each keyword is constantly and automatically adjusted based on up-to-the-minute data to find and maintain its most efficient position. Not only does this type of tool make sure the campaign is operating as efficiently as possible, but it also lets the marketer maintain much larger keyword lists, increasing response while lowering their average order/conversion cost. This level of effectiveness is well beyond the typical campaign strategy based on position or click costs alone.

Of course, an effective tool shouldn't limit the agency, professional, or marketing team. The tool has to be able to administer the campaign, optimize the listings, and report the results in a consolidated manner. A truly effective system will even help the agency allocate the client's media budget across the engines to ensure that the client's campaign is yielding the lowest possible CPO.

Flexibility in tracking is also important. Many agencies and marketers already use third-party tracking or web analytics services to monitor results for their clients' campaigns. Available campaign optimization tools can "hook into" and use many of the most popular third-party tracking systems and optimize around a broad array of metrics, which makes them easy to set up.

A successful search engine campaign is the result of a close working relationship among the marketing team, the search engines, and the chosen optimization tool. Even the best tool cannot substitute for the knowledge and experience of professionals on the marketing team (internal or external). But if their strategy is sound, and the tool is capable of correctly implementing this strategy, they are sure to succeed. Conversely, if the tool is inadequate, no strategy, however brilliant, can succeed because it will fail in the execution stage.

What Are the Functions of Campaign Management?

Campaign management can be broken down into three basic functions. The first is *tracking* or collecting the data. The second is the *bidding logic* that adjusts your keyword bids based on this data. And the third is *reporting*. No one would argue that anything will work right if the data you're collecting is inaccurate. But whether you're using third-party tracking or the services of a campaign management firm using its own tracking system, getting the keyword conversion data you need and being able to have confidence in its accuracy is not a difficult task. Also, while the reporting is the fun part of campaign management, such reporting has little or no effect on your results. Effective campaign optimization requires making decisions in real time. No client should be using reports to make decisions. By then it's way too late. Any good campaign management system should be capable of making correct decisions long before a user sees a report.

That point leads us to the bidding logic portion of the system. This is the module that actually makes the bidding decisions. It spends your marketing money as it sees fit. Needless to say, it's the most important function in campaign management. Yet, almost nobody talks about bidding logic, because the algorithms are widely regarded as some form of secret, or marketers are presumed to be math phobic.

My firm has developed several styles of bidding logic over the years, and we find most of the bidding engines we've developed to be very effective. Although I can't detail what our competitors' bidding logic is, I will go through the basics of how ours operates in one unique situation.

Let's model a situation that happens thousands of times a day and step through the decision tree. Say we're running the phrase *callaway golf club* on Yahoo, and we're tracking results all the way through to the sale. Our current bid is $1.52, and we're in position 3. We have set a target CPO at $30. We've had 9 clicks come in, and we just got an order on the 10th. We know that the order cost us $15.20, which is 10 clicks × $1.52 per click price. This cost is well below our target cost per order of $30. So what do we do? Should we raise the bid to get to position 2? The answer is maybe.

If there is a budget cap in addition to an ROI target, there may be cheaper orders elsewhere, meaning the marginal cost of the next order is less somewhere else in the campaign. Or perhaps the historical data has determined that for this keyword the conversion rate actually goes down as you move up the list, particularly at top positions where the "compulsive clickers" find themselves interacting with listings they don't even want. Knowing how each keyword conversion rate reacts to position is essential in determining what your next move should be. It's easy to see that no matter how accurate the tracking data is, the system must also make proper use of historical data. Whether it's human smarts or machine intelligence, whether you thrive or even survive in the competitive search landscape will be determined by your cunning.

Do You Need Bid Management?

If you are spending less than $1,000 a month, or your marketplace is very noncompetitive and the conversion events you seek to optimize around are often difficult to track (store visits and phone calls), you may not need bid management at all. It's possible that the functionality provided by the search engines with respect to ad scheduling and budgeting may be sufficient to get you quite far along the path to optimal profitability. The whole idea of bid management is to pay as much as you can afford for clicks that are highly valuable and as little as possible for clicks that aren't valuable.

It may seem like a campaign's success or failure hinges on killer bid management. Although bid management is a campaign's foundation, other factors can be more important. Don't focus too myopically on bid management at the expense of other profit-enhancing strategies and tactics.

The engines' algorithmic changes result in less clarity of the bid landscape and cause and effect of bid changes, and the implementation of API charges (fees levied on technologies that manage bids through an application programming interface) reduces the need for overactive bid management systems. The search engine bid landscape is becoming more complex for reasons that have less to do with bidding and more to do with targeting. Complex campaigns clearly must be managed through automated means to tap their full potential. Human oversight can and will continue to play a critical role as well.

Two of the big three search engines (Google and Yahoo) have rolled out rudimentary bid management systems, and every indication is that Microsoft will do so as well, perhaps before you read this book. Some marketers may be tempted to rely on these tools to manage campaigns to direct-response metrics (cost per actions, or CPAs). However, engine-provided bid management technology isn't right for everyone who needs bid management.

Google's Conversion Optimizer

Google Conversion Optimizer is essentially a bid management product, which is in beta at the time of this printing. You set a CPA and use the Google conversion tracking pixel on your site's conversion (thank you) page. The system will then, hypothetically at least, manage to your CPA goal. Google describes the Conversion Optimizer as "an AdWords feature that manages your advertising costs around specific conversion goals." Interestingly, Google has supposedly added some fairly advanced logic into its system that only some high-end bid and campaign management technologies provide. For example, many off-the-shelf bid management systems don't factor in conversion differences by match type, geographic location, and Google network partner, whereas Conversion Optimizer does.

Although the Google system may seem ready to rock, other Google features in your campaign or bid management system are incompatible with the Conversion Optimizer, including Position Preference, Budget Optimizer, Site Targeting, Advanced Ad Scheduling, and Preferred Cost Bidding. Plus, if you are using Google Analytics, you currently still have to use a separate conversion pixel on your site specifically for the Conversion Optimizer and reporting within the AdWords interface.

Yahoo's Campaign Optimizer

Yahoo's Campaign Optimization requires the Yahoo customer solutions department to enable the feature. Similar to the version Google launched, the Yahoo system optimizes around success metrics that you set. The engine boasts of efficiency gains that are probably excessively optimistic. According to the site, "Campaign Optimization can help you spend your campaign's budget as efficiently as possible based on your business objectives (i.e., if you want to achieve a certain cost-per-click or return-on-ad-spend figure) or guidelines (e.g., the value and importance of impressions, clicks, and conversions/revenue)."

I actually take issue with the claim "as efficiently as possible" since it is difficult to prove, and there are some amazing third-party bidding and campaign optimization technologies that might challenge Yahoo's assertion right along with me. Besides, an advanced marketer looking at the simplicity of the Yahoo Campaign Optimizer system would likely find it lacking.

What Are the Elements of Bid Management?

In the earlier days of campaign and bid management, the marketplaces were not opaque. You could see the bids around you in the bid landscape. This resulted in protracted bidding wars for position where marketers would escalate bids on a minute-by-minute basis. Now, with nearly opaque bid landscapes and Quality Score–driven ranking algorithms at Google and similar systems in place at Yahoo and Microsoft, the bid volatility is reduced. However, due to the importance of day-parting, a certain amount of volatility is still in place under the surface. If you are bidding manually and find yourself making frequent daily bid changes, you are probably in a volatile market. It never hurts to understand how your bidding system or campaign management solution deals with volatility or at least the philosophy your technology vendor uses to approach a volatile marketplace.

The automated bid-management systems by Google and Yahoo are one-size-fits-all solutions. But great campaign management goes far beyond managing bids. Even businesses in the same industry category often have significantly different success metrics and key performance indicators, so any standard tool will generally not be customizable enough.

There are many ways of writing a bid management algorithm that manages to a CPA. As someone who was intimately involved in developing one of the first bid management systems and witnessed the bid landscapes evolve, I've tested and incorporated dozens of different approaches into bidding algorithms. Here are some questions to ask when evaluating such systems:

- What level of statistical confidence do you want to ensure for a system that detects a conversion rate decline?

- How rapidly do you want a bidding system to react if conditions seem to be trending positively based on the most recent data?

- If certain patterns repeat, can the system learn or be programmed to take advantage of the repeating patterns?

- Does the system work as well in volatile keyword markets as it does in stagnant ones?

- Can the system detect or test the elasticity of your marketplace to determine if upside opportunities exist at a very low incremental marginal predicted cost (entailing slightly higher CPAs)?

- Does the system play well with some of the settings you might want to use within the campaign management web interfaces, such as day-parting, bid boosts (raising of bids based on specific factors being in place), or ad scheduling?

Conspiracy theorists argue that giving Google or Yahoo the ability to change bids is the equivalent of writing them a blank check (subject to budget constraints or IOs [insertion orders] that are in place). The issue is really broader than that, because search is increasingly being regarded as just one part of more complex integrated marketing plans.

Even if these questions were answered, there are systemic questions that relate to using each engine's pixel to control that engine's spending/bidding. Each of the pixels will have a different attrition rate due to cookie deletion. This means that the same metrics will never fully reconcile with reality. It's also possible to double count if the searcher uses more than one engine's network. Media interaction effects may also be of interest as well as understanding the last click (media and search may have both been involved in steering the user to conversion within a single cookie's duration).

How Important Is High Visibility?

High visibility in the search results is a means to an end. Bid management is all about gaining high visibility when it matters most. More valuable prospects and customers produce more valuable clicks right before they become customers. Better bid management solutions are all about getting the valuable clicks for you when they matter, and these clicks are easier to get if you have top position.

Although it is possible to run a business using what might be called a "bottom-feeding strategy" consisting of running your ads in lower positions hoping to be noticed, the real opportunity comes with high positions. Google has made achieving top positions even more difficult through a variety of changes to its platform. The first wild card is Google's Quality Score, which not only impacts the price you have to pay to achieve a position but can also impede your ability to take a slot above the organic results. Google requires a nonpublished minimum Quality Score and a minimum bid price (by keyword) to let ads be eligible for the coveted spots above the organic listings. That's why bid management can't work in a vacuum. Your ads have to be relevant and tested and your landing pages appropriate.

When Do You Need an Agency?

If you are running a large campaign in-house, you risk the defection of your in-house expert. Given the constant flow of strategic and tactical work associated with a search marketing campaign, getting help from an outside agency or agency with technology tools may make sense. The value they add may more than make up for their fees. It's always best to evaluate these kinds or relationships "all-in," meaning that both costs and incremental revenue and profit are counted.

Choosing vendors based solely on management fees makes sense only if you believe you're buying a pure commodity and the following factors have no role in success or failure:

- Technology
- Staff skill level and training
- Staff hours allocated for production and strategy

If you spend several hundred thousand dollars a month on a highly complex campaign in a highly competitive marketplace where you aren't the number-one player, the failure of any important element within the search campaign can have highly material consequences.

But because the focus on cost versus overall profitability and business benefit can lead to a productive discussion, let's do the math to see whether choosing a vendor this way makes sense. To simplify the model, we won't cover all the aspects of a PPC SEM campaign that are highly positive but more difficult to measure or manage. These factors might include offline conversions, the branding impact of search, and the benefits of acquiring an online customer with a high long-term lifetime customer value. We'll do the calculations based purely on immediate, observable ROI. To make it interesting, we'll also model the opportunity cost implications of selecting vendors that have better technology against those that may be more or less skilled at search or perhaps more or less willing to aggressively staff an account after bidding the lowest to win the business.

The first assumption is that not every vendor will do as well as its competition. After 13 years in the search business, I can attest to there being a wide diversity of performance levels in the marketplace, not only among my competitors but even within some agencies. It can make a huge difference which team you get—making team headcount far less important than who your strategist or account manager happens to be. I'm not talking about five percent variation, either. It's fairly common to see performance variation in excess of 25 percent, much more so if the agencies have different pedigrees or capabilities.

Clearly, SEM isn't a commodity service. But let's assume the short list in this instance includes agencies of similar size, age, and technological capabilities. Let's also assume that variation between the best and the worst performer is 20 percent. (I'd bet that in a sample set of 10, there'd be a 20 percent variation from the mean in both directions.)

Depending on the business category, the margin on retail products sold online ranges between 5 percent and 60 percent. Let's assume a margin of 40 percent with a short-term, online-only, highly tracking-centric campaign, where it wouldn't be unusual for a marketer to assign a net search profit of half the margin. That's an ROAS of 5, meaning you can spend up to $20 to generate $100 in revenue and still be left with a net search profit of $20. To look at this correctly, you would want to factor in the cost of the agency in the spending, not just the media cost.

Since this is an example of a fairly large search spender where some economies of scale are present, let's assume the full-service SEM agencies are bidding a media management fee range of 5 percent to 15 percent of spending. The variation in fees as it relates to the spend under management for an ROAS of 5 and an assumed $20 spend to generate the $100 is from $1 on the low end to $3 on the high end.

Yet we are making the conservative assumption that the best and worst agencies are 20 percent apart in efficiency in spending money, because it's very likely that there is a correlation between price paid

Note

Calculating the impact on true ROI, and therefore the opportunity costs of doing something in a suboptimal manner, will reveal much higher costs.

and quality of service delivered (not a perfect correlation, perhaps). However, since we used a very conservative difference in agency performance, let's assume the cheapest agency is the poorer performer. Could the media savings outweigh the performance loss?

Table 11.1 shows a comparison of agency performance variances. Factoring in their own cost, the agencies don't really get to spend $20 of each $100 because they aren't counting their fees. The agency with a 5 percent fee spends $19 on search media, the one with the 10 percent spends $18, and the one charging 15 percent spends only $17 on clicks. Yet when you include a conservative *performance variance* (ability to extract revenue from the search spend) of 20 percent, you see that the low-performing agency generates $95 in revenue from its $19, whereas the top performer (which is also highly likely to be the most expensive or at least at the top of the range) generates $102 in revenue with a media spend of $17. In effect, this agency is able to achieve an ROAS of 6 (a 20 percent improvement), even though its invoice (or bid for the business) is three times more than the lowest bidder, making the more expensive vendor choice a far better business decision.

Table 11.1 Agency Fees Comparison

Measurement	Formula	Low-Fee Agency	High-Fee Agency
Profit margin on all goods sold online	(assumed)	40%	40%
Gross media spend	(assumed)	$20	$20
Agency fee	(assumed)	5%	15%
ROAS	(assumed)	5	6
Agency fee per $20 spent	Gross media spend × Agency fee	$1	$3
Net media spend	Gross media spend – Agency fee	$19	$17
Gross revenue	Net media spend × ROAS	$95	$102
Net search profit	(Gross revenue × Profit margin) – Gross media spend	$18	$21

Although this example is simplified and doesn't take several less-material factors into account, the calculations should show that this multichannel merchant is very likely setting itself up to fail—or at least fail to achieve its true potential, even though someone's going to get a pat on the back for saving the company money during tough economic times. You might wonder whether this same company, if audited by the IRS, will be picking a tax audit specialist accounting firm in the same way it's selecting an SEM agency! In both cases, millions of dollars are on the line.

Although management fees are a consideration when choosing an SEM vendor, it's more important to consider technology, staff skill level and training, and staff hours allocated for production and strategy, among other factors. Making money can be much more profitable than saving money.

Entering into Performance Deals, or Not

Should any company selling goods or services online be using a performance marketer to represent them in the paid-search space? Let me rephrase that question: What type of questions should an online seller be asking his performance marketer?

By *performance marketer*, we mean companies promising to deliver orders for an agreed-upon allowable. When search engines use the phrase *pay-for-performance*, they mean clicks and traffic—not orders, revenue, and leads.

The earliest web-based performance marketers or performance marketing agencies were affiliate networks, which were initially set up to deliver banner advertising originating from thousands of second- and third-tier websites. Because the quality of the traffic was impossible to measure or assess, marketers demanded that the only way they would agree to pay for their banners to be displayed on these sites was to pay for that traffic on a PPO (pay per order) or commissioned basis. These host sites now became *affiliates* or partners of the marketer, getting paid only when they delivered orders. These entities expanded their coverage to email and eventually to search marketing.

Many merchants and marketers set up their own affiliate networks like Amazon and such, but it was a lot of work. You had to do the requisite programming, find the affiliates, track the orders, remove the fraud, and make the commission payments. This barrier created the market for third-party companies—affiliate managers—to step in and manage the process. They would cultivate the network of affiliate sites, remove fraud, and step in the middle of the transaction. In other words, you pay them on a per order basis and they in turn pay the affiliate a reduced commission. The "spread" between what they get paid and what they pay out becomes their gross profit.

Now let's get to the question at hand. Should these performance guys be playing in the paid search business? The answer is sure; it's a free country. However, I don't think they are doing right by their clients. I can see their role in eliminating the risk of doing business with thousands of second-tier sites by shifting the risk onto those sites themselves. After all, the sites deliver tons of traffic but only get paid when they deliver an order. It's the only way for a marketer to do business with these thousands of small publishers, but paid search is different.

Paid search is an open real-time marketplace—with the right tools, you know your position and keywords, as well as often knowing (at least in some cases) your competitors' positions and keywords.

So who's taking the risk? The paid search engines aren't taking the risk. They get paid when they deliver the traffic, not when they deliver an order. So the risk now shifts dramatically to the performance company. It gets paid only when it delivers an order, but it has to pay for traffic. Well, that's its business. Sounds pretty risky to me.

Which takes us to the second question. Should any online marketers be using these guys to represent them in the paid search space? The answer is yes, but only if that marketer is willing to leave tons of orders on the table and endure huge lost opportunities in the most effective online media to date only to avoid assuming a small, controllable, temporary risk.

If a marketer is willing to pay its performance company $50 per order, how much of that $50 do you think it is going to spend on search media? First you have to knock off its margin. Let's assume it's between 30 percent and 40 percent. This leaves approximately $30. Not bad! But how does the performance company make sure that it doesn't spend more than $30 to get that order? By trading off volume. That's the dirty little secret. It can bid low for any terms and basically guarantee a lower volume of cheap orders that protect its margin.

Only the marketer loses. By giving up the little risk of advertising directly on the engines, he has given up huge opportunities. Of course, why should we believe that a performance marketer is willing to assume the risk of advertising your product on paid search when you are not willing to assume that same risk? Does he know something about your product that you don't know? The only thing he knows is that he can control the keyword bids and the volume to guarantee his margin. He's taking no risk at all. It's good business, if you can get it!

Which take me to the third and last question. What type of questions should an online seller be asking his performance marketer? I can only think of four important questions:

- What percentage of my per-order fee is going to be spent on search media?

- What number of orders can you guarantee you will deliver me per month? (After all, the performance marketer has to assume some risk. It's why you want to do business with it.)

- What is its monthly media-spending budget for your account?

- As keyword prices go up, what is its strategy to keep order flow high?

If their answer to any of these questions is "it depends," it's clear that the performance marketer doesn't want you to know what its margin is or how it plans to do the best job it can in paid search on your behalf. Is this what you want? With any other agency or a direct relationship with the search engines, you'll know exactly where your money is going and what your opportunity costs are by not raising your allowable CPO. Search marketing campaigns can be executed in ways that deliver maximal control to you, the marketer, giving you the upside.

My advice is to bite the bullet. Open an account on Google, Yahoo, and Microsoft, and hire a good search management firm or an agency that uses a technology that will minimize your risk and quickly maximize opportunity. You stand to reap the rewards of the most effective media the Internet has to offer. Leave the performance guys to their affiliate networks. It's what they do best.

Using Your In-House Team

Should marketers manage search in-house or outsource it? Conference sessions are devoted to this question, research analysts weigh in about it during briefings, and white papers have delved into it.

Some in the SEM agency community and some in-house SEM practitioners are engaged in a war of words over this point. Complicating the picture is campaign-enhancing technology, including bid management, landing-page testing, click segmentation systems, and supporting web analytics.

Perhaps each side is solidifying its career prospects. Reality lies far from the rhetoric presumably aimed at CMOs (chief marketing officer), marketing VPs, and the executive suite in general. After all, the livelihood of both in-house and agency SEM practitioners depends on what the executive decision-makers believe to be the optimal scheme.

What are the merits of outsourcing SEM compared to those of managing SEM (both PPC search and SEO) in-house? The answer depends on multiple factors that must be evaluated before selecting a strategy.

Even the definition of *outsourced SEM* can vary. For example, my team services some clients who believe they aren't outsourcing search because the partnership keeps certain roles and responsibilities on the client side, even though my team provides services beyond technology and tech support. Other clients receiving the same level of service consider such an arrangement to be outsourcing. It's more important for marketing executives to determine the specific needs and campaign objectives, then decide how best to achieve those goals.

The search marketing industry is barely a dozen years old. CMOs should consider other key business processes, such as legal and accounting functions, that are carried out in-house or by outside firms. Large corporations and even some midsize entities have in-house counsel but still rely on outside law firms, particularly when special external skills and knowledge best serve the enterprise. Likewise, managing accounting functions in-house doesn't preclude the use of an external accounting firm. Within marketing, the same continuum exists for traditional advertising and public relations services.

A CMO must determine the balance of skills and expertise required to accomplish search marketing objectives. This may include whether to retain a combination of in-house staff and external expertise, such as production expertise, strategic experience, and analytical savvy.

As with legal and accounting services, an enterprise's SEM needs may change over time. When a major lawsuit looms, even a well-staffed in-house legal department will generally call in reinforcements from outside. Within media and search marketing, factors influence the staff hours required to accomplish campaign objectives, including:

- A campaign's age
- A campaign's size, including engines, keywords, and segmentation groups
- Competitiveness of an industry segment
- Speed at which the search engines make changes to their offerings, including algorithms and types of media
- Frequency of change in product/service mix
- Seasonality of an industry
- Current employee team size

- Current employee team skills mix and level of experience

- Likelihood of employee turnover, driven by a shortage of SEM experience in the marketplace

- Changing technology needs

- Level of aggressiveness and willingness to test

At times in the campaign lifecycle, there may be significant opportunities that can only be captured by deploying significant production resources, uncovering knowledge through careful statistical analysis, or applying expertise. To build an in-house team for every stage of a campaign isn't optimal. Even the staunchest in-house SEM advocates may miss huge opportunities and should consider a partnership during a campaign.

Within paid search, exchange-traded (auctioned) media presents another important factor in determining the enabling technology's fit. Technology decisions occur within a "build versus buy" continuum, as do the services and expertise side of search. Technology can do more than automate mundane aspects of real-time auction media marketplaces. In some cases, it can be more effective than human effort alone. Yet technology poses challenges depending on the amount of customization and training required.

One challenge is the technology's level of customizability and its power are often correlated with the level of training required to fully tap its capabilities, making the level of support from your technology vendor particularly important. Bells and whistles you'll never use are worse than worthless and clutter the user experience.

If you're a CMO or other senior executive overseeing search marketing, consider the point on the continuum between in-house and outsourced that will best serve your organization now and for the next 6 to 12 months. Then revisit this mix if you determine that you're either missing profit/growth opportunities or overspending on services for your current needs.

 **PART III**

Beyond the Big Three Engines

Part III

Introduction

Consumers use their favorite primary search engine to find everything. Most even use search engines as a form of navigation, even when they know exactly where they are going and don't really need to search at all. You might be tempted to ignore the other forms of keyword-targeted traffic. However, there are all sorts of places you can buy clicks that add tremendous value to your core paid search advertising campaign. Some of these forms of media, while keyword targeted, are not even considered by purists to be search engine advertising. However, since the traffic can be highly valuable, and most marketers classify these second-tier traffic sources as search traffic, I've devoted an entire section to the subject. Every form of advertising isn't right for every marketer in the same way that every keyword doesn't belong in every campaign. However, some of these advertising sources deserve a good look and full evaluation. You may find that your competition has completely ignored some traffic sources and that at the right price this traffic is quite profitable.

Chapter 12

Additional Search Traffic Sources

Although general purpose search engines—Google and Yahoo, for example—will likely account for the bulk of visitors to your website, it's important not to overlook additional sources of traffic. These sources—comparison shopping engines, online Yellow Pages, and vertical and international search engines—can present opportunities for you to get in front of customers when they are in the mood to buy. You may also be able to take advantage of the lower level of advertiser competition within these sources, making them more cost-effective contenders for your search advertising dollar.

Marketing On Comparison Shopping Engines

Unlike general purpose search engines that cater to a broad audience and therefore must satisfy a wide range of search query types, *comparison shopping engines* are special purpose search engines designed to aid shoppers and prospective buyers evaluate products, prices, and vendors (**Figure 12.1**). Because these engines are so focused, they attract visitors with a high degree of purchase intent. They also give merchants a way to avoid the high CPC prices associated with highly competitive listings on general purpose engines.

Figure 12.1

Comparison shopping engines, such as NexTag, provide consumers an easy way to search for products, compare them, and easily come to a purchase decision.

The "big three" search engines, Google, Yahoo, and Microsoft, have each developed comparison shopping engines as adjuncts to their main search engine services. In addition, there are hundreds of third-party sites, each of which provides similar functionality.

How Do They Work?

Comparison shopping engines gather information about products and prices in a variety of ways. Some use crawlers to gather information from external vendors' websites; others rely on data feeds supplied directly by the vendors. Many engines rely on a combination of crawling and feed inclusion to keep their product and price lists up to date. Comparison shopping engines often bring in ancillary data, including seller ratings, to provide shoppers meaningful information on the fitness of sellers.

Merchant advertisers typically have a range of options for placing product information within comparison shopping engines. Merchants can complete product information forms, which is practical when they have only a handful of products to list. Larger product lists can be uploaded via a web interface or via FTP.

Some comparison shopping engines deliver clicks to the merchant for free, whereas others require fees for the shopping engine operator, either in the form of a cost-per-click payment or a flat fee typically for position on a specific page or keyword/product search.

Shopping Engines from the "Big Three" Search Engines

The "big three" search engines have each rolled out comparison shopping engines that serve as adjuncts to the information they include within their primary search results. The shopping results may require that a searcher specifically select the shopping/products tab. Or if the search engine decides that the searcher would be best served seeing product search results, those results may be given priority placement within the general search results page using a concept commonly called *universal search*, where the search engine selects results from one or more supplemental databases and mixes those results into the main search results page.

- **Google Shopping/Product Search:** Formerly known as Froogle, Google's Product Search is free. According to a study of online merchants conducted by DoubleClick in late 2008, Google

Product Search was the most frequently used comparison shopping engine, with 63 percent of respondents reporting they had used it. Merchant advertisers can list products with Google Product Search one by one, or submit a data feed, using a related Google product, Google Base. Free merchant listings appear in Google Product Search (**Figure 12.2**) within the "organic/natural search results" area of the SERPs. Text ads are served via Google AdWords to other (paid) areas of the SERP but being an advertiser is not a requirement for having listings appear within Google Product Search. For more information, check out www.google.com/base/help/sellongoogle.html.

Figure 12.2
Google Product Search (formerly Froogle) incorporates comparison pricing, links to merchant reviews, plus ads placed through Google AdWords.

- **Yahoo Shopping:** Unlike Google Product Search, getting exposure through Yahoo Shopping must be paid for. Yahoo runs a CPC auction with minimum bids varying per product category (Yahoo Shopping currently has 1,200 categories). Merchants can additionally choose to build a storefront within Yahoo Shopping entitling them to a 20 percent discount off the marketplace's rate card. Having a storefront also frees merchants from having to supply a data feed, because Yahoo simply pulls product data directly from the merchant's store. Like Google Product Search, Yahoo Shopping (**Figure 12.3**) lets merchants place ads around product and category pages. For more info, go to http://searchmarketing.yahoo.com/shopsb/index.php.

Figure 12.3

Yahoo Shopping offers comparison pricing, links to product reviews, plus ads placed through Yahoo.

■ **Live Search cashback (Microsoft):** In 2007, Microsoft acquired Jellyfish, a comparison shopping engine, added an incentive program, and called it Live Search cashback (**Figures 12.4** and **12.5** on the following pages). Searchers who buy products through it are rewarded with rebates that the merchant can specify. Merchants are charged only when searchers actually purchase a listed product, making cash-back's revenue model truly cost per action (CPA). Merchants can get started with cashback fairly easily. The requirements for participation include the ability to supply a standardized data feed, plus the ability to place a traffic conversion pixel on the merchant website's "thank you" page. This *traffic conversion pixel* communicates with Microsoft's servers that a conversion has taken place. For more information, go to http://advertising.microsoft.com/advertising/cashback.

Figure 12.4

Microsoft's Live Search cash-back provides comparative product pricing but no links to product or merchant reviews.

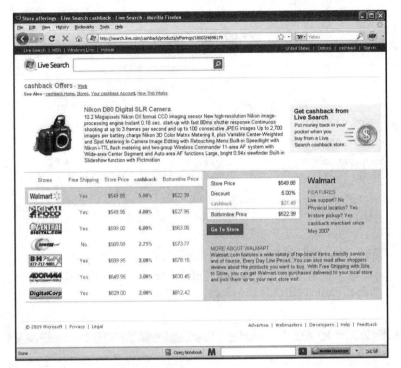

Figure 12.5
The cashback program rewards searchers who buy products through it with rebates the merchant can specify.

Third-Party Comparative Shopping Engines

Hundreds of third-party comparative shopping engines are currently in operation. Because preparing and maintaining product lists can be time consuming, it's best to focus on those engines providing the highest volume of qualified traffic. **Table 12.1** on the next page lists some popular comparative shopping engines, with traffic data compiled by Quantcast, a competitive analytics service. Be aware that several of these engines use the term *performance-based* when describing how their ad programs work. However, some will bill you for a click, whether or not such a click results in a conversion, whereas others will only bill you if a conversion (sale) occurs.

Table 12.1 Popular Comparative Shopping Engines

Shopping Engine	Estimated Monthly Traffic: U.S. Users (Quantcast)	Ad Model
NexTag.com	17.8 million	CPC
PriceGrabber.com	8.1 million	CPC
Pricerunner.com	1.4 million	CPC
Pronto.com	11.1 million	CPC
Shopzilla.com (formerly BizRate)	14.3 million	CPC
Shopping.com	7.0 million	CPC
Smarter.com	10.8 million	CPC

Comparison shopping engines often provide customer reviews to provide a snapshot of current popular sentiment towards a listed vendor (**Figure 12.6**).

Figure 12.6

Comparison shopping engines frequently incorporate links to customer reviews in their results pages. This information can provide critical information that can make or break a purchase decision.

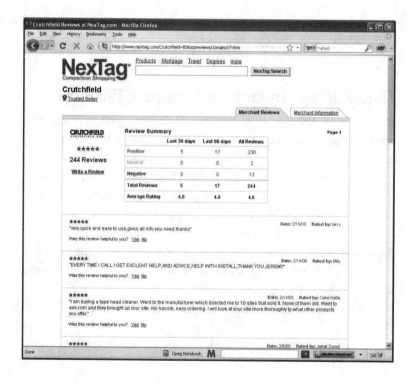

Marketing on Internet Yellow Pages

Internet Yellow Pages (IYPs) may not be as popular as the bigger general purpose search engines, but they have been designed to be particularly user friendly when a searcher wants to limit a search to a narrow geography. Both local marketers and national advertisers with a local presence are present in the IYPs and use the advertising options provided.

IYPs have been providing search inventory and search-based sources of traffic for years. Their results are compiled from databases typically served by a major data vendor. These vendors have the same role as the major search engines' algorithms. Their mission is to have complete, up-to-date data on businesses, classified by category, subcategory, and geography. IYPs, like comparison shopping engines, frequently incorporate user reviews of merchant advertisers, as shown in **Figure 12.7.**

Figure 12.7
Internet Yellow Pages provide another source of traffic to a website. They let users search through merchants grouped by several categories.

IYPs started out selling search result inventory much the way they sold print display advertising. The advertiser paid a fixed cost per month on an annual contract. In the case of SuperPages.com (Verizon's IYP), this cost was billed in a monthly phone bill. Costs were determined by ad size, format, elements included, categories included, geographies covered, and a tier. The higher the tier, the higher the listing appeared in the results. Other IYPs launched with similar plans. Many placements and plans included small graphic elements or logos. Recently, many IYPs have embraced auction-style pay-per-click (PPC) search listings.

If local advertising is important to you, and you need more opportunities to display listings for your business to a locally-minded audience, consider IYPs. A sample of major players includes the following:

- **Verizon SuperPages (www.superpages.com):** SuperPages listings are purchased from Verizon and powered by customized FindWhat.com technology. The tiered results are replicated via syndication agreements with other portals, including MSN, but the PPC listings are not. SuperPages' ad model is CPC; ad display options include plain text ads plus enhanced (graphics and/or video) formats.

- **Yahoo Yellow Pages (http://yp.yahoo.com):** Yahoo's Yellow Pages uses a tiered approach. Monthly fees are based on the tier and category. Additionally, merchants can place PPC ads via Yahoo Local advertising programs.

- **YellowPages.com (www.yellowpages.com):** This service sells listings directly by category. Merchants can choose among a wide range of enhanced advertiser programs, including Video Profiles, which let advertisers post promotional video content, Premium Inventory Listings, which include "tile ads" and "priority local listings" that boost visibility, YPclicks (a SEM campaign management program), and YP Site Solutions, a website building and hosting program.

- **CitySearch (www.citysearch.com):** CitySearch is like an IYP, but it's organized around content and editorial. Text listings are sold directly on a pay-for-performance basis. Yahoo results (standard, non-geo-targeted) are also displayed.

Marketing on Vertical Market Search Engines

Many local marketers and niche businesses have a difficult decision to make with regard to paid search. Nearly every major industry sector has one or more vertical directories, vertical search engines, or *vortals* (vertical portals). Often those vertical directories/vortals are buying paid search listings, and some of them may also have a reasonably high organic position for the same or similar keywords. If you are a local or niche marketer, the decision boils down to the following courses of action (which are not necessarily mutually exclusive):

- Buy a directory listing based on whatever ad revenue model the directory uses in order to get either the visibility within the directory or clicks from the directory to your site.

- Buy paid search listings and compete with both your competitors and the vertical directory, selectively buying the clicks that are most valuable to you.

- Engage in SEO for the terms of interest, competing for position with both your direct competition and the vertical directory.

- Decide the glut of competition is escalating the price and reducing the ROI so dramatically that alternative media options will have a higher predicted ROI.

If you are wondering why the vertical portals exist, a primary driver was a supply/demand skew between spots in the organic and paid search results and the number of businesses within a major metropolitan region looking to advertise.

The data you should look at when making a decision with respect to the possible choices includes the competitive landscape, how the directory charges, the demonstrated value of the directory clicks or impressions compared to the clicks you can buy directly, and perhaps other value the directory provides beyond clicks to your site. Each of the vertical directories has its own business model and way of charging you for a listing, profile page, or participation. The typical vertical directory pricing models include:

- **Annual membership:** Memberships may be tiered and include a la carte features that may be in the list that follows or may be highly specific to the industry sector being covered.

- **CPC (cost per click):** Some directories charge on a CPC basis. If you are considering participating in one of these directories, it is more important than ever to consider the source of their traffic because you are paying for clicks originating from somewhere else and ending up at a directory. If the directory gets its traffic from organic placement on the "big three" search engine databases (which power far more search engines through syndication deals), the clicks you get as a directory customer are essentially delayed clicks from organic engine placements. If the directory buys many of its clicks from questionable sources, those clicks are mixed in with your paid directory clicks. If the directory ranks high for your most coveted keywords in the organic listings, you can make a compelling case for the clicks since they are essentially delayed clicks from organic positions you'd find hard to replicate.

- **Sponsorships by region or specialty:** Banner or text link sponsorships are sold on a fixed-fee basis.

- **Banner advertising:** Targeted on a run-of-site basis or based on registrant/visitor behavior.

- **Cost per lead:** Some directories choose to ask their visitors for information in order to match those leads with advertisers. The biggest challenge for this business model happens when the leads are non-exclusive, meaning that many of your competitors are also receiving the same leads at the same time.

To understand how these business models come together, it may be useful to pick an example from the legal field, which is a highly competitive sector with many vertical segments. A recent search for *New York lawyer* in Google, Yahoo, and MSN turned up the following directories in the paid and organic results:

- **LawyersinNewYork.com:** This directory sells a landing page banner program for $900 annually, plus a $199 listing. However, it offers no specific performance guarantees, and the search engine used is a Google CSE (Custom Search Engine) deployment. So, you'd need good SEO on top of paying to be included in its CSE result.

- **Lawyers.com:** Run by LexisNexis, a division of Reed Elsevier, Inc. Lawyers.com is an example of what happens when a powerhouse within an industry decides to build and run the industry's online directory as well. This type of scenario has both positives and negatives. The positives are the resources that the parent group can bring to bear. The downside is that your competitors are far more likely to be participating here than in a directory with fewer marketing and sales resources.

- **FindLaw.com:** This directory has a diversity of packages, and nearly all are sponsorship- or fixed fee–based as far as I can tell from reading the descriptions. It seems to have adopted a style similar to the Yellow Pages model of having something that appeals to everyone at many price points.

- **LegalMatch.com:** As its name suggests, this directory allows the consumer or business to fill out a form and then the participating lawyers get the leads to follow up on. As with most lead generation–oriented directories, a combination of lead quality and level of competitiveness combine with the price per lead to determine whether participation is warranted.

Similar directory models exist in a wide diversity of industries. The easy thing is finding the directories. A simple search in the top search engines for your profession's keywords will reveal all your options. For example, ServiceMagic.com is a frequent player in the contracting and home services area, and there are dozens of vertical directories in the healthcare industry.

Often these directories can be used in conjunction with a highly targeted and profit-centric PPC campaign to enhance visibility for your business. I highly recommend you at least check to see which directories cover your industry, if only to know who you are up against in the organic and paid search results.

Chapter 13

Contextual Keyword Targeting

What is contextual advertising? Well, the word *context* is an old word whose Latin root (contexere) means "to weave together." In its modern usage, *context* refers to the linguistic parts that surround a given term and therefore convey its meaning. So it's useful to think of contextually targeted advertising as advertising that is woven together with editorial content in a way that is relevant because the theme of the advertising matches the theme of the content. If you are reading a blog post about Caribbean cruises for singles, there is a distinct possibility that you might be interested in that type of vacation. Google, Yahoo, and Microsoft are joined by a host of other providers who specialize purely in matching text ads contextually based on the content being displayed to a reader. The key distinction to keep in mind about contextual advertising is that the reader has not yet chosen to search and therefore may not have as great a desire to transact within a short time frame. Yet, if a relevant ad appears next to content, readers may find their curiosity tweaked and select the ad, perhaps your ad.

The search engines have hundreds of thousands of advertisers, from the biggies down to the very niche businesses. Many of those advertisers suffer from a shortage of searchers (meaning not enough people are looking for their products or services). Contextual ad inventory is one way that search advertisers broaden their campaigns to generate awareness and perhaps even purchase intent.

Exploring Contextually Targeted Advertising

In the early days of online advertising, the targeting of advertisements to different types of content pages was crude. Targeting was first done on a "run of network" (RON) basis, which means that it rotated throughout a given site. Category-specific targeting came later; this gave advertisers the ability to only run ads in particular areas of a given site, for example, in the business, lifestyle, or other sections. This type of targeting is still used widely in online advertising, both on sites offering their own advertising programs and on ad networks, which run ads through a group of websites participating in the ad network.

Contextually keyword-targeted advertising represents a genuine leap beyond RON and category-level ad targeting, because it lets advertisers select individual pages or articles whose content is more germane to the products and services advertised, based on keywords appearing in those pages and articles. When it's done correctly, this form of advertising provides a win-win scenario for marketers (whose ads, because they are judged by viewers to be relevant to their interests, are more likely to be acted upon by viewers) and the people exposed to such advertising (because they perceive such ads as being aligned with the theme of the editorial matter surrounding them).

Google had a big role to play in the advancement of contextually targeted keyword advertising when it launched its AdSense program in 2003 using technology acquired from a company called Applied Semantics. Today, Google has the largest contextually targeted advertising network in the world, with billions of pages served daily across thousands of websites.

For search engines such as Google, the value proposition for offering contextually targeted keyword advertising is based on a simple premise. Although people use search engines a lot, they don't spend nearly as much time searching as they do surfing websites, reading and writing e-mail, and engaging in other nonsearch activities.

It was a logical step for search engines to become big players in contextually targeted keyword advertising. Advertisers who had become comfortable selecting and buying keywords could leverage their efforts to reach a much wider audience just by clicking a few buttons. Advertisers quickly learned, however, that the results they got from using contextually targeted keyword advertising rarely matched those gotten from search-based keyword targeted advertising. Read on to find out about why these two channels are so different.

Contextually Targeted Keyword Targeting vs. Search Advertising

Contextually targeted advertising shares several characteristics with search-based advertising. Marketers bid for keywords that serve as triggers for the display of their ads and pay either by the click or by the impression. (Contextual targeting can also occur by targeting categories of content, which is known as *placement targeting*.) Unlike search, however, contextually targeted advertising doesn't appear on SERPs (search engine results pages) but on pages of third-party websites.

This is an important distinction because people browsing websites are in a very different frame of mind from people entering queries into search engines. Searchers typically arrive at a search engine with a defined need in mind and the expectation that a result, either paid or organic, will meet this need. It's useful to describe these searchers as being in *hunt mode*. People surfing websites or reading lengthy articles are in a different mental state. Instead of being in *hunt mode*, they are *grazing* for information, and although they may have inner, unmet needs, these needs are in the background, not the foreground. Furthermore, the way that contextually targeted ads are displayed to the user is profoundly different from search-based ads. Instead of appearing prominently (either on top or on the top-right of SERPs), an ad blends in with the editorial material around it, making it much less noticeable.

The result is that consumers of contextually targeted advertising do not respond to it as avidly as they do with search-based advertising. Click-through rates are lower, often much lower than with search-based ads. At the same time, click prices for contextually targeted ads are typically lower than for search-based ads, making this channel a good choice for marketers seeking increased reach at relatively low incremental costs. Additionally, unlike search ads, content networks supporting contextually targeted ads offer marketers options beyond the simple text ad. These networks typically support a wide range of ad formats, including text, image, rich media, and video that brand marketers often prefer over plain text ads. The result is added flexibility for marketers whose creative impulses are throttled by the tight character restrictions of text ads.

How Contextual Targeting Works in Google

Contextually targeted advertising typically works across a network of websites whose owners have elected to become part of such a network, and there are literally hundreds of vendors providing this kind of service, some of which will be enumerated in this chapter. But because Google currently provides the world's largest contextual network through its AdSense program, it's useful to start with a discussion of how Google does it. Additionally, the way that Google handles contextual ads is very similar to the way that Yahoo and Microsoft adCenter do, so the same advice for best practices applies.

Thousands of websites belong to Google's AdSense program; some are large and well-known, others small and highly-focused on a particular content niche. Google actively encourages the owners of websites to participate in AdSense, does not have minimum traffic requirements, requires that such sites do not market prohibited products (such as gambling or adult services), do not infringe on copyrighted material, and abide by other policies designed to ensure that they have displayed valid editorial content to users. The result is a very large network that Google claims now receives 4.3 billion daily page views from 705 million monthly visitors. **Figure 13.1** is an example of Google's AdSense program serving up some contextual keyword targeting ads.

Figure 13.1
An example of contextual keyword targeted advertising running on a third-party site.

Google uses a system that crawls websites participating in its AdSense program and subsequently analyzes the content of each page in which advertising space is made available through the inclusion of a short snippet of JavaScript code. Although Google does not disclose precise details about how its contextual algorithm works, it's clear that the keywords on each site's page and the formatting assigned to them are important factors in determining what each page is about. Google claims that its algorithms are smart enough to distinguish ambiguous terms such as *Windows* (which might refer to the Microsoft operating system or to glass windows) or *Java* (which might refer to the place, or to the slang term for coffee, or to the programming language) based on the context in which each term is used on each page.

After analyzing such pages, Google adds them to its inventory of available contextual ad placements, making them available to marketers who have elected to use contextual targeting in their AdWords accounts. Marketers can select contextual targeting by selecting the appropriate Content Network radio button in the AdWords console interface, which **Figure 13.2** shows. The Content Network checkbox is actually turned on by default, and marketers who do not want this option will need to deactivate it to prevent their ads from being served in the Content Network.

Figure 13.2
Google's AdWords console shows selections for a campaign running through search and through Google's contextually targeted Content Network.

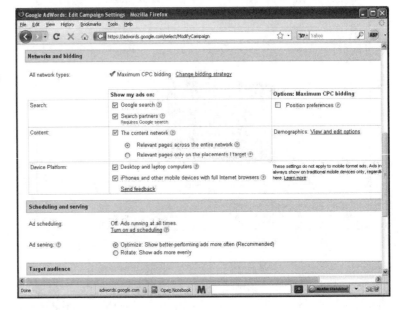

Contextual Targeting in Yahoo

Like Google, Yahoo maintains a content network across which marketers can buy contextually targeted ads. Yahoo's network is much smaller than Google's, but the individual sites in its network are much larger. Currently, no site is eligible for inclusion in Yahoo's network that does not have at least 20 million page views per month. Prominent members of Yahoo's network include USA Today, CitySearch, eBay, NBC's online properties, iVillage, Salon.com, and many other large publishers. Like Google, Yahoo's contextual matching system doesn't use keywords alone to determine which webpages that ads are served on, but it considers keywords, along with ad title, description, and landing page content. Yahoo similarly recommends that you maintain ads for Yahoo's search and Content Match separately to simplify because the performance of each channel differs so widely.

Contextual Targeting in Microsoft adCenter

Microsoft adCenter has a content network similar to Yahoo's, in that it has a small number of partners whose sites are large. Many of these partners are actually part of Microsoft's content empire, including Hotmail, MSN Entertainment, MSN Health & Fitness, MSN Autos, and MSN Money. External partners include The Wall Street Journal, Fox Sports, and CNBC.com. The same best practices (which we'll explore in a moment) for running contextual campaigns in Google and Yahoo apply to running contextual campaigns running in Microsoft adCenter.

Using Best Practices for Contextual Keyword Targeting

Building and running a campaign through Google's Content Network is similar to running a search campaign. You select keywords relevant to your product or service, add negative keywords to suppress the ad from being triggered by inappropriate searches, compose an ad, and direct it to a landing page. But there are some important nuances you'll need to understand to make sure your ad appears on pages providing a good match with the keywords you select.

Use Keyword Themes

Unlike search ads, Content Network ads aren't triggered by individual keywords but by groups of them (Google calls such groups *themes*) within a given ad group, along with the ad text you specify. To ensure the maximum likelihood of having ads matched to an appropriate content page, Google recommends that you create at least three thematically related lists of between 15 and 30 keywords residing in at least three ad groups.

Table 13.1 includes some examples that Google uses to illustrate its recommended approach for a hypothetical pet goods supplier.

Table 13.1 Hypothetical Ad Group Themes

	Ad Group 1	Ad Group 2	Ad Group 3
Theme	Direct product theme (dog supplies)	Complementary products theme (pet supplies)	Audience theme (dog owners)
Keywords	dog supplies dog products dog food dog treats dog bones dog crates dog collars dog beds leashes dog shampoo -cat -fish -pet -training -adoption -guide	pet supplies cat supplies fish food cat food pet products animal products -training -adoption -obedience	dog day care dog walkers kennels dog training

(Source: www.google.com/adwords/learningcenter/text/76856.html)

Why create multiple thematically distinct ad groups instead of just one? The idea here is to cast a wide net so that your ads have the greatest chance of appearing next to articles that might be relevant. Although the individual keywords you specify have an impact on whether Google decides to serve your ad beside a given article, so does the entire group, along with the wording in your ad.

Keep Contextual Campaigns Separate from Search

Keeping your contextually targeted ad campaigns separate from your search campaigns is a highly recommended practice, both because you need to think about keywords differently, and because click-through rates (CTRs), conversion rates, and costs per click (CPCs) will also be markedly different. Many marketers who have experimented with the content networks of search engines have subsequently decided to not participate in the content network at all. It's also more convenient to keep reporting for search and contextual campaigns separate to better analyze each. Even the best advertising copy (titles and descriptions) for the same exact keyword may differ dramatically when that ad is in a contextual environment instead of a search engine results page. For these reasons, if you decide to use contextual targeting, make sure you manage your campaigns separately.

Consider Placement Targeting

Placement targeting provides a way for marketers to specify, on a categorical, topic-based, or site-specific way, where their ads appear. Google's placement targeting provides a way for marketers using contextually targeted advertising to exert more control over where their ads appear on Google's Content Network. Placement targeting can provide you a way to focus your marketing efforts on sites or audience segments most likely to respond to your ads. Google's Placement Targeting tool (**Figure 13.3** on the next page) provides an easy way to specify additional parameters that control where and to whom your ads are shown. The tool lets you browse categories and subcategories, describe topics, list URLs, or select demographics. If you already have a good idea of who your audience is and where they spend their online time, it's a great way to target them.

Figure 13.3
Google's Placement Targeting tool lets you home in on sites, topics, URLs, or audience segments you are most interested in reaching.

Handling Contextual Advertising Issues

Although contextually targeted advertising and search are closely related, there are issues pertaining to contextual advertising that you should know about before embarking upon a contextual advertising campaign.

Click Fraud

One very nettlesome problem that has afflicted marketers using contextually targeted advertising is the issue of click fraud. Click fraud can affect search networks if competitors click maliciously on each others' ads to cost each other money. But because contextually targeted advertising occurs across third-party sites, the risk is elevated, because unscrupulous site publishers can either on their own or through third parties generate clicks that do nothing more than make them money, given that they are paid a share of each click billed by the search engines.

How bad is the click fraud problem? No one seems to agree. According to third-party auditing firm, Click Forensics, 28 percent of clicks on third-party networks such as AdSense and the Yahoo Publisher network are fraudulent. Google has stridently objected to such assertions, criticized Click Forensics' methods, and stated that no more than 10 percent of AdSense clicks aren't bona fide. (Google eschews the term *click fraud*, preferring the more neutral term *invalid clicks*.)

It can take a lot of work and vigilance on the part of marketers to establish whether they have been victimized by click fraud. The search engines do their best to police their third-party publishing networks to weed out the malefactors, but these efforts are less than 100 percent effective. Even if fraudulent (or invalid) clicks constitute only a few percentage points, this can add up to a lot of money given a sufficient level of spend. If you're concerned about click fraud, the best course for you may be to simply deselect the Content Network, leaving the problem for others to settle.

Imperfect Content Matching

Matching ads to appropriate content pages is difficult, and results do not always provide a good match. You may have observed cases where attempts by automated content matching systems to serve ads against editorial content do a poor job. Some articles, for example, "how to" articles on how to choose a flat-screen television, provide excellent opportunities to place ads for such appliances. A news article on the future of the flat-screen television industry would likely be a poorer choice, because it would likely be read by investors instead of consumers.

Algorithms, even the best ones, do not always make the right choices, and some level of human intervention may be necessary to screen out poor editorial venues for serving contextual ads. For example, with Google, it might be necessary to use placement targeting to limit your ad's exposure to sites offering "how to" articles rather than those offering industry news or other material.

Poor Click Quality

Contextually targeted campaigns do not yield the same levels of CTRs or conversions as search campaigns. This is due to the audience of each type of campaign being so different. Searchers, who are in hunt mode, are highly motivated to find an answer to a compelling personal need within a very short time frame. Consumers of editorial material are in browse or *information gathering* mode and may only have a casual interest in consuming products or services, making them less likely to click or convert.

Is Contextual Advertising For You?

There is no reason for you not to experiment with contextually targeted advertising, because it can give your campaigns additional reach. Just be aware that search and contextual advertising are two completely different animals addressing completely different audiences, so don't expect that your campaigns will deliver you the same response level or click quality as search campaigns. Whether you decide to add contextual advertising to your online marketing toolkit largely depends on whether the generally lower costs of this channel outweigh its comparative disadvantages vis-à-vis search. The only way to know if the contextual route is the right one is to focus not on the traffic this channel will bring you but on whether the conversions you get from this traffic is worth the money you'll spend to attract it.

Considering Third-Party Contextual Advertising Vendors

Beyond the big three search engines, hundreds of vendors offer contextually targeted advertising services. Some support only search-style text ads; others support a full range of ad formats, including text, graphical, and video. Two vendors, Kontera and Vibrant Media, provide a unique form of ad unit called the *in text* unit. In text units consist of underlines that are superimposed on a keyword or phrase within an editorial unit; when users roll the pointer over this word or phrase, an ad unit pops up over the page.

Although it is beyond the scope of this chapter to enumerate all the vendors of contextually targeted advertising, **Table 13.2** lists some significant players.

Table 13.2 Third-party Contextual Advertising Vendors

Vendor	Targeting Methodology	Billing Model	Reach (Monthly Unique Users)	Supported Ad Formats	Notable Publishers in Network
AdBrite	Placement	CPC, CPM	85 million	Text, graphical	LinkedIn, Drudge Report, Alexa, Chicago Sun-Times
Ask.com	Keyword	CPC	72 million	Text	C|Net, Citysearch, Match.com, Dogpile, Excite
Chitika	Placement, keyword	CPC, CPM	60 million	Text, graphical	ConsumerSearch.com, MobileMag.com, Coolest-Gadgets.com
Kontera	Keyword, placement	CPC	75 million	In text	n/a
Quigo	Placement	CPC	54 million	Text, graphical	AOL Money & Finance, TMZ.com, Engadget, CNNMoney.com, TIME.com, People.com, ESPN.com
Vibrant Media	Keyword	CPC	120 million	In text	n/a
Miva	Keyword, placement	CPC	Unknown	Text, graphical	C|Net, Reunion.com, Eurekster.com
Pulse360	Keyword, placement	CPC	Unknown	Text, graphical	MSNBC.com, USAToday.com, IMDB.com, Comcast.net, Weather.com
ContextWeb	Keyword, placement	CPC, CPM	100 million	Text, graphical	SmartMoney.com, Investor's Business Daily, The Parenting Group
Looksmart	Keyword, placement	CPC, CPA	Unknown	Text	Ask.com

Chapter 14

Extending Search with Behavior

Behavioral targeting (BT) is a broad term that includes several different methods and technologies. The fundamental idea behind BT is to use online behavior to help sufficiently identify individuals to group them within an audience segment. Once a user has been so identified, such an audience segment is sold to advertisers bidding for it. Tracking and ad serving technology let advertisers "follow users around" as they travel the web from site to site. This form of targeting is very different from the targeting contextual advertising uses, which is limited to a particular page or site.

BT lets advertisers buy "buckets" of users whose behavior is similar. Such buckets might include online gamers, frequent shoppers, or lonely hearts. Additionally, BT-style targeting allows an additional level of personalization, which its proponents claim improves relevancy. For example, users who have read an article on San Francisco and have searched for airline fares can be served an ad for a hotel in that city, even though they have not yet searched or otherwise specified a desire for such a service.

What Is Behavioral Targeting?

Why did behavioral targeting come along? Well, as you saw in Chapter 13, "Contextual Keyword Targeting," one major problem with contextual advertising is that people exposed to it usually do not respond as frequently or as avidly as they do when exposed to search advertising. The result is that advertising isn't very effective, publishers carrying such ads don't earn much, and users regard such ads as undesirable clutter.

Advocates of behavioral targeting claim that response rates from well-designed behavioral targeting campaigns provide much higher response rates. This is one reason that marketers have embraced it in recent years (see **Figure 14.1**).

Figure 14.1
Percentage of marketers reporting use of BT technologies (Source: JupiterResearch Advertiser Executive Survey).

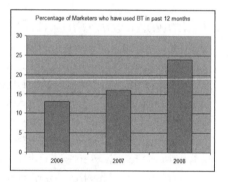

The main reason that interest in BT is high is that behavioral targeting has the potential to benefit all the major commercial constituents of online publishing: web publishers (who can charge more by selling desirable audience segments to advertisers), advertisers (whose ads are responded to more frequently by those exposed to them), and web surfers (who will be exposed to fewer but more highly targeted ads perceived as being better aligned with their personal interests).

At the same time, the term *behavioral targeting* has raised red flags from privacy advocates and government regulators such as the Federal Trade Commission (FTC), which has accused its proponents of glossing over the fact that behavioral targeted advertising relies on tracking users as they surf around the web or within individual websites, but that few targeted users seem to be aware of the practice or know what to do to remove themselves from such targeting if they object to it. Additionally, concerns have been voiced that participants in BT do not employ policies that adequately protect tracking data from falling into the hands of other parties who may not sufficiently respect privacy concerns. The frightening idea that such personal data might be used to infringe on peoples' privacy evokes the all-pervasive surveillance systems cited in George Orwell's *1984*.

What exactly is behavioral targeting? What role should it play in your online marketing mix? Read on (and fear not—this is a book, so you can turn to any page without fear that we're going to sell this data to anyone).

Two Main BT Types

There are two main types of behavioral targeting technologies in use today: *cookie-based* and *packet-based*. The first method (also known as *onsite behavioral targeting*) is widely used by many different ad networks and by the "big three" search engines. The second (also known as *network-based behavioral targeting*) is far more controversial, for reasons we'll discuss in detail.

Cookie-based behavioral targeting

Cookies are at the heart of most behavioral targeting systems today. Cookies are small text files that are exchanged between a person's web browser application and a web server. Cookies provide a range of highly useful functions when using websites, including storing users' passwords (so they don't have to reenter them each time they visit), remembering where the user was in a given process (such as moving through an online shopping cart system), or saving preferences the user might have expressed about the way that the website should perform.

When a person visits a website that is set up to send and receive cookies, the cookie is deposited on the person's hard drive. When at a later point in time the user returns to the same website, the cookie is retrieved, thus allowing the website to recognize this returning user as the same person who came by earlier.

Cookies provide a convenient way for online marketers to identify a web surfer and to track his or her online activities. Cookies can be deposited or dropped on the user's computer by websites and even from banner advertisements and search ads. Unless you've deliberately prevented your browser from accepting cookies, it's likely that you have many of them residing on your PC right now (see **Figure 14.2**).

Figure 14.2

Cookies provide the means to track user's activities across the web.

Although cookie data alone is insufficient to provide detailed personal information about a web surfer, such data, when aggregated, allows ad networks to create profiles based on such tracking. These profiles are then sold to marketers seeking to buy different audience "bundles," such as people who have read car review articles, accessed auto review sites such as Edmunds.com, and then entered search queries such as *compare Ford Focus with Honda Civic*. A web user demonstrating such online behavior might be deemed a likely car buyer who marketers might want to serve customized ads to.

Cookies aren't a perfect means to identify users because they can be deleted or blocked completely using the web browser's security and privacy features. Various studies have been done on cookie deletion rates, and their findings have pegged these rates from 30 (comScore 2007) to nearly 40 percent (JupiterResearch 2005). This means that roughly one in three web users deletes cookies regularly, which markedly undermines the effectiveness of cookie-based behavioral targeting.

Packet-based behavioral targeting

Unlike cookie-based behavioral targeting, which depends on the exchange of data between browser application and web server, packet-based behavioral targeting occurs at the packet level, which constitutes the basic building blocks of all information exchanged on the Internet.

Packet-based behavioral targeting occurs at the ISP (Internet service provider) level. All packet traffic from subscribers is collected, analyzed, and used to create the same kind of user profiles sold to advertisers by cookie-based behavioral targeting entities.

Here's the difference: ISPs, unlike the proprietors of online ad networks or search engines, know exactly who their users are (because they maintain subscription records for each customer who pays them each month). Consequently, any ISP using this technology is theoretically capable of both snooping on someone's online activities and knowing exactly who the targeted user is at the same time.

Although advocates for packet-based behavioral targeting, including representatives of such firms as NebuAd and Phorm, aver that the tracking data gathered from users is masked and anonymized, thus shielding the ISP (or anyone else) from ever knowing the exact identity of web surfers, packet-based behavioral targeting schemes have not gone very far. Many consider them to be potentially far more intrusive than tracking systems using cookies because the ad networks do not have personally identifiable data available to them for such correlations.

Regulation and Self-Regulation of Behavioral Targeting

The FTC has long expressed concerns about the overaggressive use of behaviorally targeted advertising technologies. In 2007 and 2008, the FTC held a series of workshops designed to air concerns from important constituents in online advertising, including BT technology vendors, consumer and privacy groups, and the search engines.

The result was a set of principles designed to help self-regulate the industry:

- **Transparency and control:** "Companies that collect information for behavioral advertising should provide meaningful disclosures to consumers about the practice and choice about whether to allow the practice."

- **Security and limited data:** "Companies should provide reasonable data security measures so that behavioral data does not fall into the wrong hands, and should retain data only as long as necessary for legitimate business or law enforcement needs."

- **Material change:** "Before a company uses behavioral data in a manner that is materially different from promises made when the company collected the data, it should obtain affirmative express consent from the consumer."

- **Sensitive data:** "Companies should obtain affirmative express consent before they use sensitive data—for example, data about children, health, or finances—for behavioral advertising."

Note

The FTC has traditionally favored industry self-regulation rather than direct regulation from Washington.

Although it appears that self-regulation of behavioral targeted advertising will prevail for the near-term future, a reasonable possibility exists that some forms of it may eventually be regulated, because self-regulation works only if there are no "bad actors" flaunting self-regulatory principles. The online ad world has historically been a wild and wooly environment, so concerns about marketers respecting self-regulatory boundaries are well-founded. In 2009, two important FTC officials, including former commissioner Pamela Jones Harbour and incoming chair Jon Leibowitz, expressed doubts that the industry can effectively police itself. "Self-regulation has not yet been proven sufficient to fully protect the interests of consumers with respect to behavioral advertising specifically, or privacy generally," said Harbour. The industry is approaching "a day of reckoning," warned Leibowitz, unless it can collectively abide by BT best practices.

How Search Engines Offer Behavioral Targeting

Search engines are in a unique position to offer behavioral targeting to marketers using their ad platforms. Behavioral targeting requires a lot of data to work correctly. It can take a lot of time, and money spent, to develop enough information about a user's online activity to make valid inferences about what audience segment he or she truly belongs to.

Search engines, of course, have extensive data on their user base, both from cookies deposited on users' hard drives and from data disclosed by users joining Google, Yahoo, or Microsoft in order to enjoy special free features such as Google's Gmail email service, Yahoo's email or financial services, and Microsoft's email and online group service.

The wealth and depth of data gives them a real advantage. Additionally, cookies deposited by search engines will likely be deleted less frequently than those deposited by other sites and services, which means that searchers will likely see relevant BT-generated ads for a longer period.

The "big three" search engines have similar but distinct implementations of behavioral targeting technologies. Here is a summary of what each one offers to marketers interested in running behavioral targeted campaigns.

Google

Until 2009, Google had deployed only a very limited implementation of behavioral targeting on its search network (that is, Google properties, not Google's content network). In March of 2009, however, it announced a more ambitious plan to serve behaviorally targeted advertising across the ad-serving networks it acquired through its DoubleClick acquisition and also through its AdSense network. Google dubbed its new program *interest-based advertising*, perhaps to avoid the stigma that behavioral targeting has been traditionally associated with.

On its search properties, Google uses prior search behavior occurring within the same search session to determine if additional relevant ads should be served. For example, if a user searched for *car rental* and subsequently searched for *San Diego*, Google's system might conclude that this user should be served an ad targeted at users searching for *San Diego car rentals* (see **Figure 14.3**).

Figure 14.3

In this instance, a user whose last search query was for *car rental* is served an ad for a San Diego–based car rental company after he searches for *San Diego*. Google's system has concluded that such an ad is relevant based on prior search queries.

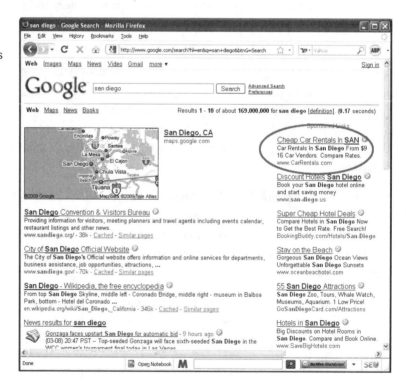

The interest-based advertising program involves running behaviorally targeted ads across its ad network using cookie-based tracking. To address concerns voiced about personally identifiable information being gathered and shared, Google noted that "throughout this process, Google does not know (the user's) name or any other personal information about her. Google simply recognizes the number stored in (the user's) browser, sees that it falls into (the user's interest category), and shows more (ads targeting this interest). Google will also not use sensitive interest categories, such as those based on race, religion, sexual orientation, health, or sensitive financial categories."

It appears that Google crafted its approach to take account of and abide by the FTC's principles of self-regulation. Additionally, Google offers users exposed to BT ads an easy way to opt out of the program and to modify the interest areas the system has (see **Figure 14.4**).

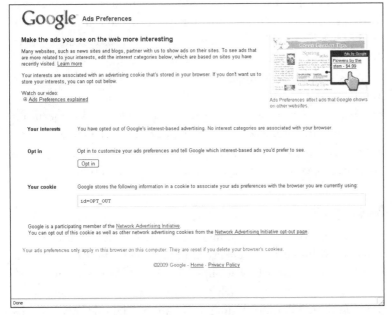

Figure 14.4
Google's Ad Preferences provides users exposed to behavioral targeted advertising a convenient way to opt out of the program or change interest categories associated with their behavior.

Marketers can also take advantage of behavioral targeting in Google through its DoubleClick Advertising Exchange. This form of behavioral targeting would more likely be retargeting current site visitors.

Yahoo

Yahoo has long been an proponent of behavioral targeting, and its 2007 acquisition of BT firm BlueLithium added a powerful arsenal to its array of BT-like targeting tools.

In February of 2009, Yahoo made a major announcement of a new BT product suite applicable to both its search and display network. Two behavioral targeting products were included in Yahoo's announcement. Search Retargeting for Display Ads allows marketers to run display ads whose targeting is based on a user's past search activity. Enhanced Retargeting for Display Ads lets marketers generate targeted ads on-the-fly, such as ads containing specific offers for specific products, based on users' activities on third-party sites within the Yahoo publisher network.

Yahoo is in a strong position to offer and profit from behavioral targeted advertising. Its various services have millions of subscribers who have disclosed their demographic information. It also has millions of pages within its own sprawling site where it does not ordinarily sell premium-priced advertising, plus a large ad network resulting from its absorption of Right Media, an online advertising company. Yahoo's search engine remains popular as well. The result is an environment in which behavioral targeting may well provide a means for Yahoo to better monetize its properties. For marketers, the fact that Yahoo is increasingly bringing powerful behavioral targeting technologies to bear on its large audience is a very good thing.

Microsoft

Like Yahoo, Microsoft's online properties constitute a large online audience. Millions of people use Hotmail (the Microsoft free online email service), use MSN groups, or use its search engine, Live Search. Microsoft's approach to BT appears to blend behavioral data with other data, including demographic data self-disclosed by users and search query data. Microsoft claims that this combined approach has improved conversion rates by up to 76 percent in internal tests. Retargeting is also available through Microsoft's adECN, which is being integrated into their main offering.

Other BT Vendors

It's clear that the search engines are leading the charge toward behavioral targeted advertising, but they aren't the only game in town. Many third-party firms offer BT on their own site networks. The following is not intended to serve as an exhaustive list, but it points out some of the major players in BT ad serving today.

24/7 Real Media

www.247realmedia.com

24/7 Real Media is an audience segmentation firm owned by WPP, an ad agency holding company. It serves behavioral ads against a large network it claims reaches 135 million unique users per month; notable network partners include The McGraw-Hill Companies, Cygnus Business Media, Nielsen Business Media, and Reed Business Information.

Audience Science (formerly Revenue Science)

www.audiencescience.com

Audience Science runs a large network of some 10,000 sites with a claimed reach of 385 million unique Internet users, against which it applies behavioral targeting. Notable network publishers include the Financial Times, Gannett, Jumpstart Automotive Media, New York Times Digital, NikkeiNet, Reuters.com, The Guardian.co.uk, Univison.com, and Wall Street Journal Digital.

Blue Lithium

www.bluelithium.com

Blue Lithium, purchased by Yahoo in 2007, now applies its behavioral targeting technologies across Yahoo's sizeable content network of some 500 million monthly users.

Didit (my firm)

www.didit.com

Didit uses a unique hub-centric method to create behavioral targeting segments across display media exchanges, including Yahoo's Right

Media, Microsoft's adECN, and Google's Advertising Exchange, plus a couple of up-and-coming online media exchanges. By working across many real-time media exchanges at the same time and bidding in real time at the impression level for individuals who fit a particular behavioral profile (such as retargeted recent searchers), Didit is able to deploy limited marketing budgets very efficiently.

Specific Media

www.specificmedia.com

Specific Media runs a network consisting of some 450 "brand name publisher" sites, including ABC, ABCNews, the Gannett Newspaper Group, ESPN, FoxNews, FoxSports, the sites of Major League Baseball, NBC, the New York Times, and others. It sells behavioral segments to advertisers, including automotive, B2B, consumer software, entertainment, family, finance, food and drink, health and beauty, home and garden, magazine, news and media, portal, real estate, shopping, sports, and travel.

Tacoda

www.tacoda.com

Tacoda, acquired by AOL in 2007, is a pioneer in behavioral targeting. In 2008, its behavioral targeting technologies were incorporated into AOL's Platform-A advertising platform, where they now serve to deliver BT ads across AOL's popular sites, including AOL News, Sports, Money & Finance, Moviefone, and MapQuest. Additionally, this network includes thousands of high-traffic third-party sites that are part of the Advertising.com network.

Tribal Fusion

www.tribalfusion.com

Tribal Fusion maintains an ad network consisting of some 1,200 popular sites, whose reach it claims is some 129 million unique users per month. It offers both behavioral ad targeting and technology providing for dynamic ads whose creative elements can be customized for individual audience segments.

ValueClick

www.valueclick.com

ValueClick maintains a network of some 13,500 sites and has been deploying and upgrading behavioral targeted ad technologies since 2005.

Is Behavioral Targeting For You?

If you're running search campaigns, you're already participating in a marketing channel that makes use of some aspects of behavioral targeting. After all, the queries entered into search engines reveal a great deal about the past and future behavior of such searchers. Now that each of the major search engines has embraced behavioral targeting and included it among the targeting levers they offer, there's no reason for you not to learn about it and apply it to your online marketing campaigns. Although some claims about the performance improvements that BT can offer online campaigns are quite likely overhyped by BT proponents, even modest improvements in CTR provided by this form of targeting can make huge differences in campaigns with sufficient scale and spend levels.

Tying It All Together

Like it or not, consumers and business people about to make a purchase or a purchase decision are hunting for solutions to their commercial needs. You probably use the search engines in much the same way. That's what makes search engine advertising and SEO such a critically important component of any marketing plan. Potentially hundreds of media and marketing touch points and impressions from both you and your competition are driving consumers to search for products, services, and solutions. The marketers who know how to leverage the power of search engine marketing will find themselves benefiting and taking more than their fair share of search visitors, turning them into customers.

If you are just getting involved in search engine advertising now, you have some catching up to do. Some of your competitors may have been at paid search for years and if they are smart, those competitors have been testing and refining their campaigns the entire time. That means they are reaping the rewards of an investment of time, energy, and money. Don't despair, if search engine advertising is going to work for you, you'll know fairly soon after implementing a campaign. Just don't expect to get it perfect the first time out. I didn't, and no one I know has, and that includes marketers who have hired top agencies like my firm Didit or others to set up and manage campaigns for them. But using a professional services firms will get you closer to an optimal campaign faster since they have seen what works and what doesn't across dozens or perhaps hundreds of campaigns.

PPC search is a test-and-learn laboratory. The more you test and learn, the better your campaign becomes. Auction marketplaces that force you to bid for clicks that turn into customers provide constant pressure to innovate and improve. Some words of wisdom as you put this book aside to either manage your campaigns or instruct your agency as to your objectives:

- Be clear about both goals and objectives.

- Make sure your site is ready for the traffic and presents your company, products, and services in a good light.

- Know how much an average customer is worth but also know what a great one is worth to you and your business.

- If possible, don't simply track online behaviors but offline behaviors as well, including store visits and phone calls. Even if you can't tie them to a specific keyword or click, offline tracking provides a basis for a budgetary fudge factor.

- Look at what your competitors are doing. The longer a competitor has been at PPC search advertising, the more likely they are to have discovered things that are working.

- Stay educated. This book is only part of your education. If you are doing your own campaign management, delve into the Google, Yahoo, and Microsoft help/support documents.

There are dozens of reasons why it's important that you become familiar with and competent in paid search at the strategic and possibly even at the tactical level. Perhaps the biggest reason is that there's ample evidence that more forms of media may be auctioned off in the future in some kind of marketplace or exchange. The lessons learned in one advertising auction will apply to many of the other media auctions we will see develop over the next several years, particularly digital advertising beyond paid search text link ads.

Once you've had a chance to immerse yourself into paid search and by extension other forms of auction-based media, I hope you'll be as enthusiastic as I am about the power of search engine advertising to give you a leg up on your competition.

More Than Just a Glossary

In search engine advertising, as with many industries, there are lots of acronyms and buzzwords that may seem unfamiliar to traditional marketers and business owners. In addition to seeing some use of acronyms and buzzwords in this book, you are likely to encounter similar unfamiliar terms when reading industry news, blogs, instructional materials, and even the search engine online tutorials and help files. This glossary helps you make sense of them all.

ad   Advertisements a searcher sees after submitting a query in a search engine or website search box. In paid placement campaigns, these ads are usually text, with a title, description, and display URL. In some cases, a keyword the searcher used in his or her query appears boldfaced in the ad. Ads can be positioned anywhere on a search results page; commonly they appear at the top—above the natural or organic listings—and on the right side of the page, also known as the right rail. Keyword-targeted ads may also be shown in a contextual nonsearch environment.

ad copy   The main text of a clickable search or context-served ad. Some in the industry define the ad copy as exclusively referring to the content between the ad title and the display URL. Others use the broader definition of the overall ad.

ad title   The first line of text displayed in a clickable search or context-served ad. Ad titles serve as headlines. The industry standard for the title length is currently 25 characters, including spaces.

affiliate   An individual or company that markets a merchant's products or services and is paid only a sales commission fee.

affiliate program   A program that allows other companies or individuals to market a company's products or services for a commission fee per item sold.

algorithm   A formula or set of formulas used by a search engine to rank paid or organic listings in response to a query. The relevancy of a listing and, in the case of paid search ads, the revenue factor heavily into the algorithms of all the search engines.

application programming interface (API)   This is a standard set of protocols that allows two or more computers to communicate with each other to automate data sharing or tasks. In a search marketing context, engine APIs allow advertisers, agencies, or technology providers to create computer programs to automate the management of their search engine marketing (SEM) campaigns, bypassing the search engines' web-based interfaces.

bid The maximum amount of money an advertiser is willing to pay each time a searcher clicks on an ad meeting a specified set of targeting parameters, including keyword but also geography, match type, syndication partner, and in some cases demographic targeting variables such as age, income, or gender. Bid prices can vary widely depending on competition from other advertisers and keyword popularity. Most advertisers set bids based on historically observed post-click conversion data.

bid boosting A form of automated or pre-sent bid management that lets you increase your bids when ads are served to someone whose individual profile meets a specific set of targeting criteria, including perhaps demographics, geography, day-parts, or days of the week. Microsoft adCenter was the first to enhance demographic focus and add bid boosting in its web-based interface.

bid management software Software that manages paid placement campaigns automatically, called either rules-based (with triggering rules or conditions set by the advertiser) or intelligent software (enacting real-time adjustments based on tracked conversions and competitor actions). Both types of automatic bid management programs monitor and change bid prices, pause campaigns, manage budget maximums, adjust multiple keyword bids based on click-through rate (CTR), position ranking, and more. Larger advertisers in particular tend to use bid management solutions, although some small marketers managing complex campaigns can benefit as well.

black box algorithms Black box is technical jargon for cases when a system is viewed primarily in terms of input and output characteristics. A black box algorithm is one where the user cannot see the inner workings of the algorithm. All search engine algorithms are hidden in both the organic and paid placement models. However, the search engines share a bit of information about the algorithms to facilitate marketers' ability to understand and improve the relevance of results.

buying funnel Also called the buying cycle, awareness funnel, and sales cycle. Buying funnel refers to a multistep process of a consumer's path to purchase a product. Steps include awareness, education, preference, intent, and final purchase decision.

click-through rate (CTR)   A percentage representing the number of clicks that an ad gets, divided by the total number of times that ad is displayed or served (total clicks ÷ total impressions for a specific ad). For example, if an ad has 100 impressions and 6 clicks, the CTR is 6 percent. All other things equal, search engines prefer ads with a higher CTR, as high CTRs tend to correlate with the perception of relevance by searchers.

click fraud   Non-authentic clicks on a pay-per-click advertisement that are motivated by something other than a search for the advertised product or service. Click fraud may be the result of malicious or negative competitor/affiliate actions, or a network publishing partner of the search engine may be fraudulently inflating click counts. Generally the search engines do an OK job of policing click fraud because the poor quality fraudulent traffic dilutes the quality of clicks causing savvy marketers to bid less for those clicks. However, many in the industry believe that technology and human resources should be deployed at the advertiser or agency level to monitor click quality and potential fraud, especially for large campaigns.

contextual advertising   A form of ad targeting that uses the content on a page to determine which ads to show. This form of advertising is most commonly associated with keyword targeted advertising and is often an additional option within a search marketing campaign in a search engine. Stand-alone contextual ad providers also exist.

cost per acquisition (CPA)   Sometimes called cost per action. CPA can either be a target metric or a calculated result. For example, if a campaign cost $80 and resulted in 4 conversions, the CPA is $20 ($80 ÷ 4). It cost $20 to generate one conversion. Similarly, a campaign could be managed to a target CPA of $20. If any portion of the campaign does not achieve that target result, bid price changes or other actions would be taken in an attempt to bring the campaign into line with the target CPA.

cost per click (CPC)   The amount billed by or bid for a click from a publisher or search engine in exchange for delivering a consumer through an ad to a website. There is often a difference between the bidded CPC and the billed CPC to take a variety of factors, including auto-discounters that the engines use in the black box auction system, into account.

cost per lead (CPL)   Also referred to as CPA, the target or actual metric that you are paying to receive a lead.

cost per order (CPO)   As with cost per acquisition (CPA), this can be both a target metric or a calculated result.

cost per thousand impressions (CPM)   Acronym for ad serves or potential viewers. Compare to cost per click (CPC) pricing—CPM is a standard billing and monetization model for offline display ad space, as well as for some context-based networks serving online search ads to, for example, web publishers and sites.

contextual advertising   Advertising that is served or placed on a web page based on the page's content, keywords, and phrases. The sites that serve these ads are considered part of a contextual network or content network, in contrast to a SERP (search engine results page) ad display, which occurs only in a search advertising network (network of search engines). Advertisers are often given the option of expanding their keyword-targeted ad campaigns to include contextually targeted ad opportunities. Generally, the visitors responding to a contextually placed ad are not as close to making a purchase decision. This lowers the measured conversion rate, and therefore many marketers prefer to limit their keyword advertising to search results.

conversion rate   The percentage of visitors from a particular ad, keyword, or campaign who convert (take one or more desired actions at your site). For example, if an ad brings in 100 click throughs and 12 of the 100 clicks result in a desired conversion, the conversion rate is 12 percent ($12 \div 100 = 0.12$). Higher conversion rates are an indication of better quality traffic and better targeting and, depending on the price paid for the click, may result in better ROI.

day-parting   The ability and process of specifying times of day when a specific campaign is running or a way of changing the price you are willing to pay based on the time of day. This function targets searchers more specifically. The term *day-parting* is sometimes used to describe the same process of specifying days of the week for differing bid prices or ad-serving rules.

display URL   The web page URL that you actually see in a pay-per-click (PPC) text ad when a URL is displayed (sometimes they are suppressed). Display URLs usually appear at the bottom line in the ad.

Dynamic Keyword Insertion (DKI)   The insertion of the specific keywords a searcher included in his or her search into the displayed ad title or description. Essentially, this feature can customize an ad based on the exact search query used by the searcher. This is a fairly advanced tactic and tends to be applicable to larger advertisers, but it has its place even in some smaller campaigns.

effective cost per thousand (eCPM)   An important metric for the search engines because it measures the predicted revenue generated by an ad option and is determined by multiplying the cost per click (CPC) by the predicted click-through rate (CTR), and multiplying that by one thousand: (CPC × CTR) × 1,000 = eCPM. All the search engines use some form of eCPM optimization to rank ads because they only get paid by the click and must factor in the predicted CTR to calculate expected revenue for an ad.

geo-targeting   The ability to target ads against the geographic location of the searcher or, in the case of nonsearch ads, the surfer. Geo-targeting can improve profitability of a campaign through localization and personalization of the ad to specific regions.

impression   One view or display of an ad. The number of times your ad was served/displayed by the search engine when searchers entered your keywords (or viewed a content page containing your keywords).

keyword/keyword phrase   The specific word or combination of words a marketer selects within a campaign to trigger the display of an ad. This also describes the word or combination of words entered by the searcher.

lifetime value (LTV)   The value of a customer over the length of that customer's purchases. Knowing the LTV or this profit total helps marketers know the value of a new customer acquisition.

organic results   Results on a search engine results page that occur specifically due to the search engine formulas and algorithms that calculate relevance to a search query. The engines do not collect revenue for clicks occurring on true organic results. However, at the current time Yahoo still has a paid inclusion program that some in the industry consider monetizes organic results due to the fact that the algorithm is the same even though the clicks are paid.

paid inclusion   Refers to the process of paying a fee (annual fixed or cost per click) to a search engine in order to have specific pages or content included in that search engine or directory. Also known as guaranteed inclusion. Paid inclusion does not alter rankings of a web page; it merely guarantees that the web page itself will be included in the index.

pay-per-click (PPC) advertising   PPC advertisers pay only when their ad is clicked on.

Quality Score   A relative score, which quantifies the relative quality of one ad over another, assigned by Google to a paid ads listing. The Quality Score is used together with maximum bidded cost per click (CPC) and predicted click-through rate (CTR) to determine each ad's rank and search engine results page (SERP) position. Quality scores reflect an ad's historical CTR, keyword relevance, landing page relevance, page load speed, and other factors proprietary to Google. Yahoo refers to the Quality Score as a Quality Index. And both Google and Yahoo display three- or five-step indicators of quality evaluations for individual advertiser listings. Advertisers with higher quality scores can generally achieve higher positions at lower bid prices.

return on advertising spending (ROAS)   Ratio of the revenue generated by ad campaign per dollar spent on advertising expenses. Calculated by dividing advertising-driven revenue by ad spending. So if an ad generated $100 in revenue, and the spend on that ad was $20, the ROAS would be 5.

return on investment (ROI)   Acronym for the amount of money (generally profit but could be revenue) you make on your ads compared to the amount of money you spend on your ads. For example, if you spend $100 on pay per click ads and make $150 from those ads, then your ROI would be 50 percent. The calculation is ($150 − $100) = $50 ÷ 100 = 50%. The higher your ROI, the more effective your advertising is.

search engine results page (SERP)   The page a searcher sees after entering a search query into an engine. Often a SERP contains both paid ad (sponsored) and organic listings in varying layouts.

tracking URL   A specially designed and/or unique URL used within a campaign to track inbound clicks for the purpose of tying those clicks to subsequent conversions or other actions. In some cases, the tracking URL is provided by an external tracking and campaign management service, or it may be an internal URL generated as part of the existing website technology. The URL is often coded to allow conversion data to be tied back to specific ad listings.

Index